"Jeremy Evans, a clear-thinking young Christian philosopher, has written an excellent treatise on the problem of evil. This volume is a work of both breadth and depth. It effectively expounds on the key themes pertaining to evil, and it provides important insights and wise guidance regarding the most troubling question we as human beings face, both intellectually and emotionally."

*Paul Copan*
*Professor and Pledger Family Chair of Philosophy and Ethics*
*Palm Beach Atlantic University, West Palm Beach, Florida*

"In this well-written volume, Jeremy Evans covers an extensive range of difficult challenges regarding what is widely held to be the most difficult subject facing theists. Turning the table on the critics time and again, Evans works his way systematically through numerous labyrinths, accumulating an abundance of great responses. I regularly found myself in agreement with his reasoning and highly recommend this text."

*Gary R. Habermas*
*Distinguished Research Professor*
*Liberty University and Theological Seminary*

# The Problem of Evil

The Challenge to Essential Christian Beliefs

**B&H Studies** in Christian Apologetics
Robert B. Stewart, *General Editor*

# The Problem of Evil

The Challenge to Essential Christian Beliefs

JEREMY A. EVANS

B&H
ACADEMIC
NASHVILLE, TENNESSEE

The Problem of Evil: The Challenge to Essential Christian Beliefs
Copyright © 2013 Jeremy Evans

Broadman & Holman Publishing Group
Nashville, Tennessee

All rights reserved

ISBN: 978-1-4336-7180-7

Dewey Decimal Classification: 170
Subject Heading: GOOD AND EVIL \ THEOLOGY \ ETHICS

Unless otherwise noted, all Scripture quotations are taken from The Holy Bible, New International Version®, NIV® Copyright © 1973, 1978, 1984, 2011 by Biblica, Inc.™ Used by permission. All rights reserved worldwide.

Scripture quotations marked ESV are taken from The Holy Bible, English Standard Version Copyright © 2001 by Crossway Bibles, a division of Good News Publishers. Used by permission. All rights reserved.

Scripture quotations marked HCSB are taken from the Holman Christian Standard Bible®, Copyright © 1999, 2000, 2002, 2003, 2009 by Holman Bible Publishers. Used by permission. Holman Christian Standard Bible®, Holman CSB®, and HCSB® are federally registered trademarks of Holman Bible Publishers.

Scripture quotations marked NKJV are taken from the New King James Version. Copyright © 1982 by Thomas Nelson, Inc. Used by permission. All rights reserved.

Scripture quotations marked NRSV are taken from the New Revised Standard Version Bible, copyright 1989, Division of Christian Education of the National Council of the Churches of Christ in the United States of America. Used by permission. All rights reserved.

Printed in the United States of America
1 2 3 4 5 6 7 8 9 10 • 17 16 15 14 13
VP

# Contents

B&H Studies in Christian Apologetics . . . . . . . . . . ix
Acknowledgments . . . . . . . . . . . . . . . . . . x

### CHAPTER ONE
The Problem of Evil: Introductory Issues. . . . . . . . 1

### CHAPTER TWO
The Logical Problem of Evil . . . . . . . . . . . . . 15

### CHAPTER THREE
The Evidential Problem of Evil . . . . . . . . . . . 23

### CHAPTER FOUR
The Defeat of Good and Evil . . . . . . . . . . . . 43

### CHAPTER FIVE
Divine Hiddenness . . . . . . . . . . . . . . . . . 61

### CHAPTER SIX
The Problem of Hell. . . . . . . . . . . . . . . . . 81

## CHAPTER SEVEN
Natural Evil: Comparing Theism and Naturalism . . . . . . . . . . . . . . . . . . . . 113

## CHAPTER EIGHT
Prolegomena to the Deontological Problem of Evil . . . . . . . . . . . . . . . . . . . . . . . . . . 133

## CHAPTER NINE
Moral Evil: Comparing Theism and Naturalism . . . . . . . . . . . . . . . . . . . . 137

## CHAPTER TEN
The Relationship between God's Will and God's Commands . . . . . . . . . . . . . . . . . . . 157

## CHAPTER ELEVEN
Is God Morally Arbitrary or Morally Irrelevant? . . . 177

## CHAPTER TWELVE
Evil and the Worship-Worthiness of God . . . . . . 197

Concluding Thoughts . . . . . . . . . . . . . . . . 217

Name Index . . . . . . . . . . . . . . . . . . . . . 221
Subject Index . . . . . . . . . . . . . . . . . . . . 223
Scripture Index . . . . . . . . . . . . . . . . . . . 225

# B&H Studies in Christian Apologetics

B&H Studies in Christian Apologetics is a series of academic monographs on subjects that are central to the apologetic task. Christian apologetics involves the defense of the Christian faith (negative apologetics), rational and evidential support for the basic tenets of the Christian faith (positive apologetics), and the effective communication of the basic tenets of the Christian faith (contextual apologetics). These books will address each of these tasks, though obviously in different ways and to differing degrees, as the subject matter dictates. The books in this series are both academically rigorous and pastorally practical. The authors are all recognized experts on the subjects that they address. They are also evangelical Christians. Though each volume is written by a committed Christian, every book in the series may be profitably read by both Christians and non-Christians alike, since subjects are presented accurately and fairly. None of the books in the series misrepresents the views that they address and intend to refute. Straw men are not welcome inside the covers of these volumes.

The first draft of each book has been read by the general editor of the series and at least one outside reader. We have commented on the contents to the authors. Nevertheless, the authors have the final say on what they have done in light those comments. All of these books are suitable for university or seminary courses on the subjects they address. Though they are monographs, many of the books in this series are also suitable for use as secondary texts in general courses in apologetics, philosophy, theology, world religions, cults, or biblical studies. Additionally, they will prove beneficial for working pastors and educated lay readers. All of them have been written with an eye to the defense and promotion of doctrinal orthodoxy as well as to the building up of the faith of believers. As such they are intended for both the academy and the church. One of the greatest needs in the church today is to bring heads and hearts together in such a way that Christians are better equipped to serve the Lord Jesus. We hope and pray that the B&H Studies in Christian Apologetics series is a step in that direction.

*Soli Deo Gloria,*
Robert B. Stewart
General Editor

# Acknowledgments

Throughout the duration of this project I have been blessed to have the insights and assistance of a number of great thinkers, among whom are (in no particular order) Bob Stewart, John Depoe, John Churchill, James Noland, Allen Gehring, Hugh McCann, Scott Austin, C. E. Harris, James Aune, Greg Welty, and Heath Thomas. I am appreciative for the time and efforts you spent thinking with me about the contents of this book. I am also thankful for the team at B&H Academic (Chris Cowan and Ray Clendenen). Your editorial assistance makes this volume a better work than it otherwise would have been. Last but not least, many thanks to Bob Stewart for giving me an opportunity to flesh out some of my thoughts regarding the problems of evil and suffering. Bob is a real friend—may his tribe increase.

CHAPTER ONE

# The Problem of Evil: Introductory Issues

## What Do We Mean by Evil?

Christians have generally agreed that evil is not a substance or a thing but instead is a privation of a good thing that God made. A privation of a good is the corruption or twisting of a created thing's essence or substance.[1] Evil, since it is not a thing in itself, is parasitic on the good. There can be good without evil, but there cannot be evil without there being a good upon which it preys. The concept of evil as a privation of the good has been essential in undermining at least one argument against the existence of God from evil, namely that God *caused* evil. The thought is as follows:

- God created only actual things (or substances).
- Evil is not an actual thing (or substance).
- Therefore, God did not create evil.

As a corruption or twisting of what is good, evil is the absence of something that *ought* to be; it is the absence of what fulfills a thing's nature or essence. Evil, as such, is not a *mere lacking* of some quality or characteristic. A snake, for example, lacks arms, but we would not say a snake is deprived of arms. Aquinas explains:

---

[1] See, for example, Thomas Aquinas, *De Malo*, trans. Jean Oesterle (Notre Dame: University of Notre Dame Press, 1995); *Summa Theologica*, trans. by Fathers of the English Dominican Province (London: Burnes and Oates Publishers, 1942); Joseph Bobik, *Aquinas on Matter and Form and Elements: A Translation and Interpretation of the De Principiis Naturae and the De Mixtione Elementorum of St. Thomas Aquinas* (Notre Dame: University of Notre Dame Press, 1998).

> As the term good signifies "perfect being," so the term evil signifies nothing else than "privation of perfect being." In its proper acceptance, privation is still predicated of that which is fitted by its nature to be possessed, and to be possessed at a certain time and in a certain manner. Evidently, therefore, a thing is called evil if it lacks the perfection it ought to have. Thus, if a man lacks the sense of sight, this is an evil for him. But the same lack is not an evil for a stone, for the stone is not equipped by nature to have the faculty of sight.[2]

The potentiality for sight is present in a human but not in a stone; accordingly, since humans have the potentiality for sight, the inability to see is expressed as a privation of sight—it is a perfection that should be in accord with the nature of a particular thing.

While the inability to see is a physical privation, moral failures such as gossiping and slander are expressions of an evil relationship—the privation of rightly relating to one another. Perversion is a state of being due to persistence in moral wrongdoing, which reveals that evil can be in a nature.

A more thorough treatment of the nature of causation and free will are forthcoming in this work. Suffice it to say at this point that the metaphysical view of evil that is expressed here is derivative of the privative view of evil found in Augustine and Aquinas, among others.

## CATEGORIES OF THE DISCUSSION: MORAL AND NATURAL EVIL

### Moral Evil

The first type of evil, and the one most discussed in the relevant literature, is moral evil. Moral evil occurs when free persons misuse their freedom in such a way that the content of their will and/or actions violates a moral standard. The first component of moral evil is the intention formed in the agent to perform an immoral action. An intention is different than a desire. A person can desire something and never intend for the contents of their desires to be a course of life for themselves. For example, having a sexual temptation is not the same thing as having formed an intention to commit an immoral sexual action. The type of desire being described is akin to what Scripture calls a temptation, and being tempted should not be considered the same thing as committing a sin;

---

[2] See Thomas Aquinas, *Compendium Theologia*, trans. Cyril Vollert in *Light of Faith: The Compendium of Theology* (Manchester: Sophia Institute Press, 1993), 114, 125–26.

Jesus was tempted in the same way that we are, and this was not reckoned unto him as sin (Heb 4:15). Forming an intention to commit immoral actions is a hardened concept from a mere desire. A person can, for example, have a desire to act virtuously and never *decide* to act on the desire. When the agent forms an intention, she is moving from having reasons to perform an action to deciding for herself that this is the action she will take.[3] Moral evil is then to be understood as having occurred when an agent intends to perform an action of moral disvalue.

Simply intending to commit an action does not mean that the action necessarily occurs, for there may be an intervening factor that prohibits the action from ever obtaining. For example, when Lynette "Squeaky" Fromme attempted to assassinate Gerald Ford in September of 1975, she never worked the action of her pistol to ensure that a bullet was in the chamber of the gun. When she pulled the trigger nothing happened, as all of the bullets were still in the magazine of the gun. No doubt Fromme had a settled objective to murder President Ford but failed in the endeavor of murdering President Ford. The failure in the act does not mean that her intentions were any less immoral, as the old adage "no harm no foul" might indicate. The moral failure consisted in the forming of the intention to murder. The tactical failure consisted in her not working a gun properly. The same could be said of Sarah Jane Moore, who attempted to assassinate Ford a mere two weeks later and failed to accomplish the attempt because the sights on her gun were off by several inches.

Even though moral evil is first to be categorized as when a person forms the intention to commit an action of moral disvalue, moral evil also involves the content of the action itself when the content of the intention is not mitigated by an intervention of some kind. Suppose, for example, that Squeaky Fromme had chambered a bullet or that Sarah Jane Moore had corrected the sights on her .38. Even though a moral wrong occurred in forming the intention to murder, *suffering* is what occurs when the actions resultant from intended evil are brought about. Suffering has many manifestations. If Ford had been assassinated, his family would have experienced emotional suffering; he would have, perhaps, experienced emotional and physical suffering.

---

[3] The topic discussed here is nuanced, and there are different views about what desires, reasons, intentions, and so forth are. My point here is to take some less controversial features of agency and flesh out their expression in Scripture. For more thorough treatment of these topics, see Hugh McCann, *The Works of Agency* (Ithaca: Cornell University Press, 1998); Timothy O'Connor, *Persons and Causes: The Metaphysics of Free Will* (Oxford: Oxford University Press, 2000), or *Agents, Causes, and Events: Essays on Indeterminism and Free Will* (Oxford: Oxford University Press, 1995); Robert Kane, *The Significance of Free Will* (Oxford: Oxford University Press, 1996); Randolph Clarke, *Libertarian Accounts of Free Will* (Oxford: Oxford University Press, 2003).

The distinction between evil and suffering is an important one, for these terms are not coextensive. There can be evil without suffering, as when the objectives of evil intentions are thwarted. There can be suffering that is not evil, as when a person is imprisoned for committing a serious enough crime to warrant the imprisonment. So a distinction is in order. While the imprisonment of a criminal is a not a *happy* state of affairs, neither is it a *wrong* state of affairs. When a person suffers for a morally sufficient reason, we can agree that the suffering is bad but are not entitled to conclude that it is wrong. Arguments to the extent that the problem of evil is one that reduces to the experience of pain or suffering are not entirely on point, for such reductionist views fail to capture this important distinction. Likewise, there are goods in states of affairs that are not necessarily right. For example, persons that commit adultery usually do so for emotional and physical satisfaction, among other things. Emotional and physical satisfactions are good things, but when they are satisfied through adultery they are *wrong*. Genesis describes the forbidden fruit as "good" for food and desirable for gaining wisdom (Genesis 3). Partaking of the forbidden fruit, though providing these goods, was wrong because it violated a divine command. Moral evil, as such, occurs when an objective moral requirement is vitiated through the intentions (free will) of a person, the *usual* result of which is the suffering of others.

**Natural Evil**

The second category of evil typified in the relevant literature is natural evil. Natural evil is generally accepted as evil resultant from nonhuman causes such as earthquakes, hurricanes, and tornados. Arguments from natural evil against the existence of God usually emphasize the *nonhuman* element in the definition, as it removes free will in the explanation of these events occurring. Such arguments then center the discussion on God's bringing about these states of affairs rather than humans, the intention of which is to indict God for authoring evil.

This understanding of natural evil is admittedly unsatisfying. A hurricane that moves from the African coastline into the Atlantic without ever making landfall or affecting human life in any discernible way is not usually considered to be *evil*. It might be considered bad weather but not evil. So these events are not in themselves evil but take on the label of being evil when they cause human or animal suffering. It is the suffering of sentient beings resulting from these events that might be understood as evil; hurricanes or earthquake are not evil. Perhaps a better understanding of natural evil is to redefine the categories of its expression to include the following:

- There are violent, natural states of affairs that produce human suffering, and human suffering that is not connected to one's personal misconduct is wrong.
- There are violent, natural states of affairs that produce human suffering, and human suffering that is derived from these states of affairs *that are also connected to human misconduct* is bad but not necessarily wrong.
- There are violent, natural states of affairs that never affect any human in any negative way that are caused by the misuse of human free will.
- There are violent, natural states of affairs that never affect any human in any negative way that are not caused by the misuse of human free will.

A larger taxonomy is, no doubt, available. These distinctions, however, help clear up some issues attendant to the problem of natural evil, at least as far as how natural evil is to be conceived. Nature, as an impersonal force, does not commit evil. One question concerns how nature responds to human evil, including humans abusing the earth and the effects that yields. Another question concerns other agents that might be a factor in nature's behavior that produce human suffering. For example, in Job 1 Satan causes a great wind that destroys the house Job's children are in, effectually causing their deaths. In the same chapter a lightning strike kills sheep and their attendants (v. 16). Free will must be factored in as a possible explanation of natural evil at least some of the time. When free will is at issue, then nature becomes a means by which moral evil is brought about; a hurricane in the hands of an evil agent such as Satan is as efficient for destruction as a gas chamber in the hands of Hitler.

We will return to the topics of moral evil and natural evil in later chapters. Suffice it to say at this point that the words "natural evil" are unsatisfying, for they fail to take a range of issues into consideration. The chapter on natural evil will address this problem.

## DISTINGUISHING BETWEEN A DEFENSE AND A THEODICY

Scholars traditionally distinguish a defense from a theodicy.[4] A theodicy is an attempt to justify the ways of God in light of the vast amounts of evil

---

[4] This distinction received its clearest expression in Alvin Plantinga, *God, Freedom, and Evil* (Grand Rapids: Eerdmans, 1974).

we find in the world. A theodicy, as it were, attempts to answer the question "why." Theodicies are thus offensive rather than defensive in approach. It is generally true that when people are suffering they want an answer to the question why. Taking the approach of a theodicy implies accepting the burden of proof concomitant with the intention of the project. The theodicist is not so much claiming "it might be the case that" as she is claiming "it is the case that." The strength of this claim reveals how high the bar is raised, for it is purporting to express God's own thoughts about the matter and not just what the theodicist supposes are God's thoughts about the matter. This is not to say that only one line of thought is permissible in developing a theodicy, such that, for example, the free will theodicy is the only legitimate theodicy. As will be noted in a moment, there are inferential relationships among several theodicies. The point here is simply to express the scope of the project in theodicy and why some are suspicious that such a case will never be offered on this side of heaven.

A defense, as one might guess, is not an attempt to explain what God is up to in permitting evil, but instead tries to provide rationally compelling reasons to question the soundness of the argument from evil against the existence of God. Rather than make suggestions about God's reasons for permitting evil, a defensive strategy generally arrives at the conclusion that the atheist's objection from evil is either inconclusive or logically fallacious. Accordingly, the primary strategy for defenses is to undermine an argument, and only secondarily is a defense interested in offering answers to the "why" question.

In the following sections I will develop the rationale behind several theodicies. It is not my intention to argue for any one of these theodicies but to provide a descriptive survey as a resource for some of the most prominent lines of thought in the Christian tradition. Indeed, my view differs from each of these in a number of respects, but that is an issue that will be taken up at a later time.

## The Punishment Theodicy

The first theodicy we will consider is the punishment theodicy, according to which some suffering is a result of divine punishment for sin. Brief consideration of Scripture may warrant such a perspective. In Exodus we find "I will punish them for their sin"; Isaiah explains, "I will punish the world for its evil"; Jeremiah warns of God punishing Israel "as your deeds deserve."[5] Moreover, traditionally attendant to this view is the doctrine of hell, whereby God's wrath is poured out on those who reject Christ. Paul says:

---

[5] Exod 32:34; Isa 13:11; Jer 21:14. All biblical quotations are taken from the NIV unless otherwise noted.

He will punish those who do not know God and do not obey the gospel of our Lord Jesus. They will be punished with everlasting destruction and shut out from the presence of the Lord and from the glory of his might on the day he comes to be glorified in his holy people and to be marveled at among all those who have believed.[6]

Michael Murray and Michael Rea explain that defenders of the punishment theodicy provide several reasons punishment can be good, including rehabilitation, deterrence, societal protection, and retribution.[7] Rehabilitation, for example, results in the sinner coming to grips with the wrongness of her actions and transforms her character from that way of life to a morally transformed life. Supposedly this is the principle under which the American judicial system functions when detaining persons for criminal misconduct. In any case, the greater good of punishment for the purpose of rehabilitation is that it benefits the wrongdoer first and secondarily the society in which he or she lives.[8] Through punishment moral transformation is made possible.

As for deterrence and societal protection, the punitive benefits are not for the criminal per se but for those who are harmed or could possibly be harmed by the criminal. If we take punishment to be action-deterring, it could be that deterrence occurs in others who would have been likely to perform the same actions (e.g., there are death penalty arguments made on the principle of deterrence). Considering the fate that has befallen others who have invested in wrongful deeds leads the would-be wrongdoer to consider whether or not she wants the same fate to befall her if she were caught. In a literal sense, the wrongdoer that is punished is deterred as well, especially if the punishment is death. The difference between strict deterrence and rehabilitation is that deterrence is not so much directed at character formation as it is consequence avoidance.

A third benefit of punishment, like deterrence, is geared more toward the benefit of others than that of the wrongdoer. If criminals are incarcerated, and appropriate measures are taken, then presumably their ability to exact more wrongs is limited given their confinement.[9] An extension of this argument has an eschatological ring, in that hell is often considered a place where the

---

[6] 2 Thess 1:8–10.

[7] Michael Murray and Michael Rea, *An Introduction to the Philosophy of Religion* (Cambridge: Cambridge University Press, 2008), 170.

[8] See William Alston, "The Inductive Argument from Evil and the Human Cognitive Condition," in *Philosophical Perspectives*, vol. 5 of *Philosophy of Religion*, ed. James E. Toberlin (Atascadero, CA: Ridgeview, 1991): 29–67.

[9] Murray and Rea, *Introduction to the Philosophy of Religion*, 171.

viciousness of humanity's depravity is quarantined so that the harmful intentions of the reprobate cannot be carried out on another person. This requires, of course, that hell is a place of isolation and that the benefits of societal protection are not to include the wrongdoer himself, for presumably the wrongdoer can still harm himself in hell. The telling feature of hell is that one may make an argument from it (the greater) to other instances of lesser suffering, and in doing so undermine other arguments from evil which suggest that the amount and intensity of suffering are beyond what is needed for any divinely appointed purpose. This issue will be addressed in the chapter on hell.

As for retributive theories of punishment, when people commit crimes they usually incur in penalty more than what was taken in the act itself. Theft, for instance, often results in a fine that is greater than the amount stolen in the first place, if not resulting in incarceration.[10] Part of the rationale behind the retributive theory of justice is that when a criminal act occurs, more than just the obvious harm is actually done. It is not so much that $500 was stolen from the house during the burglary, but a sense of violation and insecurity of well-being in the house after the invasion normally follows. Exacting an extra measure beyond what is directly evident in wrongdoing goes to insure justice will be served.[11]

The idea of punishment has explanatory power, and since an all-powerful, knowledgeable, good God is the exactor of punishment, then the pitfalls that usually attend the human judicial system do not apply. God knows how to fit the penalty to the crime. In fact, part of the argument from evil against the existence of God hinges on the problem of divine justice. Why do the wicked prosper, and why do the righteous suffer? Implicit in such questions is a principle of justice, presumably conjoined with the belief that the wicked should be punished and the righteous rewarded. If this is correct, then intense suffering that results from human sin is a live option in theodicy—the only detail is discerning its place of application.

## The Free-Will Theodicy

The second theodicy is the free-will theodicy. According to the free-will theodicy, God is justified in permitting evil and its consequences because "he has to do so if he is to bestow on some of his creatures the incommensurable privilege of being responsible agents who have, in many areas, the capacity

---

[10] Ibid.
[11] Ibid.

to choose as they will, without God, or anyone else (other than themselves), determining which alternative they choose."[12] When Adam partakes of the fruit in Genesis 3, the most severe charge brought against God is not that he caused Adam to sin, but that in making Adam significantly free God brought about the possibility that Adam might misappropriate his freedom and choose a course of action that is morally wrong. God is not responsible for Adam's choices given that Adam was endowed in creation with self-determining free will. The ground for denying God's causing evil is that human freedom is conceptually incompatible with divine determinism (not divine sovereignty). Otherwise stated, determined choices are not free.

Solidifying a free-will theodicy usually requires assent to the idea that being significantly free is intrinsically valuable rather than fleshing out the value of freedom from how people exercise it, that is, from freedom's instrumental value. If it is intrinsically better to be significantly free than not, then questions concerning divine decisions in creation are asked and answered; objections from the abuse of freedom are derived from a category confusion regarding freedom's intrinsic value with the ends that come as a result of misappropriating it.

Even so, we value human freedom instrumentally in that it enables us to choose a path for our lives, allows for unique contributions to the human story, and is the source and origin of relationship development. The dissonance about freedom is that we love its benefits and hate its deficits, at least as far as instrumental value is concerned. If we center the discussion on the consequences of freedom rather than what freedom is, it is far from clear that God has not faltered in his providence. After all, God could allow immoral actions and then remove the harmful consequences of those actions. Freedom is preserved, and intense suffering is avoided. While such a view agrees that freedom is valuable, it denies that allowing actions to have harmful consequences justifies permitting the free act.

For example, if I freely burn down my neighbors' house while they are on vacation, God can miraculously rebuild the house so that my neighbors never knew or dealt with the ramifications of their house being burned down. Freedom is preserved, and consequences are avoided. Consider the rape and murder of a five-year-old girl. There is nothing logically problematic with asserting that God permits the rapist to commit the rape and to succeed in her subsequent murder, during which God disables the girl from ever being conscious of her rape and strangulation—and revives her upon her death without her ever knowing anything happened to her. Freedom is preserved, and consequences

---

[12] Alston, "Inductive Argument from Evil," 48–49.

are avoided. Since the visceral reaction against the free-will theodicy centers on the negative consequences of freedom's application, let us call this new construal of God's activity a "nonconsequence world."

Several problems attend a nonconsequence world. First, the objection does not address the free-will theodicy at all but questions the lack of divine intervention. Notice that each suggestion indicates something *God* can do to mitigate the effects of free decisions, which says nothing at all about the nature of human freedom or the agent performing the act in question.

Suppose, for the sake of argument, that we allow the question about divine intervention to remain, and we suggest that God override the consequences of our actions while still permitting our freedom to exist full force. The scenario envisioned here makes our world much like the famous pleasure machine scenario—where all of our experiences are either directly pleasurable or transformed into a pleasurable experience. In such a world we would not have any recourse from committing horrendous evils because we would not know the seriousness of the ensuing harm from acting in such a way. Admittedly the moral status of actions is not governed solely by the ends of our actions; however, we certainly deliberate about the consequences of our actions upon the well-being of others and ourselves. In other words, the suggestion that God stamp out bad consequences, albeit a freedom preserving proposal, undermines our ability to make significant moral choices.

Proponents of a nonconsequence world should expect God to make acts such as rape a pleasure for the victim either directly through the sex act or indirectly through psychological manipulation. In doing so, another critique is leveraged; the proposal effectually strips the moral accountability between the perpetrator and his victim as well as what the definition of rape entails.

To use a less chafing example, suppose I steal my neighbor's birdfeeder after a squirrel breaks my own. Before choosing to steal the birdfeeder I recognize that my action is morally wrong—I am not confused about the moral status of the action. Sometime after I steal the birdfeeder, my conscience gets the better of me; I return the birdfeeder to my neighbor (with a bag of birdseed as a gesture). The only discernible response I should receive from my neighbor upon my returning the birdfeeder is one of utter perplexity; for if God replaces the stolen birdfeeder to prevent the material and emotional harm caused by the action, then my ability to set things right will be completely undermined. My neighbor will have no concept of ever having been wronged or perceive any need for apology or remuneration.[13] What is more, it is hard to see how

---

[13] Murray and Rea, *Introduction to the Philosophy of Religion*, 174.

I could ever actually discern that my action was worthy of reproach to begin with, for if God "undoes" the negative consequences of evil choices, then presumably the wrongdoer will benefit from this undoing as well. The line of thought is as follows: one of the harmful consequences of my choices is the effects these choices have on me. Not only is it true that malformed decisions adversely affect my character; the ability to concede one evil action makes it more probable that I will make another concession in my future deliberations and choices. In an effort to stall this decline of character, God must undo the harmful effects of my own choices on me. Such an action would be a literal divine recreation of my character such that any of my future wrong decisions would have nothing to do with my previous deliberations and choices. For this suggestion to pass muster, God would have to be the ultimate revisionist historian. These reasons, and more, provide compelling grounds to question the claim that God can undo the harmful nature of free decisions while guarding the integrity of freedom itself.

## THE NATURAL-LAW THEODICY

A third theodicy is called the natural-law theodicy, according to which there is a double effect from human participation in a lawlike natural order. In his excellent work *Evil and a Good God*, Bruce Reichenbach explains that from the natural law:

> The possibility arises that sentient creatures like ourselves can be negatively affected by the outworking of these laws in nature, such that we experience pain, suffering, disability, disutility, and at times the frustration of our good desires. Since a world with free persons making choices between moral good and evil and choosing a significant amount of moral good is better than a world created without free persons and moral good and moral evil, God in creating had to create a world which operated according to natural laws to achieve a higher good. Thus, his action of creation of a natural world and a natural order, along with the resulting pain and pleasure which we experience, is justified. The natural evils which afflict us—diseases, sickness, disasters, birth defects—are all the outworking of the natural system of which we are a part. They are the byproducts made possible but that which is necessary for the greater good.[14]

---

[14] Bruce Reichenbach, *Evil and a Good God* (New York: Fordham University Press, 1982), 100–101.

As it were, the same fire that produces heat in our homes and cooks our food can also burn us if we put our hands in it, and as such may serve as a theodicy for *natural* evil.

It has also been argued that the natural law provides the conditions for the exercise of human freedom. The natural order can be regular enough to "provide the degree of predictability required for morally significant choice even if there are exceptions to the regularities."[15] Even if God can "put aside" the regularities via miraculous intervention and save a suffering animal, he could not intervene in every instance of suffering wrought from the natural law without thereby undermining its predictability. God saving a dying fawn from being burned by forest fire started by a lightning strike by no means indicates that he could intervene in every such occurrence of natural evil; God has strong reason in each case from doing this; for if he didn't, he would have no reason for letting nature usually take its course.[16] What atheists must then express is a justification for their belief that God would have a morally sufficient reason to make an exception to the natural law; providing such an account can be quite daunting, given that our range of perception on individual events and their relationship to the whole is aggravatingly limited. We can speculate about the logical possibility of God's intervention without giving careful attention to the metaphysical implications of God's intervention, and it is the metaphysical structure of reality that is of interest here. Consider William Alston's clarifying point:

> To use a well-worn example, it may be metaphysically necessary that the chemical composition of water is $H_2O$ since that is what water essentially is, even though, given the ordinary use of the concept of water, we can without contradiction or unintelligibility, think of water as made up of carbon and chlorine. Roughly speaking, what is conceptually or logically (in a narrow sense of "logical") possible depends on what things are like in themselves, their essential natures, regardless of how they are expressed in our thought and language.[17]

Determining what is logically possible may not be too difficult. Determining metaphysically possible "alternative systems" of the natural order may be a project beyond our abilities. Can there be conscious, volitional, sentient beings that are also unable to feel pain but still appreciate those experiences that are pleasurable or produce happiness? As Alston and others propose, suggesting

---

[15] Alston, "Inductive Argument from Evil," 53.
[16] Ibid.
[17] Ibid., 55.

that we have so much as a clue about these kinds of questions betrays our ignorance of the depths of the questions involved.

## THE SOUL-MAKING THEODICY

John Hick has championed a view known as the soul-making theodicy. Proponents of the soul-making theodicy predicate their view on the "creation of humankind through an evolutionary process as an immature creature living in a challenging and therefore person-making world."[18] This assumes a two-stage conception of the creation of humankind; mankind was first created in the image of God, and later into the likeness of God.[19] The first stage is the progression of *Homo sapiens* through the gradual process of evolution, which produced a more complex brain, moral awareness, and more successful adaptive measures than found in other animals. This stage of human existence was a "potentiality" for knowledge of God and having a relationship with him unlike being created from the start as fully mature and moral beings.[20] The second stage is the current stage of *Homo sapiens*, where the process of evolution has produced an intelligent, moral, and spiritual animal that bears the likeness of God.[21]

Hick's soul-making theodicy is a drastic shift from previous theodicies, for unlike the free-will theodicy, it does not start with morally responsible beings but concludes that through this process we become morally responsible beings—our souls are, as the argument suggests, *made* through trials and tribulations. So why does God create humans in this immature state? Hick contends that the hard-won virtues are the virtues worth having, and it is in the "relationships with human beings with one another, in a context of this struggle to survive and flourish, that they can develop higher values of mutual love and care, of self-sacrifice for others, and of commitment to a common good."[22] The divine plan through which this occurs involves four conditions:

1. The divine intention in relation to humankind, according to our hypothesis, is to create perfect finite personal beings in filial relationship with their Maker.

---

[18] John Hick, "A Soul-Making Theodicy," in *The Philosophy of Religion Reader*, ed. Chad Meister (New York: Routledge, 2008), 538.
[19] Ibid., 539.
[20] Ibid.
[21] Ibid., 540.
[22] Ibid., 545.

2. It is logically impossible for humans to be created already in this perfect state because in its spiritual aspect it involves coming freely to an uncoerced consciousness of God from an epistemic distance, and in its moral aspect, freely choosing the good in preference to evil.
3. Accordingly the human being was initially created through the evolutionary process, as a spiritually and morally immature creature, and as part of a world which is both religiously ambiguous and ethically demanding.
4. Thus that one is morally imperfect (i.e., that there is moral evil), and that the world is a challenging and even dangerous environment (i.e., that there is natural evil), are necessary aspects of the present stage of the process through which God is gradually creating perfected finite beings.[23]

The messy and time-consuming nature of this endeavor in soul making will likely not be fulfilled on this side of heaven, thus if the "unity of humankind in God's presence is ever to be realized it will have to be in some sphere of existence other than our earth."[24]

Other than some nonintuitive features of the basic argument, several ideas contained in this view are invoked on a consistent basis. The virtue of patience is developed through circumstances in which our patience is tested. The virtue of courage is developed in the face of danger. The virtue of loyalty is developed through trials that test our commitments to family and friends. The experience of evil is inextricably connected to the development of these character traits and, as such, provides a morally sufficient reason for God's permitting the evil that pervades our world.

## CONCLUSION

It is not my intention to endorse any one of the theodicies described in this chapter but to provide the reader with some idea of the major developments pertaining to the problem of evil and the problem of human suffering. As the argument progresses in this book, each of these theodicies will have its place. Indeed, it is my contention that no one theodicy suffices to answer the problem of evil, but that each theodicy has its application in particular domains of the conversation. I will allow this line of thinking to develop with the flow of the book.

---

[23] Ibid.
[24] Ibid., 547.

CHAPTER TWO

# The Logical Problem of Evil

The problem of evil, or the argument from evil, suggests an incompatibility between the perfect-making properties of God and the fact that evil exists. In this chapter we will respond to one of the earliest and potentially most devastating arguments from evil, commonly referred to as the logical problem of evil (LPE). Consider the following summary of J. L. Mackie's famous argument:

> In its simplest form the argument is this: God is omnipotent; God is wholly good; yet evil exists. There seems to be some contradiction between these three propositions such that if any two of them were true, the third would be false. But at the same time all three are essential parts of most theological positions; the theological, it seems at once, must adhere and cannot consistently adhere to all three.[1]

Why not? Mackie continues:

> Is God willing to prevent evil, but not able? Then he is impotent. Is he able, but not willing? Then he is malevolent. Is he both able and willing? Whence then is evil?[2]

To make the argument as precise as possible, Mackie is claiming that it is *logically* impossible for all of the following to be true at the same time (called the theistic set):

---

[1] J. L. Mackie, "Evil and Omnipotence," *Mind* 64 (1955): 200.
[2] Ibid.

1. God is all-powerful.
2. God is all-knowing.
3. God is all-good.
4. Evil exists.

The concepts that theists are deploying simply do not cohere with the presence of evil. If God were truly all knowing, powerful and good, evil would not exist at all. However, evil exists; therefore, the traditional doctrine of God espoused by Christians contains a contradiction.

If the argument made by Mackie is successful, then belief in God is as logically false as if we were to believe that a square contains only three sides. If the propositions contained in (1) through (4) are logically inconsistent, we may conclude that it is *necessarily* the case that God does not exist.

## ALVIN PLANTINGA AND THE FREE-WILL DEFENSE

What we can see from Mackie's presentation is that there is the appearance of a contradiction in affirming the theistic set. After all, Mackie's claims are intuitive. However, what does it mean to say that the beliefs contained in the theistic set are inconsistent? One possibility is that the set contains an explicit contradiction. For example, it is logically impossible to affirm that I both exist and do not exist in the same time and in the same way.[3] Applying this principle to the theistic set, we can see that the theist has not committed any such contradiction. We have not, for example, affirmed that God is both omniscient and yet not omniscient. Indeed, beliefs such as these are explicitly contradictory. Nor has such a logical blunder occurred in affirming God's power or goodness.

Another possibility, and one that is more promising for Mackie's argument, is to elicit an implicit contradiction from the theistic set. To envisage an implicit contradiction consider the following set of propositions:

(8) George is older than Paul.
(9) Paul is older than Nick.
(10) George is not older than Nick.[4]

The sense in which this set of beliefs is inconsistent is that it is not possible that all of the members of the set can be true in the same time and in the same way. In fact, it is necessarily true that

---

[3] Alvin Plantinga, *God, Freedom, and Evil* (Grand Rapids: Eerdmans, 1974), 12. I am following Plantinga's numbered propositions throughout this chapter.
[4] Ibid., 14.

(11) If George is older than Paul, and Paul is older than Nick, then George is older than Nick.[5]

Here we notice a relation of ideas that draw out the implicit, logical contradiction contained in (8) through (10), for we cannot simultaneously endorse (8) through (10) without the ideas contained in the propositions necessarily contradicting one another. Much the same reasoning is being leveled against the existence of an omniperfect God. The idea is something like the following:

(12) If God exists, he is omniscient, omnipotent, and omnibenevolent.
(13) An omniscient being has the prior knowledge of evil to prevent evil.
(14) An omnipotent being has the ability to prevent evil.
(15) An omnibenevolent being has the desire to prevent evil.
(16) Therefore, if there were a God, there would be no evil.
(17) There is evil.
(18) Thus, necessarily there is no God.

The argument is valid; if we assume the truth of the premises then the conclusion follows from those premises. However, the question is whether or not the argument is sound; that is, are there sufficient reasons to reject what is given in the premises?

Earlier we noted two possibilities for a belief set to be contradictory—that it contains either an implicit or explicit contradiction. So, if the very concept of God, when conjoined with the existence of evil, yields one of these types of contradictions, then it is impossible (logically) to affirm the existence of God. This is why the conclusion in (18) is worded so strongly. The nonexistence of God, if the argument passes muster, is necessary.

So what must the theist provide to circumvent this full-on logical assault? The answer is that the theist must provide an account whereby all of (12) through (17) are maintained and yet the existence of God is shown to be *possible*. In order to accomplish this task, it must be shown that the theistic set above is a logically consistent set of beliefs, in this case providing an explanation that makes the coexistence of evil and God possible. Before turning to this task, three provisos are important regarding what is needed to be successful to defeat the LPE: (1) Theists need not prove that their response to the LPE is true; it only needs to be possibly true. (2) Theists are not required to believe

---

[5] Ibid.

their explanation as to how evil and God can logically coexist. (This sounds counterintuitive, but we are dealing with logical relationships between ideas, not our beliefs.) (3) Only one explanation is required if it shows that the existence of God and evil are compatible; that is, if one suggestion proves that God and evil may possibly coexist, then it is not impossible that God and evil coexist.

Admittedly, it is an added perk if we can prove our suggestion to be true and that we believe what we are saying in response, but such is not required for the task at hand. We are merely providing what the burden of proof requires, which in this case is a defense. Rather than justifying the ways of God in light of evil, it will be sufficient to demonstrate that the argument against belief in God does not work. In *God, Freedom, and Evil* Alvin Plantinga provided the logical leverage for the theist to claim that evil does not serve as a disproof of the existence of God. This leverage is derived from what is known as the free-will defense (FWD).

According to Plantinga, God has a morally sufficient reason for permitting the evils that surround us, namely that he created humans significantly free, and freedom is of great intrinsic value. Moreover, given that he created us free, it opened up the possibility that something might go wrong in the exercise of that freedom. To quote Plantinga:

> A world containing creatures who are significantly free (and freely perform more good than evil actions) is more valuable, all else being equal, than a world containing no free creatures at all. Now God can create free creatures, but he can't cause or determine them to do only what is right. For if he does so, then they aren't significantly free after all; they do not do what is right freely. To create creatures capable of moral good therefore, he must create creatures capable of moral evil and he can't give these creatures the freedom to perform evil and at the same time prevent them from doing so.[6]

In essence, to eliminate evil God would have to eliminate significant freedom as well. More pointedly, what Plantinga elicits is a specific kind of freedom, what is traditionally called libertarian freedom. According to libertarianism, in order for an agent to be free with respect to an action, it must be within that agent's power either to perform or to refrain from performing that action. Accordingly, there was nothing necessary about Adam's act of eating the forbidden fruit.

---

[6] Ibid., 30.

Thus, under Plantinga's definition of freedom, it becomes logically impossible for the theist to affirm both that God created humans significantly free and that God would eliminate evil when free creatures exercise their freedom in a morally repellent way. God's creation of humans with significant freedom only means that he created a set of circumstances whereby evil may occur; it does not mean he determined it to occur. By parity of reasoning, we do not incarcerate parents for murders that their children perform under the auspices that by conceiving the child they therefore brought about the murder.

But one wonders why free creatures cannot always choose what is right. After all, since we are dealing with logical possibilities, isn't it possible for God to create humans significantly free such that they always exercise their freedom in a morally positive way? There is nothing incoherent about this suggestion, for significant freedom does not entail that actions of negative value must be chosen, only that they might be. Consider a world in which God created humans and they always choose what is right! Mackie suggests:

> If God had made men such that in their free choices they sometimes prefer what is good and sometimes what is evil, why could he not have made them such that they always freely choose the good? If there is no logical impossibility in a man's choosing the good on one, or on several occasions, there cannot be a logical impossibility in his freely choosing the good on every occasion. God was not, then, faced with the choice between making innocent automata and making beings who, in acting freely, would sometimes go wrong; there was open to him the obviously better possibility of making beings who would act freely but always go right. Clearly, his failure to avail himself of this possibility is inconsistent with his being both omnipotent and perfectly good.[7]

It is important to draw out some principles that are implicit in Mackie's argument. Clearly, what Mackie has in mind about freedom is different from what Plantinga has given attention to defend. Recall that Plantinga's argument is that God could not have created creatures significantly free and eliminated the possibility of moral evil without at the same time eliminating a greater good (in this case, creatures having libertarian freedom). Mackie's suggestion here indicates a compatibilist view of human freedom. If we ask, "Could God have created creatures to prefer always what is right?" (as indicated in the Mackie quote above) even the theist must respond, "Yes." God could have causally determined all desires, thus guaranteeing that every decision would

---

[7] See Mackie, "Evil and Omnipotence," 209.

be morally right. Insofar as this is a possible world, Mackie wonders why it isn't the actual world. Why didn't God create a "compatibilist world" where our desires are determined beyond our control, and yet we are still considered free insofar as we always choose something according to our greatest desire?

Though the conversation is nuanced, when we speak of possible worlds we are describing a complete set of states of affairs from the way the world is to the way the world could have been. What this means is that there are states of affairs ranging over worlds that are mutually exclusive from one another (in terms of the choices made and the values pertaining to those choices). For example, in the actual world (call it $W_1$). Oswald shoots Kennedy on that infamous November day in 1963. However, in another world (call it $W_2$), no such action ever takes place; Kennedy passes by the Texas Schoolbook Depository with nothing but fanfare. What is true of both $W_1$ and $W_2$ is that both are possible worlds in the logical sense, but only $W_1$ is actual.

Why is it helpful to speak of possible worlds? It helps because it explains how human choices might be characterized as free and how the propositions that capture human choices can be understood (both in terms of their truth values and when comparing one world to another). Consider Michael Peterson:

> Possible worlds contain some interesting features. For example, a proposition p is possible if it is true in at least one world and impossible if true in none. A proposition p is necessary if it is true in all possible worlds. Another feature of possible worlds is that persons as well as other things exist in them. Clearly, each of us exists in the actual world, but we might also exist in a great many worlds distinct from the actual world. These other worlds are simply possible, but unactual.[8]

With all of this in mind, we must ask whether God, the all-good, all-powerful, all-wise Creator can actualize (bring about) any possible world. Deterministic worlds aside, we must wonder if God could actualize a world of significantly free creatures each of which always chooses the right course of action. If in fact God has created us significantly free, then God has chosen to make us in such a way that he will not violate that freedom. As such, God does not cause us to choose what is right, anymore than he causes us to choose what is wrong. Literally construed, he creates us with the ability to choose and confers existence on the content of our choices. But in doing so, he has limited himself in terms of the states of affairs that even he can bring about.

---

[8] Michael Peterson, *God and Evil: An Introduction to the Issues* (Boulder, CO: Westview Press, 1998), 38.

Consider again our earlier case study of Oswald shooting Kennedy. Let's say that if Oswald is offered the job at the depository in $W_1$, and accepts, then he will shoot Kennedy. Further, let's say that in $W_2$ Oswald is offered the job at the depository, and he declines the job and does not shoot Kennedy. What we have in $W_1$ and $W_2$ are worlds that are identical except in how Oswald responds to the job offer and the subsequent shooting (or nonshooting) of Kennedy. If Oswald rejects the job offer and does not shoot Kennedy, then even God cannot actualize the states of affairs in $W_1$. Of course, this is no more an indictment against God's power than his inability to create circular squares. That being said, consider the magnitude of the divine task of deliberating over possible worlds of creation and discerning the likelihood that there is one world where nothing goes wrong for an indefinite amount of time, ranging over a multitude of moral options. This makes the next idea from Plantinga seem more reasonable, namely that every human possibly suffers from transworld depravity. Transworld depravity is defined accordingly:

> If an essence *E* suffers from transworld depravity, then it was not within God's power to actualize a possible world *W* such that *E* contains the properties *is significantly free in W* and *always does what is right in W*.[9]

It is not Plantinga's claim that transworld depravity is true, only that it is possible—and that it is possible that for every world God could have created, every essence in every world possibly suffers from transworld depravity. If transworld depravity is possibly true, then not even God could make it the case that significantly free creatures always do what is right in every possible world.

## Conclusion

Let us recall that the argument provided by Mackie is deductive, which means the conclusion necessarily follows from the premises if the argument goes through. It is the task of the theist to provide an account whereby it is possible for a perfect God and evil to coexist. Plantinga suggests that it is possible that God created humans significantly free; therefore, it cannot be true both that these creatures are significantly free and that he prevents them from choosing and acting in a morally repellent way. Free will makes the existence of evil possible. However, if God intervenes on these choices and actions, then the agent cannot be considered significantly free. Such a proposal, by every standard of measurement, makes the possibility of evil and God tenable.

---

[9] Plantinga, *God, Freedom, and Evil*, 53.

Suppose, though, that you do not endorse Plantinga's model of freedom; you think that we are determined in all we choose. Such a claim is beside the point. As we have noted, Plantinga's defense must only be *logically* possible; it does not have to be true to counter the claims of Mackie. If it is purported that God and evil are impossible to reconcile, simply offer a possibility for their reconciliation. Defending the truth of the suggestion is icing on the cake.

In this chapter we developed the logical problem of evil and provided the most formidable response to this objection, namely the free-will defense. It should be noted that the LPE is a relic of the past. Even J. L. Mackie, who formulated the LPE in its most precise form, decidedly rejected his own thesis in his later work, effectually conceding that the problem of evil does *not* show that the central doctrines of theism are logically inconsistent with one another given the reality of evil.[10]

---

[10] J. L. Mackie, *The Miracle of Theism* (Oxford: Clarendon Press, 1982), 150.

CHAPTER THREE

# The Evidential Problem of Evil

It is almost universally agreed that evil is logically compatible with the existence of God. However, the more troubling arguments from evil against theism take a different shape than the logical problem of evil. Rather than purporting to show the logical problems that surface from evil, evidential arguments (EA) from evil intend to show that the pervasiveness of evil makes it *less likely* that God exists. It is claimed that the amount of evil and the apparent existence of gratuitous evil provide rational grounds for rejecting theism as a viable option for rational belief.

The best expression of the EA is from William Rowe, who makes the following argument:

1. There exist instances of intense suffering which an omnipotent, omniscient being could have prevented without thereby losing some greater good or permitting some evil equally bad or worse.
2. An omniscient, wholly good being would prevent the occurrence of any intense suffering it could, unless it could not do so without thereby losing some greater good or permitting some evil equally bad or worse.
3. Therefore, there does not exist an omnipotent, omniscient, wholly good being.[1]

To solidify this argument we are invited to consider two kinds of evil we find throughout our experience, namely the suffering of humans and animals. As for human suffering, Rowe recounts the story of "Sue,"[2] a five-year-old girl who was raped and beaten by her mother's boyfriend. For our purposes, the entire report is worth noting:

---

[1] William Rowe, *Philosophy of Religion: An Introduction* (Belmont, CA: Wadsworth Publishers, 1978), 87.
[2] This is not her real name but was assigned to her by William Alston.

> [Consider] a little girl in Flint, Michigan who was severely beaten, raped, and then strangled by her mother's boyfriend on New Year's Day of 1986. The girl's mother was living with her boyfriend, another man who was unemployed, her two children, and her nine-month old infant fathered by the boyfriend. On New Year's Eve all three adults were drinking at a bar near the woman's home. The boyfriend had been taking drugs and drinking heavily. He was asked to leave the bar at 8:00 p.m. After several reappearances he finally stayed away for good about 9:30 p.m. The woman and the unemployed man remained at the bar until 2:00 a.m. at which time the woman went home and the man to a party at a neighbor's home. Perhaps out of jealousy, the boyfriend attacked the woman when she walked in the house. Her brother was there and broke up the fight by hitting the boyfriend who was passed out and slumped over a table when the brother left. Later the boyfriend attacked the woman again, and this time she knocked him unconscious. After checking the children, she went to bed. Later the woman's five-year-old girl went downstairs to go to the bathroom. The unemployed man returned from the party at 3:45 a.m. and found the five-year-old girl dead. She had been raped, severely beaten over most of her body, and strangled to death by the boyfriend.[3]

This story recounts a state of affairs that is, as proponents of EA argue, intrinsically evil. Even if the rape and murder of the little girl leads to some greater good, we are left to wonder whether the ends justify the means, for presumably God could attain those ends without her being attacked and killed. The story of Sue represents not only the problem of human suffering; it represents the problem of moral evil as well.

In the second instance of evil, we are invited to consider the case of Bambi, an innocent fawn that gets trapped under falling timber that is burning as a result of a lightning strike somewhere in the forest. It is not only true that Bambi is burned, but he remains trapped under the fallen trees for several days before being relieved of his suffering through death. The story of Bambi not only represents the problem of animal suffering; it also represents the problem of natural evil.

What these two cases purportedly show is that the suffering involved in each circumstance is unnecessary. There either is (1) no morally sufficient reason for which these evils are permitted, or (2) even if there is a morally sufficient reason for permitting these evils, God could attain those ends without the requisite suffering supposedly necessary to bring about those ends. It is not

---

[3] Documented in Bruce Russell, "The Persistent Problem of Evil," *Faith and Philosophy* 6 (1989): 123.

just the extent of the suffering involved that is troubling. There is the further concern that proposing a model of divine providence that justifies these actions in light of an end that results from them treats the victims as means toward that end, rather than as ends in themselves.

Let us return to the argument proposed earlier and how that plays out regarding these two cases. The first premise of the argument has garnered most of the attention in the literature due to the fact that it makes a claim about how the world really is. According to Rowe, there are instances of gratuitous evil. This is not a claim that there *might* be instances of gratuitous evil; in fact, *there are* instances of gratuitous evil, that is, evil that is not necessary for the attainment of a greater good, or for which no greater good ever obtains. Since Rowe contends that gratuitous evil is incompatible with the existence of a perfect and provident God, then one instance of gratuitous evil rationally counts against the tenability of theism. So why does Rowe think there are gratuitous evils? Reflecting on the cases of Bambi and Sue, he writes that these instances of horrific suffering permit the following judgment:

> [P] No good state of affairs we know of is such that an omnipotent, omniscient, wholly good being's obtaining it would morally justify that being's permitting [Bambi] or [Sue].[4]

According to Rowe, we have *good reasons* to think that P is true, and not "just that we can't see how some good we know about (say, my enjoyment of smelling a fine cigar) would justify an omnipotent being's permitting" Bambi and Sue to suffer.[5] The essence of P is that we can see "how such a good would *not* justify an omnipotent being's permitting" Bambi or Sue to suffer.[6] For example, God does not need Sue to be raped and murdered if the morally sufficient good in mind is that she be united with God in heaven. God could, in the tradition of Elijah or Enoch, whisk her away to heaven without her ever having to experience these horrors at all. As Rowe claims, "The good states of affairs I know of, when I reflect on them, meet one or both of the following conditions: either an omnipotent being could obtain them without having to permit [Bambi] or [Sue], or obtaining them wouldn't morally justify that being from permitting" their suffering.[7] So even if heaven is the outweighing good, as

---

[4] William Rowe, "Ruminations about Evil," in *Philosophical Perspectives,* vol. 5 of *Philosophy of Religion* (Atascadero, CA: Ridgeview, 1991), 69–88. Rowe refers to these cases as E1 and E2, but I am substituting the nomenclature to simply "Bambi" or "Sue" for easier reference (following William Alston).
[5] Ibid., 72.
[6] Ibid.
[7] Ibid.

even Rowe concedes it is, then God is still not right in allowing her suffering because there are other ways through which this end can be attained—failing both conditions. If this is true, then Rowe believes he has sufficient grounds to conclude:

> [Q] No good state of affairs is such that an omnipotent, omniscient being's obtaining it would morally justify that being in permitting [Bambi] or [Sue].[8]

Q, as Rowe notes, is tantamount to premise 1 in the earlier argument. So if we are justified in accepting Q, then we are justified in accepting premise 1 in the earlier argument.[9] As I have noted, premise 1 indicates (factually) that there likely are gratuitous evils in the world. If we are justified in accepting P and have sufficient grounds to infer Q from P, then we are justified in accepting premise 1 in the original argument. Accepting premise 1 in the previous argument concedes that there is at least one instance of gratuitous evil in the world, which, as Rowe has claimed, makes it very unlikely that God exists. This is the logic behind the EA.

The question is "are we justified in accepting P?" If P is not acceptable, then obviously we are not justified in inferring Q from P. If we are not justified in inferring Q from P, then we are not permitted to accept premise 1 as having been established. If premise 1 is not established, then the atheist has no way, other than through sheer say-so, to suggest that there are, in fact, pointless evils in the world. So as a first point for discussion, I will investigate whether the inference from P to Q is acceptable, after which I will address some concerns about premise 2.

## QUESTIONING PREMISE 1

In the introductory chapter of this book we surveyed several dominant lines of thought that theists have proposed as morally sufficient reasons for God's permitting evil, including free-will, natural-law, and soul-making theodicies, among others. Indeed, the morally sufficient reason for God's permitting a particular evil may vary or be some admixture of views. But as a first line of response to premise 1, William Alston argues that the theist might have sufficient evidence for belief in God *independent* of any considerations of the

---

[8] Ibid.
[9] Ibid., 72–73.

problem of evil whatsoever.[10] If we assume, as proponents of EA have, that we are justified in taking what our experience indicates is true, then a person may have *prima facie* reason to believe in God as derived from a religious experience. Or perhaps the arguments for the resurrection of Jesus are so compelling that they provide, independent of the issue of evil, evidence for the truth of theistic belief—the resurrection specifically evidencing Christian belief. The important feature of this maneuver is that it undermines the platform from which the EA advances. Rowe's claim that evil provides rationally compelling evidence for theism hinges on the rational starting point for theism and atheism being exactly equivalent; the equal equivalence in probability as a starting point for rational inquiry obtains when we "put aside" any positive evidence for theism.[11]

Why in the world would theists want to put aside the positive evidence already extant for the rationality of their views? The problem of evil is one facet of a larger conversation about a broad range of phenomena that require explanation. Other phenomena requiring answers include: why is there something rather than nothing; the presence of objective moral values; the presence of conscious, sentient beings that are *able* to experience pleasure and pain; and, the reports of religious experiences. Which view best explains all these things? In any event, Alston's first point rightly draws the "equal probability" starting point into question. Moreover, it undermines the atheist claim that theists are obligated to provide a response to the problem of evil in order to solidify the rational footing of their views. If the problem of evil is to count against the rationality of theistic belief, it must do so when complementing the broader project of explaining all of these other phenomena, for which theism has tremendous explanatory power.

A complementary point worth mentioning comes from Jonathan Kvanvig. The EA, he notes, is predicated on how we make rational inferences, and

> The normal pattern of inference for theists is not from the claim that every evil has a point to the claim that God exists, but rather the opposite. The existence of God, as traditionally conceived, entails, we can grant, that every evil has a point. So the theist can infer that every evil has a point in the same way that ordinary folk reject the Cartesian demon hypothesis. In the case of Descartes's evil demon, the usual grounds for inferring that

---

[10] See William P. Alston, "The Inductive Argument from Evil and the Human Cognitive Condition," in *Philosophical Perspectives*, vol. 5 of *Philosophy of Religion* (Atascadero, CA: Ridgeview, 1991), 31.

[11] William Rowe, "The Evidential Argument from Evil: A Second Look," in *The Evidential Argument from Evil*, ed. Daniel Howard-Snyder (Bloomington, IN: Indiana University Press, 1996), 265.

such a hypothesis is false are from the fact that it is reasonable to believe that ordinary plants, animals, and other people exist. One does not have to show first that it is reasonable to believe that no Cartesian demon exists in order for the more ordinary claims to be reasonable; the order of inquiry can be, and ordinarily is, opposite while still being fully rational.[12]

If Kvanvig's argument is correct, then the theist can rationally believe that every evil has a point while being under no obligation to provide an account of what the point actually is. It is not only an a priori inference from the attributes of God that he has a point for which he permits evil; it is also correct to say that there can be a point for which an instance of evil is permitted and we *never know* what it is. The old adage in logic is one man's *modus ponens* is another man's *modus tollens*. The evidential argument evinces the following form and conclusion:

1. If God exists, then gratuitous evils do not exist.
2. Gratuitous evils do exist (or, there is at least one gratuitous evil).
3. Therefore, God does not exist.

Theists, on the other hand, make rational inferences in a strikingly different way.

1'. If God exists, then gratuitous evils do not exist.
2'. It is very likely that God exists.
3'. Therefore, it is very likely there are no gratuitous evils.

The question at hand is not whether these arguments are valid. The question centers on which second premise (2 or 2') has more compelling evidence for its acceptance. Theism may then point to arguments for rational theistic belief previously mentioned as evidence for 2', while using 1' through 3' as an a priori defense against EA.

A third line of response to EA, and one garnering the lion's share of attention, is a view called theistic skepticism. That is to say, adherents to this view accept theism as true, but they are skeptical that if there is a greater good for which God permits evil that we would be in the right cognitive position to (1) know or (2) understand what the point might be. As Alston explains, each theodicy provided as a response to evil reveals "limits to our cognitive powers, opportunities, and achievements in arguing that we are not in the right

---

[12] Jonathan Kvanvig, *The Problem of Hell* (Oxford: Oxford University Press, 1993), 7.

position to deny that God could have that kind of reason for various cases of suffering."[13] He categorizes and describes the cognitive limits as follows:

1. *Lack of data.* This includes, inter alia, the secrets of the human heart, the detailed constitution and structure of the universe, and the remote past and future, including the afterlife if any.
2. *Complexity greater than we can handle.* Most notably there is the difficulty of holding enormous complexes of fact—different possible worlds or different systems of natural law—together in the mind sufficiently for comparative evaluation. . . .
3. *Ignorance of the full range of possibilities.* This is always crippling when we are trying to establish negative conclusions. If we don't know whether or not there are possibilities beyond the ones we have thought of, we are in a very bad position to show that there can be no divine reasons for permitting evil.
4. *Ignorance of the full range of values.* When it's a question of whether some good is related to E in such a way as to justify God in permitting E, we are, for the reason mentioned in 4, in a very poor position to answer the question if we don't know the extent to which there are modes of value beyond those of which we are aware. For in that case, so far as we can know, E may be justified by virtue of its relation to one of those unknown goods.
5. *Limits to our capacity to make well-considered value judgments.* The chief example of this we have noted is the difficulty in making comparative evaluations of large complex wholes.[14]

Why is this taxonomy important? The EA claims that there are no goods, taken either individually or as an aggregate, that morally justify permitting horrific evil. The EA, as we find in P, inductively shifts from the "goods we know of" to a statement about "all *possible* goods" that *might* result from evil's obtaining. Proponents of theistic skepticism wonder how we can be sure that our knowledge of goods not only represents the goods that are *actually* in the world but also represents the *possible* goods that might result from evil.

Stephen Wykstra formalizes theistic skepticism (which he calls "the Condition Of Reasonable Epistemic Access," or CORNEA for short) accordingly:

---

[13] Alston, "Inductive Argument from Evil," 59.
[14] Ibid., 59–60. I will give attention to the problem of values ranging over parts and wholes later.

(C) On the basis of cognized situation s, human H is entitled to the claim 'It appears that p' only if it is reasonable for H to believe that, given her cognitive faculties and the use she has made of them, if p were not the case, s would likely be different than it is in some way discernible by her.[15]

So if it is reasonable to believe that if there was a greater good resultant from evil, it is *likely* that I would grasp or perceive the resultant good. If it is *likely* that I would grasp or perceive the good, and do not, then I am entitled to the claim that there is at least one gratuitous evil.

Alston's taxonomy is, of course, a partial taxonomy. But it does question the limits of our cognitive powers. What is more, theistic skepticism does not emphasize *our* powers of apprehension but compares them to cognitive powers of God. As Wykstra argues, the gap between our intellect and God's is enormous. If there is any charity to be ascribed to a situation, it must be, of necessity, to the God whose intellectual powers have no rival. Thus, "if we think carefully about the sort of being theism proposes for our belief, it is entirely expectable—given what we know of our cognitive limits—that the goods by virtue of which this Being allows known suffering should very often be beyond our ken."[16] To be fair, there is an important difference between Alston and Wykstra. Wykstra's proposal suggests that the atheist is not permitted to the claim that an instance of evil "appears gratuitous." Alston, on the other hand, thinks that the atheist is entitled to the claim that an instance of evil appears to be gratuitous but only initially so. After factoring in our cognitive limitations, no such permission is granted. Thus, if I am reading them correctly, for Wykstra there isn't even a prima facie case against theism from horrific evil, whereas for Alston there is prima facie *evidence* but no *ultima facie* case that can be made from evil.

I think theistic skepticism is a fair way of dealing with the evidential argument. However, in this chapter I will not be using theistic skepticism to refute the EA. There will be instances where I highlight some of its positive features, especially in areas where even the most vocal proponents of the EA concede it has a point. But it seems that there is another avenue for this discussion that may prove to be beneficial, and so I shall chart out into that territory.

With that in mind, let us make a distinction between goods that are instrumental and goods that are intrinsic. If the discussion is about actual and possible

---

[15] Stephen Wykstra, "The Humean Obstacle to Evidential Arguments from Suffering: On Avoiding the Evils of Appearance," *International Journal for Philosophy of Religion* 16 (1984): 73–93.
[16] Ibid., 91.

goods in an evil state of affairs, our deliberations may benefit by making this distinction between instrumental and intrinsic goods. Instrumental values, which are the governing force behind the EA, are goods the obtaining of which provide *consequential* value from our actions. For example, if Sue is going to be raped and murdered, then God must provide some beneficial consequence to Sue or to both Sue and others. On the other hand, intrinsic value concerns things that it is better to have in themselves than not, and the consequences of these values do nothing to alter the value of having this type of good. For example, it is widely agreed among theists that human freedom is intrinsically valuable to have insofar as it is a manifestation of the *imago Dei*, that is, it is a manifestation of God's own *way* of existing. Proponents of EA must concede that in most cases of moral evil there is an exercise of human freedom, Sue's case included. Attendant to human freedom, at least along theistic lines, is the account that we will give to God for our use of this freedom.[17] The important point at this juncture is that human freedom, while not being the only reason that God permits evil, is at least one instance of a justifying reason God may have for permitting evil. Moreover, if freedom is a necessary condition not only of these states of affairs obtaining but also of the moral accountability attached to our actions, then human freedom is a valuable attribute *even in its abuse*. The appropriation of human freedom does nothing to undermine its intrinsic value. This argument does not totally dismantle the EA, for we still have the question, "What amount of the exercise of evil is too much even in the interests of honoring human freedom?" I will note in a moment, and in the chapter on the defeat of evil, that the amount of evil God will permit is higher than we may think.[18]

That being said, the issue of freedom may be irrelevant, for there are acts that are intrinsically evil; and the rape and murder of a girl is one such instance. The theist needs more than just the intrinsic value of free will to remedy this concern; otherwise, the suffering is both underserved and uncompensated.[19] On behalf of Sue, Alston suggests:

---

[17] I will develop the issue of eschatology later.

[18] Since we are focused on the exercise of human freedom, I want to address some features of Sue's case that are worthy of attention. The rape and murder of Sue, while tragic, represents *layers* of bad decision making from multiple culprits. Several important facts need to be kept in mind: (1) both the mother and the murderer had been taking drugs *and* drinking, (2) the murderer expressed violence to the mother of Sue and her brother *that night* on more than one occasion, and (3) the mother never removed her children from a violent environment and influence. The rape and murder of Sue did not come out of thin air but resulted from numerous instances of bad judgment from both the mother and the boyfriend.

[19] See Eleonore Stump, "Providence and Evil," in *Christian Philosophy*, ed. Thomas Flint (Notre Dame: University of Notre Dame Press, 1990), 66. See also Alston, "Inductive Argument from Evil," 48.

Any plan that God would implement will include provision for each of us having a life that is, on balance, a good thing, and one in which the person reaches the point of being able to see that his life as a whole is a good for him.... Nevertheless, this is compatible with God having as a part of his reason for permitting a given case of suffering that it contributes to results that extend beyond the sufferer. So long as the sufferer is amply taken care of, I can't see that this violates any demands of divine justice, compassion, or love.[20]

To remedy the suffering of Sue means that her suffering is not used only as a means for other's gains; she is one of the beneficiaries of God's plan for permitting her suffering. Also, Sue must recognize the value in God's plan and endorse it.[21] In other words, subjectively Sue must come to appreciate God's plan and value it for herself. What possible reason(s) might God have that provide not only individual goods but corporate goods, the attainment of which justifies God's permission of evil?

A promising answer to this question requires some background. The EA, as predicated on Rowe's work, has given attention to several attributes of God, namely his power, knowledge, goodness, and being Creator of the world—otherwise known as restricted standard theism. It is called standard theism because these properties are those for which there is almost consensus among theistic proponents. Expanded standard theism includes these four properties but also incorporates other claims about sin, redemption, and final judgment, among others.[22] Rowe's basic argument against using expanded theism as a viable response to EA is that if the four traditional properties ascribed to theism are unlikely given evil, then any *additional* claims to the bedrock four properties are ruled out as viable candidates to justify morally God's permission of evil. As I will note, there are several reasons to caution against ruling out the explanatory power of expanded theism.

First, the "omni" attributes of God have logical extensions, as Rowe admits. God's being powerful indicates that he can do anything that is logically possible for him to do. As such, God has the power to work through miraculous healings or intervene in other human affairs. God's being powerful does not entail that he will intervene in human affairs. Deists, for example, generally affirm that God is

---

[20] Ibid., 48.
[21] Ibid.
[22] William Rowe, "Evil and the Theistic Hypothesis: A Response to Wykstra," *International Journal for Philosophy of Religion* 16 (1984): 95–100.

all-powerful but do not affirm that he is an intervener. So we are not permitted to infer from God's power alone that he will intervene in human affairs.

God's being omniscient indicates that God is maximally knowledgeable, including (ironically) that God can grasp goods beyond our ken.[23] Divine omniscience also affirms that God knows how to intervene in human affairs and the place in which his intervention will prove most beneficial. Recall that in the previous chapter it was shown that God and evil are not incompatible notions; there can be both God and evil. If there is evil, then God did not intervene to keep it from obtaining, from which we can infer that in every instance of evil God did not intervene to keep it from obtaining. As I will note, God's intervention will be in those places where it is most effective, addressing the disease of the problem and not just the symptoms. What is important to note for now is that like divine omnipotence, divine omniscience does not permit the inference that God will intervene. God could be omniscient and yet indifferent to the plights of sufferers.

God's being omnibenevolent also has several extensions. Goodness in the *moral* sense indicates agency, and agency is one property typified in personhood. So it is not just that God is powerful and knowledgeable; it is that as an agent God is intentional. Given that Rowe concedes that God, if he exists, is all-good, then we may infer that the contents of his intentions are good as well. Finally, restricted theism affirms that God is the Creator of the world. If he were not, then the problem of evil, at least for theists, is irrelevant. When we combine God's being Creator of the world with the other divine properties previously discussed, we can make the following inferences. (1) It is reasonable to suppose that God, as a knowledgeable and morally good being, created the world with an objective for it in mind—an objective that includes its ability to flourish. (2) As Creator of the world, God has certain prerogatives, including that of judging persons for the contents of their intentions and actions.

So far I have taken the four properties ascribed to God in restricted theism and given reasons to think that there are other inferences that are not independent from these properties but that are in fact derived from these properties, that bear on this discussion. The properties in restricted theism, it must be noted, are derivative of perfect being theology. They are an a priori framework from which the discussion ensues. So before I turn to another project, I want to note that the starting point of restricted theism, plus these inferences from

---

[23] I am drawing from Rowe, "Evil and the Theistic Hypothesis."

restricted theism, ground two of our previous arguments against EA. Consider again the following argument:

1'. If God exists, there are no gratuitous evils.
2'. It is very likely that God exists.
3'. Therefore, it is very likely there are no gratuitous evils.

How is our current discussion a complement to this argument? First, if God is powerful, knowledgeable, Creator of the world, and good (thus morally intentional), then there are no gratuitous evils—evils for which he has no intention in his decision to create and sustain the world. An exercise of agency is, as Hugh McCann explains, "a creative undertaking on the agent's part, to be accounted for in terms of its intrinsic features, not via the operations of other denizens in the world. Second, exercises of agency must be intentional; they have to be undertaken for the sake of some objective the agent deems worthy of attainment."[24] The major exception to these features of agency involves acts derived from weakness of will, a feature of agency not applicable to God. But if this is true of agency *simpliciter*, then these features are true of divine agency as well, and the implications for this line of inquiry are telling. We can know as basic tenets of agency that the natural progression through which actions come about are derived from the agent's intending to decide a course of action, which is a *"purposive* exertion of voluntariness."[25] The purposive exertion of voluntariness is precisely the rationale behind premise 1'.

No doubt more could be said, but this suffices to make some important points. If God exists, then God's act of creation was an intentional and thus purposeful act on his part, as is his continued act of conservation—literally his act of holding things in existence moment by moment. God's making a decision to create and sustain cannot, then, be unintended or accidental. Thus, for the features that we find in our world, both good and evil, we cannot utilize the term "gratuitous" as an appropriate label, at least as far as agency is involved.

Since God's actions are intentional, and thus directed at some objective for which he acts, then we might wonder what the objective(s) is/are. The assumption in the EA is that the objective for horrific evil is that God in some way provides an outweighing good at least for the person who undergoes the suffering, perhaps for others as well. But this working assumption is not clear

---

[24] Hugh McCann, *The Works of Agency: On Human Action, Will, and Freedom* (Ithaca, NY: Cornell University Press, 1998), 180.
[25] Ibid., 173.

at all. In fact, the foundation of this argument is incomplete. The book of Job does not claim that all of the suffering Job endured was somehow made right by God providing him with more children, wealth, animals, and land in the last several verses of the book. Nor do we look at the cross of Christ and make any suggestions that his Passion was in some way connected to an outweighing good from which *Jesus* benefited; we can see, in fact, that this is precisely *not* the case. And what, one might ask, does receiving money or even the benefits of heaven have to do with the intrinsic evil perpetuated in the rape and murder of Sue, or any other victim for that matter (including those for whom heaven is not a benefit), if we understand that remuneration (or compensation) is the proper object of divine activity?

Formulating the problem in this way begs the question, for it already assumes that *God* is attached to the situation in such a way as to be the One responsible for providing the compensation for the victim rather than the perpetrator of the act itself. It is more reasonable to accept, at least as far as the argument has been structured, that God will work in such a way as to include remedying evil by nothing short of making its perpetrator address his wrongs. Justice is good for both the victim and the victimizer, which meets both of the criteria delineated above: that both Sue, and perhaps others, including the evildoer, will benefit from God's work. Insofar as moral accountability is attached to our intentions and actions, God's holding us accountable for them is more on par with what justice demands than mere remuneration at the expense of other features surrounding the experience of evil, including how we respond to it.

This proposal is not the same thing as saying that justice is the outweighing good for which God permits evil, which is a veiled way of saying that the ends justify the means. Instead, this perspective argues that the means justify the ends, which brings us to the point of addressing divine intervention at the point of the disease and not at the sign of symptoms.

Implicit to arguments from evil is the notion that God exercises judgment about the value of human activities and how to balance those activities toward an overall good. Is it not better to suggest that God exercises judgment on *people* as to the content of their activities? The constant emphasis on outweighing goods, with its focus on God's shaping events toward an end, ignores how he might do that with *perpetrators* in mind. He may hold them accountable for their actions not only to restore justice and social order but also to foster reconciliation between the one wronged and the one doing the wrong. Without this necessary reshaping of the argument, we could have it that God provides some good for victims that never involves the perpetrator in any way, and this simply will not do. The act of rape is a manifestation of agency, for which the rapist is to be held morally accountable; further, the one responsible must be held morally accountable in such a way that responsibility is *taken* for the action. But how might this occur in such a way that Sue benefits from it and recognizes the value and endorses it? After all, Sue was not only raped but murdered. And what may be said of all the other wrongs committed that are never addressed, from vindictiveness to gossiping?

The only way that God can assure such provision is made is to do so in the afterlife. Granted, Sue's assumed participation in heaven is a great good to her. However, her participating in heaven leaves unresolved the accountability attached to being the subject of such a horrific act. The perpetrator spending a lifetime in prison may provide a social good, but it was Sue who was primarily wronged, and Sue (and God) require an accounting. Otherwise stated, God will exact in the final judgment the plans for reconciliation he gave for the here and now (Matt 18:15–20). When two persons do not or cannot come to reconciliation, a third party is invited to confirm that a wrong has been done, arbitrating between the two broken parties so that amends may be made between them. The activity of God in the final judgment works in just such a way for both the victim and the perpetrator. The perpetrator is confronted by the God whom he has wronged through acting against God's creation, and he is confronted by the victim to whom he must give account.

But what, if not heaven, is the benefit of this confrontation for Sue? If heaven is not to be counted as the outweighing good for which God permits her suffering, then what is the rest of the story? The proper activity of reconciliation is not, I suggest, in the receiving of items that have no moral connection to the wrong. Reconciliation requires both accountability and forgiveness. It requires that both the victim and the perpetrator have the proper mental attitude toward the wrong done. Sue's expectation of justice is not only right but is satisfied when God brings justice to fruition. Also, for the victim, the proper mental attitude is one of offering forgiveness. As James Spiegel notes, "suffering yields something even more fundamental in the building of Christian faith: solidarity with Christ."[26] Christ was a man of sorrows, despised and rejected by men (Isaiah 53). Christ suffered not only on the cross but daily endured temptations and the effects of the sins of others. So more than just having heaven as a facet of her life, Sue has the opportunity to appropriate her solidarity with Christ through forgiving her aggressor as Christ offers forgiveness

---

[26] James Spiegel, *The Benefits of Providence: A New Look at Divine Sovereignty* (Wheaton, IL: Crossway Books, 2005), 196.

to those who are his enemies. Admittedly, forgiveness offered is not the same thing as forgiveness received, but that is irrelevant for what solidarity with Christ is for Sue. As Spiegel explains, being part of the body of Christ, "the Christian partakes in the atoning work of Christ, his obedience, passion, death, and resurrection—Christ's righteousness becomes ours, as does his physical resurrection."[27] Thus, uniting with Christ is "to accept the whole package, from preliminary agony to final glory."[28] This proposal is not without merit. After hearing Jesus' teaching on reconciliation, Peter asked Jesus, "Lord, how many times could my brother sin against me and I forgive him? As many as seven times?" "I tell you, not as many as seven," Jesus said to him, "but 70 times seven" (Matt 18:21–22 HCSB). Forgiveness is a virtue to possess and a quality of character to exercise. Sue's opportunity to exercise this virtue, since it cannot be on this side of heaven, will be on the other.

I have avoided calling my development of thought a soul-making theodicy. Admittedly it has resonances with that view, and if one wants to put me in that category, so be it. But one thing must be clear in so doing—the language of "outweighing goods" is jargon I wish to avoid, at least in any reductionist sense of the term. How that term can be quantified is still murky business and has the unattractive feature of making it seem like God is treating people as a means to an end. I have attempted instead to provide an initial account of divine activity that reveals two things. First, when we consider agency, and the nature of intention formation, the term "gratuitous" is an inappropriate label. It suggests there is no objective toward which God directs his intentions, which is clearly false. Second, rather than emphasize remuneration or compensation as a central feature of discourse, I have given attention to the idea that God will address the problem of evil at its core, which is in the judgment of sin and the perpetrators of those sins. It is justice that makes what is wrong right, and in the account I provided the justice of God entails that the wrongdoer will take responsibility for his wrongs. Rather than emphasize justice as the outweighing good for which God permits evil, I consider justice to be God's way of addressing it.

## QUESTIONING PREMISE 2

The second premise of the argument purports to express what a perfect God *would* do in certain circumstances. More specifically, God would prevent

---

[27] Ibid., 198.
[28] Ibid.

intense suffering unless his intervention brought about the loss of a greater good or permitted some evil equally bad or worse. In other words, if an instance of evil is avoidable, God will avoid it. The second premise is not aimed at making a claim about facts in the world but instead is making a claim about the expected activities of a perfect God as derived from his attributes. Usually this is an unquestioned premise. I will not be so charitable. The speculations about what God would do are generally based on relations between ideas, namely the perfect-making properties of God and the extensions of those properties onto a state of affairs. Since ideas have entailments, this is an appropriate method for discovery.

However, another way of discovering what God *would* do is to take special revelation seriously and resolve to answer what God has done. In the parlance of possible worlds, in order for a world to be actual it must be possible. So in questioning the second premise, we will delve into the creation narrative and ponder the implications of God's granting dominion over creation to Adam and the implications of man's being entrusted with the care of creation as well as the implications this doctrine has on the prospects of divine intervention. Rather than speculate on possible divine activities, I want to address actual divine activities and the resources this provides for this discussion. I will investigate the doctrine of dominion in Genesis and will analyze some of its implications, which is an important task in diffusing arguments from evil specifically against Christianity.

After the creation of Adam and Eve, God granted dominion, or rule, to them over all the earth and the creatures dwelling on it (Gen 1:28). Dominion entails that humans have the obligation to supervise creation and to direct the affairs of nature. I do not simply mean that dominion by itself entails that humans have a special value above the rest of creation, for creation was called good before humans were ever created; instead, humans have a unique responsibility within creation. Part of the rationale behind humans having this responsibility is predicated on the verses prior to the divine command to rule and subdue—namely that humans are created in the image of God and are thus bestowed with the capacities for this task (Gen 1:26–27). If we ought to rule and subdue creation as the narrative indicates, then God has, presumably, endowed us with the capacities toward this end. Moreover, as the text indicates, it is not just that humans are given charge over creation; it is that they, in virtue of this divine command, have a position that is unique in the created order. If, as Aquinas argues, the end for which humans are created is to know and love God, then obedience to this stipulation is a part of rightly loving God and fulfilling our essence, the end of which is human flourishing.

On a broader scale, obedience to the divine command is what brings flourishing to the rest of the created order that has been entrusted to humans subsequent to God's act of creation. Contrary to some views, dominion does not mean that the fulfillment of the human essence is *using* creation as a means toward the ends of persons; instead, it means caring for creation because it has value in and of itself.[29] Rather than viewing dominion as grounds for exploitation, we must see dominion as the grounds for service. So even though Scripture affirms that humans are uniquely created in the image of God, it also affirms that proper use of the position entrusted to them is not one of being served but of serving.[30] To quote David Henderson, "Many theologians see the giving of dominion as the substance of the divine image, in which case it is all the more reason not to rule harshly over nature. For then we would be blasphemers, portraying the image of God as cruel and uncaring."[31] Dominion thus includes a human responsibility to care for every aspect of creation as God does. We will be held accountable to God as to the contents of our activities in this endeavor.

How does this excursion on dominion address the evidential argument from evil? First, it requires us to reshape the argument to factor in what God has done in his act of creation. Dominion is, at least theologically speaking, part of the created essence of humans. Exercising dominion is thus part of fulfilling the human essence for which we were created, and proper exercise of dominion entails the flourishing of nonhuman creation as well. Contrariwise, the failure to exercise proper dominion bears out its consequences both on creation and the one failing to exercise proper dominion. Using creation as a means to an end, as Sue's rapist did, is a failure to exercise this responsibility. Insofar as premise 2 is often dubbed the "theological premise" we are well served in considering how theology has informed us of the activities of God.

Second, entrusting dominion to humans, though not granting *ownership* over creation, grants *control* over creation. Control over creation has two features attendant to its proper exercise. The positive feature of control is that our activities should direct the created order in a manner that fulfills its essence. For example, Adam was entrusted with work before the fall, which means he was laboring on behalf of God's creation not as a matter of being judged for sin

---

[29] For a competing view see Lynn White Jr., "The Historical Roots of Our Ecological Crisis," *Science* 155 (March, 1967): 1203–7.
[30] See also T. D. J. Chappell, "Dominion," *Ratio* XVI (September 2003): 307–17.
[31] See David Henderson, "Creation Care," in *Taking Christian Moral Thought Seriously: The Legitimacy of Religious Beliefs in the Marketplace of Ideas*, ed. Jeremy A. Evans; B&H Studies in Christian Ethics (Nashville, TN: B&H Academic, 2011), 177–98.

but that work is fulfilling both for him and the needs of creation. He was also charged to be fruitful and multiply, which evinces that proper care of his own kind includes its propagation. The negative feature of control is that it prevents the flourishing of nonoptimal states of affairs. For example, after the fall labor was made more intense by the presence of things that work against what is good in God's original creative act. Weeds deploy resources from plants that produce vegetation for consumption, thus their flourishing needs to be prevented. Moral decay ensues from moral lapses, which requires moral instruction from virtuous persons to prevent decay from spoiling the moral center of the agent.

And so, finally, the previous precepts of dominion give us reason to think that the intervention of God in human affairs, rather than being a workaday thing that he does, instead will occur relatively infrequently. Granting control entails that God will be permissive even in decisions of great moral significance and consequence, both good and evil.

## A Missing Premise in the Evidential Argument

Perhaps the most troubling aspect of Rowe's argument is that he assumes God has moral obligations. Part and parcel to his objection from evil is that God has been derelict in his duties, and the failure endemic to the objection is one involving a moral lapse on his part. Consider again Rowe's premises (italics mine):

1. There exist instances of intense suffering which an omnipotent, omniscient being *could* prevent without thereby losing some greater good or preventing some evil equally bad or worse.
2. An omniscient, wholly good being *would* prevent the occurrence of any intense suffering it could unless it could not do so without thereby losing some greater good or permitting some evil equally bad or worse.[32]

The missing premise, one that is required for his argument to have any teeth at all, looks something like:

3. God *should* prevent any evil such that in doing so he does not lose any greater good or permit an evil equally bad or worse.

---

[32] Rowe, *Philosophy of Religion*, 87.

If we leave the argument in its original form, and without this additional premise, then the objection is profoundly incomplete. The problem of evil in all of its forms centers on *moral* failures; it is not an argument simply about the *strategic* failures God might have made. For the time being, I only provide a promissory note concerning my objection to the claim that God has any moral obligations at all. When I take up the deontological problem of evil, I will cash out this note.

## CONCLUSION

In this chapter I have given attention to the most persistent aspects of the problem of evil, namely (1) the vast amounts of evil in the world and (2) the apparent existence of gratuitous evil in the world. I shaped this chapter to fit an interaction between the two premises of the EA, providing objections along the way as to how the problem is framed. Philosophical and theological problems attend both premises in the argument, and I will not rehash here what I set out to say in the chapter. In the next chapter is my attempt to address these issues in a more constructive light. It will attempt to make sense out of the problem of evil and the suffering that results from the malformed intentions of human agents.

CHAPTER FOUR

# The Defeat of Good and Evil

In the chapter on the evidential argument, I invoked the idea of the defeat of evil. In this chapter I will develop and refine exactly what the notion of defeat entails and how it provides a more satisfying account of the problem of evil. More pointedly, even though I have asserted that God has no moral obligations to his creation, there is still the expectation that God's governance of the world is sensible and that he intends good for his creation, not harm. Earlier we noted that a purpose of suffering, even tremendous suffering, includes the participation in God's own way of life, which manifested in the incarnation includes suffering at the behest of others and suffering that results from our own misconduct. Those for whom heaven is their destiny will not only enjoy the benefits of heaven but will appreciate the nature of the sacrifice God made in Christ to overcome the ills of the world and to remedy the problem at its core; this includes reconciliation between the one who suffered and the one who produced the suffering. This proposal may appear rather strange, for in the case of Sue such reconciliation occurs only after Sue gives in a twofold way. First, in her rape and murder she is forced to give up control of her body and mental well-being; and second, in her act of forgiveness she not only participates in God's own way of life but appreciates that the act of forgiveness is the only proper means for such reconciliation. No tangible goods, as we have noted, are sufficient to rectify the wrong done, for they fail to address the problem at its source, which is the defiled heart that has such an action as its object of intention.

What the defeat of evil therefore involves is that evil must be addressed, that is, "it is a challenge to be met and, if possible, defeated."[1] The defeat of

---

[1] Hugh McCann, "Pointless Suffering: How to Make the Problem of Evil Sufficiently Serious," in *Oxford Studies in the Philosophy of Religion*, vol. 2 (Oxford: Oxford University Press, 2010), 165.

evil is not a mere means to a good, as I have noted. Instead, the evil in our world is an intrinsic part of a larger state of affairs that "constitutes a much greater good, and which would be actually less good if the evil were taken away."[2] The content of this chapter will develop and defend this view.

## THE MECHANICS OF DEFEAT

In order to comprehend the notion of defeat, consider the following items that are intrinsically good: pleasure, happiness, love, knowledge, justice, beauty, proportion, good intention, and the exercise of virtue.[3] We can also provide a list of things that are intrinsically bad: displeasure, unhappiness, hate, ignorance, injustice, ugliness, disharmony, bad intention, and the exercise of vice.[4] Bearing these distinctions in mind, a difference can be drawn between "balancing off" and "defeating." To quote Roderick Chisholm:

> It is one thing to say that the goodness—the intrinsic goodness—of a certain situation is *balanced off* by means of some other situation; and it is quite another thing to say that the goodness of a certain situation is *defeated* by means of some other situation. Again, it is one thing to say that the evil—the intrinsic badness—of a certain situation is *balanced off* by means of some other situation; and it is quite another thing to say that the evil of a certain situation is *defeated* by means of some other situation.[5]

An analogy will help make the point. Suppose, says Chisholm, that Mr. Jones is experiencing a certain amount of innocent pleasure and there is another man, Mr. Smith, experiencing the same amount of innocent displeasure—Mr. Smith is just as displeased as Mr. Jones is pleased. In this story the positive and negative values counterbalance each other.[6] If the positive and negative values counterbalance one another, then the value of the whole is *neutral*. If we *only* look at one state of affairs—for example, Jones's innocent pleasure—then the value of that state of affairs is better than the value of the whole, for it does not consider the value of the other states of affairs that occur in the world. Likewise, if we *only* look at Smith's experience of innocent displeasure, then the

---

[2] Ibid., 166.
[3] Roderick Chisholm, "The Defeat of Good and Evil," in *Proceedings and Addresses of the American Philosophical Association* 2 (1968–69): 22.
[4] Ibid.
[5] Ibid., 21.
[6] See ibid., 25.

value of that experience is worse than the value of the whole. The value of a state of affairs, independent of other features in the world, can be better than or worse than the value of the whole, which evinces the claim that a single state (one facet of our experience) of affairs bears no necessary connection to the value of the whole. The whole may be neutral in value, but a particular state of affairs (e.g., the murder of Sue) may be negative in value. If the whole is neutral, then the value of the bad part is counterbalanced. If the value of the whole is good, then the value of the bad part is outweighed. The important lesson about balancing off is that when evil is balanced off, "we may yet regret or resent *its* presence in the larger whole."[7] However, we are not entitled to make any inferences from this individual state of affairs to the value of our lives on the whole, or to the value of the world as a whole. As has been shown, the value of the parts does nothing to explain the value of the whole, and the value of the whole is not equivalent to the value of its parts.

The notion of defeat is different than that of balancing out. Chisholm provides an example that will help make this notion clear. It is possible to have either pleasure or displeasure regarding something that is bad; Jones may be pleased that Smith is displeased, or Jones may have displeasure that Smith is displeased. Taking pleasure in another's displeasure is, of course, an incorrect emotion.[8] However, insofar as it is pleasurable, there is a subjective sense in which the experience is good (to be clear, this does not mean morally good). Contrariwise, a person may be saddened by the suffering of the poor, the plight of those in need of refuge, or the slow and painful death of a loved one. While these instances are certainly states of displeasure, and the resulting sadness is also a state of displeasure, the sadness itself is a state of affairs that is good in virtue of the fact that the displeasure is one that should be felt. Indeed, we agree that if it is not felt in these circumstances something is emotionally wrong with the one who cannot feel anything. Other examples of the same point are at hand: the displeasure of fear is intrinsically bad, but fear is overcome in the exercise of courage, which is an intrinsically good attribute of character to possess; the virtuous activity of repentance includes my taking displeasure in previous wrongdoings, resulting in a whole that is better because of the bad.[9] The notion of defeat, as understood so far, means that if the suffering we experience is defeated by a whole that is good then we have reason to be thankful for the presence of the part that is bad.

---

[7] Ibid., 27.
[8] Ibid., 28.
[9] Ibid., 29.

So far we have taken some measures to clarify what is meant by defeat. It is one thing to explain these principles in abstract and yet another thing to demonstrate instances of defeat that pertain to the actual world. One instance of the defeat of evil may be found in the life of Beethoven, whose accomplishments as a composer increased in spite of his deafness.[10] As Hugh McCann explains:

> Beethoven could have reacted to his encroaching deafness by despairing of further success as a composer. Instead, he went on writing even as his hearing faded to silence, producing many of his greatest works well after he was stone deaf. Here, the evil of Beethoven's deafness is not just overbalanced by a greater good. Rather, it is addressed and, so to speak, refuted in Beethoven's accomplishment, an accomplishment that would in fact have been diminished had it not been carried off in defiance of his deafness.[11]

The example of Beethoven, and many others beside, is not that some good befalls those who suffer evil, but that those who suffer evil *participate* in its defeat. Participating in the defeat of evil requires a stance against the evil endured; we oftentimes partner with those whose abilities far exceed our own to see the task through. In fact, it is the aspect of partnership that makes the notion of defeat have even greater purchase, for it "prompts rational beings to take measures to diminish" the evil in the world.[12] We find no shortage of such actions in our own experiences. Researchers convene for the common purpose of eradicating treacherous diseases. Countries take explicit stances and offer action to stop crimes against humanity in other regions of the world with no prospects of economic or political gain from such an endeavor, but simply because it is right. Parents refuse to yield to despair as their child suffers from both physical and mental disabilities but press on in greater unity to provide a home and environment yielding a life for their child that, without those efforts and resolve, the child would never have. Evil is a parasite on the good; it distorts that which ought to be. The defeat of evil, in addressing evil *as evil*, seeks to restore the goodness of being that evil snatched away, at least as much as is within our power to do so.

The cooperative effort just mentioned has several important features. First, cooperation with others advances human solidarity.[13] Personal suffering and the suffering of others tend to "join persons in a common effort" to make

---

[10] See McCann, "Pointless Suffering," 166.
[11] Ibid.
[12] Ibid., 167. McCann uses the nomenclature of "corporate aspect" rather than cooperative effort.
[13] Ibid.

things right and reduce our alienation and isolation when a comforting presence is severely needed. We come to recognize in the cooperative effort that evil affects more than just the one directly suffering from it but elicits a proper response from the one suffering and a proper reaction from those who are "in the know" to diminish suffering when its origins are in something evil.[14] The second benefit of such an approach is that since the effort is shared, "no one individual's portion need issue in success."[15] We can be satisfied that our contributions surfaced from the abilities we have to address some measure of suffering in the world rather than abandon the project altogether due to our inability to remedy the problem in full. If nothing else, addressing the evilness of evil has already brought about a great good—a disposition that is decidedly against the promulgation of evil from within oneself and an intention to act against evil rather than embody indifference. Finally, it signifies that the essential cooperative venture occurs when we partner with those who are capable of bringing about evil's ultimate defeat. True to our experience, some of the evils in our world are beyond human abilities, even jointly, to resolve. The most that advancements in medicine will provide is a delayed death, a death that though perhaps less painful is still inevitable. The message contained within theism is that every evil has the possibility of being addressed, including the evil that is our own death. The message contained within *Christian* theism is that God was willing to partner with us in addressing this reality; and in Christ, the Father did not simply remove death, thereby pretending it has been addressed; he faced death on our behalf and defeated it in Christ's resurrection (1 Cor 15:54–57).

At this juncture it is important to emphasize some aspects of defeat for the purposes of clarity. The defeat of evil is not intending to answer the question, "Why did God permit evil?" It would be a bizarre claim indeed to suggest that God permitted evil so that it might bring about the good state of affairs of defeating the evil he permitted. God's permission of evil is predicated on the notion that he created humans significantly free, and that being free is a more valuable way of life, all things being equal, than not being free. The defeat of evil is a way of answering the question, "How might God respond to human suffering that is born from evil?" and shapes a response in such a way that it requires our doing something about it *with* him—taking his stance against the

---

[14] Not all suffering is evil. Suffering that results from our own sin or wrongdoing is not evil but is nonetheless suffering. In this case there is no obligation to alleviate the suffering.

[15] McCann, "Pointless Suffering," 167.

evils perpetrated and in so doing embodying God's own way of life. As the apostle Paul expresses:

> Blessed be the God and Father of our Lord Jesus Christ, the Father of mercies and the God of all comfort. He comforts us in all our affliction, so that we may be able to comfort those who are in any kind of affliction, through the comfort we ourselves receive from God. (2 Cor 1:3–4 HCSB)

Admittedly, the lessening through cooperative efforts of suffering born from evil is not the same thing as evil's defeat. If we recall, Chisholm said that defeat consists in a larger state of affairs that is a greater good, and of which the evil is an essential part. The essence of defeat is twofold in nature. First, as McCann says, the "defeat consists not in the lessening taken by itself, but in the larger situation in which the sufferings of some lead, by their very nature, to an improvement of the lot of others."[16] We do not surmise that the projects of today that require tremendous effort and resources are without value in virtue of the fact that no one receives immediate benefits from the endeavors themselves. Cancer research persists, and it is doubtful that anyone finds its unfulfilled objectives to be without purpose or value. Moreover, denying this principle is profoundly selfish, for it rejects the benefits we receive today from the labors of others in the past that have made the quality of our lives substantially better, either through medicine, engineering, or even the efforts of educators to overcome ignorance. Granted, most of our discussion pertains to moral evils, but the human response to natural evil has a place in this discussion as well. The tsunami that resulted from the earthquake in the Indian Ocean in 2004 speaks to such a point. Numerous countries provided resources for recovery and in responding to such needs avoided any complacency or indifference to victims' suffering. These responses provided the opportunity to break down international and cultural barriers, which is an opportunity that addresses the idol of nationalism—a wall between humans that emphasizes the needs and interests of a community at the expense of loving others, even our enemies, as we have been loved by God.[17]

The second feature of defeat "pertains not to the alleviation itself, but to the effects such efforts have on those who engage in them."[18] Even if the efforts

---

[16] Ibid., 168. See also Jean Vanier, *From Brokenness to Community* (New York: Paulist Press, 1992), esp. chap. 2.

[17] For an excellent treatment of this issue, see David Bentley Hart, *The Doors of the Sea: Where Was God in the Tsunami?* (Grand Rapids: Eerdmans, 2005), or his *In the Aftermath: Provocations and Laments* (Grand Rapids: Eerdmans, 2008), especially chaps. 4 and 11.

[18] McCann, "Pointless Suffering," 169. A complementing point is in Vanier, *From Brokenness to*

to address suffering born from evil fail, such endeavors can "almost always be counted upon to increase cooperation, mutual respect, and fellow feeling among those who participate in them."[19] In other words, in taking active measures to address evil we are also taking an active stance against it, and in so doing are appropriating not just a descriptive account of these states of affairs but a normative one. Our activities aimed at addressing evil have its defeat in mind, which indicates a defeat of evil for the person that takes such a stance. Rather than endorse horrors as something to participate in, even under the disguise of duty (as many German officers attempted to do in order to justify their WWII actions), addressing evil to defeat it strengthens the moral constitution of a person even if his endeavor to defeat some external evil fails. For the community, corporately addressing evil avoids the sense of despair that comes with believing that it must be addressed on one's own. As McCann explains, "instead of allowing the fact of suffering to drive us into isolation, we make it an occasion to forge and strengthen a common bond, and a common determination to ameliorate the condition of all."[20]

## CONVERSION AND THE DEFEAT OF EVIL

The soul-making character of the proposal thus far is rather evident. But the focal point of soul making, and the place with which I have the most agreement with McCann, is in the need for conversion. Much attention has been given to the significance of community and what it means to forge a bond with others. Given that the problem of sin is one of the major themes in the problem of evil, there is no need to think that forging a bond with God is anything less than essential to evil's defeat. The reason that conversion is the *summum bonum* of soul making is that in the act of conversion the condition of the heart is restored, "the damage wrought by sin is repaired, and the individual is made over in God's likeness, equipped with virtues modeled after God's own perfections, and anchored in that individual's role in God's creative enterprise."[21]

Cooperation with God is thus another communal element to evil's defeat, namely in the relationship between the sinner and God. As was mentioned in the previous chapter, the place in which we should expect God to intervene is at the point of the disease and not just at the symptoms. The act of conversion addresses the problem of sin directly by reclaiming a relationship between

---

*Community*, 46.
[19] McCann, "Pointless Suffering," 169.
[20] Ibid., 170.
[21] Ibid.

man and God that was broken in the act of rebellion. Conversion evidences forgiveness offered and forgiveness received, and as such manifests that amends between two broken parties has been achieved. There can be no doubt that conversion represents the highest aspect of the soul-making venture, for not only does it provide a new orientation for the person through faith and repentance; it also demands that the one coming to faith drop the illusion that a godless destiny is possible.[22] Only through conversion is fellowship with God restored, after which the process of sanctification may begin. Sanctification is in part the gradual process by which the godless life is put aside and a new character is forged. Attitudes of suspicion are replaced with trust, and the lack of objective meaning in life and life's circumstances is replaced with hope—trusting that God can bring to fruition that which on our own we are helpless to produce.[23]

The emphasis on disposition in this discussion is not an accidental one, for it helps draw to light the distinction between an action with morally good qualities and a virtuous disposition. William Wainwright makes the distinction clearer. Supposing we ask whether some virtues necessitate evil, we must distinguish, using the example of compassion, "whether one is speaking of the virtue of compassion, of compassionate responses in general, or of the compassionate responses of people who are fully informed of the relevant facts."[24] When a person possesses the virtue of compassion, he has the disposition of compassion; it is a habit of character or a readiness "to respond in a certain way if and when the appropriate occasions arise."[25] A person might respond compassionately without being compassionate. An instance of compassion does not make for a compassionate person. As the argument goes, without human suffering there would be no situations in which it would be appropriate for persons to respond compassionately. To be more precise, a truly compassionate person responds to real misfortune (not just perceived misfortune) and is informed of the circumstances that require the compassionate response. As

---

[22] A more technical treatment of the theme of sin and redemption is in Fredrik Lindström, *Suffering and Sin: Interpretations of Illness in the Individual Complaint Psalms*, trans. Michael McLamb (Stockholm: Almqvist and Wiksell, 1994), esp. chaps. 5–7 where the themes of sin and salvation are given systematic treatment, and *God and the Origin of Evil: A Contextual Analysis of Alleged Monistic Evidence in the Old Testament*, trans. F. H. Cryer (Lund, Sweden: C.W.K. Gleerup, 1983). This work is more on the theme of sin and its implications than on salvation per se, but its insights on sin are helpful, esp. chap. 3. Lindström gives significant treatment to God as the author of evil, but his sections on sin in each volume are exceptional, though technical.

[23] For a more thorough treatment of the need for divine assistance, see John Hare's excellent work *The Moral Gap: Kantian Ethics, Human Limits, and Divine Assistance* (Oxford: Oxford University Press, 1997), esp. chap. 6.

[24] William J. Wainwright, *Philosophy of Religion*, 2nd ed. (Belmont, CA: Wadsworth, 1999), 76.

[25] Ibid.

Wainwright explains, "it is necessarily true that if a person responds compassionately to another creature, he or she believes that it is in distress. It is also necessarily true that if the belief is correct, then the creature is in distress. It follows that it is necessarily true that if a person responds compassionately to another creature and is fully informed of its situation, then the creature is in distress."[26] The point is that the development of *some* virtues logically requires the existence of evil or suffering, or perhaps suffering resultant from evil, before that virtue can be possessed. The same principle holds true of other virtues worthy of possession, including bravery, patience, and even acts of forgiveness. I do not mean to indicate that *all* virtues logically require the presence of evil or suffering for their cultivation. For example, truth telling requires no such a thing. But the point here cannot be missed, for there are certain types of virtue that cannot come by any other means. What is more, the goods that *logically* require evil for their development, insofar as they pertain to this discussion, provide the grounds through which a proper exercise of human freedom and persistence in a course of action yield a disposition to respond against those evils when they arise.

Bearing this in mind, it follows that moral virtues that logically require evil cannot be cultivated in abstraction through sheer speculation on the part of the person as to "what they would do" if a certain tragedy were to occur. Without having been there, in the thick of experience, the honest person can only speak of what they *hope* would be their response if such circumstances come their way, and indeed such a hope may come about. The more pressing issue is that a person cannot have a developed *disposition*, or habit of conduct, where there previously was no relevant conduct by which the disposition comes about. So of the relevant type of virtue God has soul making as a morally sufficient reason for evil's permission; the cultivation of the relevant virtue is the manner in which that evil is addressed. One may indicate a preference for a world without evil while knowingly sacrificing these virtues on the altar of that trade. Such a world is devoid of any compassion, forgiveness, and courage. Moreover, it is likely that persons who prefer such a world are the ones most in need of the world in which these virtues may be obtained—for they are either indifferent to the value of these virtues, or relegate their gain as too costly to pursue. Indeed, such a proposal indicates an anemic view of God's power and an attitude that the one unwilling to cultivate these dispositions has already fled the field of battle in pursuit of an even more self-absorbed life.

---

[26] Ibid.

## The Disposition to Act

But one may wonder why God doesn't simply create us with virtuous dispositions, thereby casting aside any need for evil or for suffering that is derived from evil.[27] As a first line of response, it must be noted that in this proposal I first explained the significance of free will. Free will is a necessary condition for any number of goods to obtain, including the merit or demerit that attaches to our moral decision making. As such, God has a morally sufficient reason for permitting our choice of evil. Consequently, once suffering occurs as a result of evil choices, the suffering cannot be taken away. The soul-making proposal I am invoking is an attempt to show what can be done *once evil obtains*. What I am not suggesting is that God *causes* evil for the purpose of souls being developed. We are perfectly sufficient for willing evil in and of ourselves. What soul making has in mind, and the notion of defeat in particular, is that *once evil obtains* there is a course of action through which it can be addressed and overcome. It is, as mentioned before, a reclaiming of what was lost in the choice for evil. But what is more, being created with these dispositions fails to account for what is essential in the development of certain virtues, namely that they have been chosen by us. If the "virtue were not gained through our own efforts, evil would not be defeated in our achieving it."[28] The results of such choices are evident not only in how they play out in the world but for what these choices do for the one making the choice as well. A disposition to act, it must be recalled, is not the same thing as having acted in a certain way. A disposition to act is developed by persistence in what is right, only after which can we describe ourselves as morally virtuous in any relevant way. Furthermore, the suggestion that God can create us with such dispositions, though not logically bizarre, does rule out the moral aspect contained in the choices we make. If God were to choose these dispositions for us, as the objection suggests he should have done, then our choices issuing from these divinely caused dispositions would be more appropriately considered expressions of God's will than choices *we* make, leaving no meaningful moral dimension in a person's possessing a virtue. Indeed, if the disposition to act were to be completely derived from outside of persons, then no account of virtue would include their morally possessing it; they would be merely expressions of someone else's virtue independent of how they, if left to their own devices, would have chosen for themselves. This is not to say that right actions would be any

---

[27] McCann, "Pointless Suffering," 172.
[28] Ibid.

less right. It is to say that such a construal would intrinsically strip the action of its moral significance.

A second concern to the notion of defeat centers on what I call the failure critique. The essence of the failure critique is that soul making cannot be the ends for which God permits suffering, for there are numerous instances of persons that have not responded to their trials with the requisite virtue intended to be derived from it. For example, if the cornerstone of soul making is conversion, then what sense can be made of the many who do not accept Christ? This is an important question that I will address fully in the later chapter on the problem of hell, but there are other examples besides. What of the persons who recoil into despair or those who become so bent in their disposition that they take what is evil for that which is good? Do these instances provide compelling reasons to think that souls that are "not made" through suffering also indicate that soul making is a failed plan, one not worthy of God's endorsement?

Several lines of response to this objection come to mind. First, a crucial distinction to be made is between the perfection of a plan and the execution of a plan. In other words, there is a difference between a plan's possessing the right qualities for success and the plan's being executed so that the intended results obtain. Given that free will is an important feature in this discussion, there is a sense in which this objection is misdirected from the beginning. The failure, if there is any to be found, is in *our* not appropriating the divine plan. The objection is directed at the divine *plan* independent of the question regarding our appropriation of it. Second, the objection suggests that the only viable means of determining a plan's success is through the effect suffering has on the individual. Much of the suffering in our experience elicits reaction from those not undergoing the suffering but who rise up in response to it, whether the suffering is a result of immoral decisions or from natural disasters. The failure of an individual to take pro-attitudes and the necessary measures for evil's being addressed says nothing whatsoever for what attitudes they *should* have and actions they *should* take.

That being said, there is more that requires attention in this concern. It has been conceded that some virtues do not logically require the existence of evil for their development. The virtue of truth-telling, for example, has no such requirement. So the emphasis on soul making has a particular place in this discussion just as the significance of free will has its own. My intention is to locate properly the soul-making theodicy as a subset of what I have been referring to as evil's defeat. Defeat involves addressing evil both where it occurs and where it is possible. For those virtues that logically require the existence of evil for their development, the soul-making view I have proposed is the way in which that evil is addressed and defeated. The defeat of possible evil is in the person's refusal to cave in to the pressures of temptation. There is no restriction to individuals for either of these suggestions, for the virtue of courage can typify cultures, and resisting the urges in temptation is a battle normally better fought in community than on one's own. We should expect more besides, for as these virtues are developed it is hard to conceive of the resulting *dispositions* manifesting themselves in pro-attitudes toward evil or temptations to do evil.

So, is it not true that when a person responds to his circumstances in bitterness and hatred that the soul-making theodicy has been defeated? Is not such a scenario, which is an obvious feature of our experience, a defeat of defeat? Also, is not the defeat of defeat a concession that some of the evils in our world are gratuitous?

Even though responses such as these are regrettable, it does not mean that the suffering that this eventual person of vice underwent was morally unjustifiable. What is lingering behind these questions is a theory of persons much akin to Robert Adams's view of personal identity.[29] Robert Adams argues that the person we are, that is, the identity that we now possess, is due to the prior evils that we have suffered.[30] Indeed, without prior evils it is possible that my parents would never have met, nor would I have been born.[31] As Adams notes, there are no grounds for objection to evils permitted when our identities are intrinsically wrapped up in history being exactly as it was. As he notes:

> The farther we go back in history, the larger the proportion of evils to which we owe our being: for the causal nexus relevant to our individual genesis widens as we go back in time. We almost certainly would never have existed had there not been just about the same evils as actually occurred in the large part of human history. . . . My identity is established in my beginning. It has been suggested that no one who was not produced from the same individual egg and sperm cells as I was could have been me. If so, the identity of those gametes presumably depends in turn on their beginnings and on the identity of my parents, which depends on the identity of the gametes from which they came, and so on. It seems to me implausible to suppose that the required identities could have been

---

[29] Robert M. Adams, "Existence, Self-Interest, and the Problem of Evil," *Nous* 13 (1979): 53–65. See also Robert M. Adams, "Must God Create the Best?" *Philosophical Review* 81 (1979): 317–32.

[30] For a similar point see William Hasker, *The Triumph of God over Evil: Theodicy for a World of Suffering* (Downers Grove, IL: InterVarsity Press, 2008), esp. chap. 1. See also his work *Providence, Evil, and the Openness of God* (London: Routledge Press, 2004).

[31] This point is one that Hasker develops in his *Providence, Evil, and the Openness of God*.

maintained through generations in which the historical context differed radically from the actual world by the omission of many, or important, evils.[32]

One instance Adams uses to illustrate his view is Helen Keller, for she overcame tremendous obstacles in her life, and in fact became the person she was through her sufferings. Regarding Keller, Adams says:

> Would it have been reasonable for Helen Keller, as an adult, to wish, for her own sake, that she had never been blind or deaf? I think not. Let us suppose that she would have had an even better and happier life if her sight and hearing had been spared (though that is not obviously true). But whatever its excellences, that life would not have had one day in it that would have been very like any day of her actual life after the age of 19 months. Her actual life—in its emotional as well as its sensory qualities, in its skills and projects, and doubtless in much of her personality and character—was built around the fact of her blindness and deafness. The retrospective preferability of our actual lives to even better ones is based on our attachment to actual projects, friendships, experiences, and other features of our actual lives. Alas, not everyone is able now to love his life in this way. But it is clear that love for projects, experiences, and friendships that one is engaged in is highly correlated with happiness. So to the extent that the theist believes we shall all be happy in the end, he may well believe we shall all have reason to prefer our actual lives to others we could have had.[33]

In other words, wishing for a different life is equivalent to wishing that someone else existed instead of the particular people that in fact do exist. Usually referred to as the radical view of personal identity, insofar as we have the life we do resultant to certain states of affairs being true about our lives, we have no reason to complain about our circumstances being exactly as they are.

I am not committed to such a rigid view in my proposal, for what Adams's view demands is that the notion of defeat logically requires that every person must be caught up in a success story derivative from evil. The notion I have been defending offers no such requirement. Instead, I have suggested that we are responsible for our moral conduct and the effects that has on our moral character.[34] As Keith Yandell explains:

---

[32] Adams, "Existence, Self-Interest, and the Problem of Evil," 54, 56.
[33] Ibid., 60, 64 (excerpts).
[34] See also Keith Yandell, "Tragedy and Evil," *International Journal for Philosophy of Religion* 26

> No particular evils are requisite for one's participating in morally significant situations or in virtue circumstances. But given that persons sometimes freely act wrongly, and given that in any case evils are sometimes logically necessary if one is to participate in the full range of virtue circumstances, one cannot consistently be grateful that there are moral agents and bemoan the fact that there are evils. If the moral enterprise is serious, the evils will not be trivial.[35]

Thus, rather than explain our identity as being derived through circumstances over which we have no control (history, heredity), a more satisfying account requires that there are sufficient occasions "or virtue circumstances in which one participates so that one has a moral character to which one has at least significantly contributed."[36] The difference here, and one that is important in responding to this objection to the soul-making proposal offered, is that the evils are necessary only in the sense that had they not occurred the requisite virtue could not *possibly* obtain.

Before turning to one other objection, and before addressing a theological theme that gives impetus for accepting the account of defeat provided, I invite for consideration another way this view helps to shape our expectations regarding evil, whether it be addressing moral or natural evil. On this Hugh McCann, for whom I am mostly indebted for helping develop these thoughts, says:

> Instead of making the good life for one of mere passive enjoyment, it incorporates the realization that for beings made in God's image a valuable life involves facing and overcoming the challenges the world presents. It does not treat suffering as a mere causal means to a good outcome—something an omnipotent God might simply have omitted as unnecessary—nor does it justify the world's suffering simply as outweighed by a greater good. Rather, it recognizes that in its own diminishment and also in soul making, suffering is bound up in the defeating good as an integral part. In addition, this kind of theodicy recognizes the importance of suffering in reversing the damage sin does to the soul, and in reclaiming and enhancing the potential of the individual for fellowship with God. Finally, and perhaps most important, this kind of theodicy understands that through suffering all creatures are made participants in

---

(1994): 1–26; "The Greater Good Defense," *Sophia* 13 (1974): 9; "The Problem of Evil and the Content of Morality," *International Journal for Philosophy of Religion* 17 (1985): 148.

[35] Yandell, "Tragedy and Evil," 17–18.
[36] Ibid., 24.

a divine enterprise of overcoming evil—and that by their participation rational creatures are given the opportunity to prepare themselves for the knowledge of God promised to the redeemed in rational belief.[37]

A last objection to this view is worthy of attention: does not the emphasis on evil's defeat justify that we should maximize suffering in order that evil's defeat be complete? The apostle Paul addresses a strangely similar question when explaining the extent of God's grace. If God's grace is even more manifest when it remedies horrific sin, should not the worst of sin be in the world so that grace is manifest all the more? Paul responds, "What shall we say, then? Shall we go on sinning so that grace may increase? By no means! We are those who have died to sin; how can we live in it any longer? . . . For we know that our old self was crucified with him so that the body ruled by sin might be done away with, that we should no longer be slaves to sin" (Rom 6:1–2, 6). The defeat of evil is about a past reality and a present and future prospect for its address, not a future endorsement of evil in order to heighten the drama of it all. More to the point, the idea suggested here completely misses the nature of defeat, for it asks us to contribute to the already existing problem so that the process may persist. Yet such a contribution logically contradicts what the project suggests is worthy of accomplishment, which is to partner with God as an affront to what works against him. We cannot partner with him and simultaneously have as our course of intentions and actions that which is against him.

As a final note on the project of defeat, I return to the discussion in the chapter on the evidential argument concerning the sheer amount of evil. If we allow what has been offered in the admixture of soul making and defeat, the question still lingers about the amount of evil in the world. The comments in this section regard the promissory note mentioned before about defeat and theology. Earlier I noted that a rich theme in the creation narrative was God's handing of dominion over to Adam, an act that provided a type of life that involves great responsibilities and accountability for how dominion was exercised: dominion may be seen as the highest form of participation in the *imago Dei*.[38] Dominion also has a number of inferences that pertain to it. Upon the

---

[37] McCann, "Pointless Suffering," 174.

[38] A fuller discussion can be found in Christopher Wright's excellent book *God's People in God's Land: Family, Land, and Prosperity in the Old Testament* (Grand Rapids: Eerdmans, 1990), esp. chaps. 4–5. See also Oliver O'Donovan, *The Desire of Nations: Rediscovering the Roots of Political Theology* (Cambridge: Cambridge University Press, 1996), esp. chaps. 2–4. Their works are more comprehensive in scope than what I have provided here, but they each develop the theme of dominion and its application to God's interaction with creation and man's responsibility for its well-being. Each also treats the significance of redemption in Old Testament theology as to how it addresses the misuses of dominion.

granting of dominion God gave a great deal of control to humans over the affairs of the world. What is more, for dominion to be a real feature of our experience and not just an illusion, we can expect a lesser degree of divine interference than what is usually requested in arguments from evil. The expectation of less divine interference has, as a natural outflow, a way of shaping our expectations regarding the amount of evil in the world. Rather than expecting a relatively small amount of evil whose consequences are trivial, we should expect quite the opposite. Given that God is honest, the states of affairs he conserves in being provide an accurate portrayal of the depth of the sin problem, in all of its manifestations, with all of its consequences. That being said, the issuance of grievance against God from the amount of evil in the world confirms what the misuse of dominion promises to be a prevalent facet of our experience—a vast amount of suffering of a kind and variety that is limited only by the creativity with which sinners can express the depth of their sin. No doubt the manifestation of the depths of sin will bring with it actions that are morally egregious, beyond the pale of any morally justifying reason. However, if there is a point in the human narrative that is worthy of attention in this realm of the discussion, it is the choice of God to permit the first sin. Since the first sin is the act that made possible all other acts of evil, it alone counts as a sufficient quantity of evil as regards the evidential argument.[39] What we know of God's permission of the first evil is that it is bound up in a larger story about directing our freedom toward a loving relationship with him. The rest of the story, as I have tried to disclose here, is an account of how we address the consequences, both positive and negative, of how that freedom is expressed and how the notions of defeat and soul making are essential concepts in that endeavor. Toward that end I have noted that both moral and natural evil have their place in this conversation.

## Conclusion

The account provided in this chapter as a response to the evidential argument from evil, has two distinct yet related aspects to its articulation. The first aspect centers on human freedom as the source of moral evil: human freedom is a morally sufficient reason for God's permission of evil. The emphasis on human freedom is an attempt to answer *why* there is evil. The second aspect may be categorized as a postlapsarian or postfall view, and here I conjured the notion of the defeat of evil as a response to nondeductive arguments from

---

[39] I am indebted to my good friend James R. L. Noland for articulating this point. It proved to be a foundational point from which the rest of this part of the discussion ensued.

evil. The notion of defeat invites persons to recognize that once evil obtains, it cannot be undone. The proper response to this situation is to address evil as evil and to remove its hold on the content of our experience. A proper addressing of evil requires that we partner with God in this endeavor, for partnering with God overcomes the nonsense that evil can be addressed on our terms and through our means. It is precisely this kind of thinking that brought about evil in the first place. The defeat of evil, rather than merely speculating on the inferential extensions of God's power, knowledge, and goodness, attempts to provide a real-world answer to the question "what now." In other words, once we have the answer to the *why* question, we then ask *what now*. The progression of thought in this chapter is an attempt to answer this question.

CHAPTER FIVE

# Divine Hiddenness

## THE ARGUMENT FROM DIVINE HIDDENNESS

In his work *Daybreak*, the famous philosopher Friedrich Nietzsche finds the lack of certain evidence for God's existence to be troubling. He writes:

> A god who is all-knowing and all-powerful and who does not even make sure his creatures understand his intention—could that be a god of goodness? Who allows countless doubts and uncertainties to persist, for thousands of years, as though the salvation of mankind were unaffected by them, or who, on the other hand, holds out the prospect of frightful consequences if any mistake is made as to the nature of truth? Would he not be a cruel god if he possessed the truth and could behold mankind miserably tormenting itself over that truth? But perhaps he is a god of goodness notwithstanding and merely could express himself more clearly! Did he perhaps lack the intelligence to do so? Or the eloquence? So much the worse, for then he was perhaps also in error as to that which he calls his "truth," and is himself not so very far from being the "poor deluded devil."[1]

In essence Nietzsche is wondering why God takes such pains to hide himself from us, an even more troubling phenomenon when we are suffering. Indeed, "some people search for God with apparent sincerity but come away feeling unfulfilled and disillusioned."[2] Given God's unsurpassable love and care, it seems our search for him should not result in such conclusions. Rather, we might expect God to consider each request made by his children and provide a

---

[1] Friedrich Nietzsche, *Daybreak*, trans. R. J. Hollingdale (Cambridge: Cambridge University Press, 1982), 89–90.
[2] Ibid.

quick response, spare us any needless trauma, and foster physical and mental well-being, including removing mental obstacles to our understanding who he is and what our relationship with him is.[3] Daniel Howard-Snyder expresses the objector's sentiment that we expect a perfectly loving God to make it clear, right now, that he exists.[4] As Howard-Snyder explains, "love at its best desires the well-being of the beloved, not from a distance, but up close, explicitly participating in her life in a personal fashion, allowing her to draw from that relationship what she may need to flourish."[5] One might surmise that a loving God will not leave mere evidences of his existence to facilitate what is intended to be an all-encompassing relationship but will give people nothing short of himself in this endeavor. This idea is expressed by former Yale philosopher Norwood Hanson in his work *What I Do Not Believe and Other Essays*. He writes:

> Suppose—that on next Tuesday morning, just after breakfast, all of us in this one world are knocked to our knees by a percussive and ear-shattering thunderclap. Snow swirls, leaves drop from trees; the earth heaves and buckles; buildings topple and towers rumble; the sky is ablaze with an eerie, silvery light. Just then, as all the people of this world look up, the heavens open up—the clouds pull apart—revealing an unbelievably immense and radiant Zeus-like figure, towering above us like a hundred Everests. He frowns darkly as lightning plays across the features of his Michaelangeloid face. He then points down—at me!—and he exclaims, for every man, woman and child to hear "I have had quite enough of your too-clever logic chopping and word watching in matters of theology. Be assured, N. R. Hanson, that I do most certainly exist."[6]

Anthony O'Hear also agrees, in effect wondering why, if there is a God, "there are no such events, and why the miracles believers do claim either are buried in a murky and problematic past or are cures which are not unequivocally miraculous exceptions to natural regularities."[7] Given God's resources to self-disclose (knowledge, power, and goodness), we are left to wonder about the ambiguity surrounding his existence.

---

[3] Ibid., 33.
[4] Daniel Howard-Snyder, "The Argument from Divine Hiddenness," last accessed June 29, 2010, wwu.du/~howardd/theargumentfromdivinehiddenness.pdf.
[5] Ibid.
[6] N. R. Hanson, *What I Do Not Believe and Other Essays* (New York: Humanities Press, 1971), 313–14.
[7] As quoted in Thomas V. Morris, *Making Sense of It All: Pascal and the Meaning of Life* (Grand Rapids: Eerdmans, 1992), 94.

Thus, in its most precise form the argument from hiddenness is:

1. If there is a God, he is perfectly loving.
2. If a perfectly loving God exists, reasonable nonbelief does not occur.
3. Reasonable nonbelief does occur. Thus,
4. No perfectly loving God exists. So,
5. There is no God.[8]

A key conceptual component of this argument concerns what is meant by reasonable nonbelief. All God must do to make a relationship with him possible is to reveal himself in such a way that once he does, if a person does not believe in him, then that person is to blame for his nonbelief. If there is some blame in the person for his disbelief, then his failing to believe in God cannot accurately be described as *reasonable* nonbelief. However, as the argument suggests, reasonable nonbelief does occur, which rules out the possibility that a perfectly loving God exists.

It is interesting to note in advance that proponents of divine hiddenness such as J. L. Schellenberg do not take seriously the demographics of religious belief. It is no secret that the number of proponents of atheism and agnosticism are swamped in comparison to those who endorse theistic belief; some polls indicate that only about 15 percent of the world's population align themselves either with atheism or agnosticism.[9] So statements about the "many people" who find the evidence for God's existence lacking or less than compelling for belief are not accurate if we are basing "many" on actual numbers. Such a note may be beside the point though, for the argument from hiddenness indicates that if God exists, then *everyone* would believe in him, especially if it is granted that any nonbelief in God is unreasonable.

This chapter is concerned with responding to the argument from divine hiddenness (DH). I will first sketch some proposed solutions that ultimately do not succeed as a response to the problem, after which I will look into some lines of thought that have more explanatory power. The essence of the chapter is to question premise 2 of the argument above, though some aspects of the chapter will bring into question premise 3 by contraposition of 2. It will be concluded that DH does not provide conclusive reasons for nonbelief.

---

[8] J. L. Schellenberg, *Divine Hiddenness and Human Reason* (Ithaca: Cornell University Press, 1993), 83.
[9] See *The World Factbook* of the US Central Intelligence Agency, online at https://www.cia.gov/library/publications/the-world-factbook/print/xx.html.

## SOME PROPOSED AND FAILED SOLUTIONS TO DH AND AN IMPORTANT MODIFICATION

If one takes a look at certain attributes of God, an immediate inference to his hiddenness might be derived, even expected. For example, perfect-being theology generally affirms divine incorporeality, according to which God is not an embodied being but is a spirit (John 4:24). From the belief that God does not have a body one might then conclude that he is a being beyond our sensory capacities. Therefore, to expect God to be (at least normally) evident to our senses in the same way that we perceive ordinary objects such as trees is fundamentally to misunderstand not only who God is but who we are and how we relate to him.[10] Prima facie, divine incorporeality suggests the hiddenness of God.

Transcendence is another attribute ascribed to God; he is wholly other. Given God's transcendence, and that his being is not contained to the world, we may infer there is no direct experience of him in the world. Accordingly, "it should not perplex us in the least that in the ordinary course of affairs, as we live out our lives on our level of reality in this world, God is typically hidden from us."[11] Much like divine incorporeality, God's transcendence provides prima facie reason to think that God, if he exists, will be hidden.

A third attribute of God that factors into the equation involves his omnipresence. As Thomas Morris explains, "this solution to our problem begins by pointing out that for something to be an object of recognition, or perceptual discrimination, it must have a delimited presence, marked off spatially or temporally for some perceptual background."[12] Features that normally attend such distinctions include height, width, and depth, so that there may be "that-where-it-is-not as well as that-where-it-is if it is to be seen as present."[13] Taken together, divine incorporeality and omnipresence lead to a loss of the distinctive boundaries that make perceptual discrimination possible. Thus, "what seems to be a total absence of the divine is only an illusion produced by the reality of his all-encompassing presence."[14] Divine omnipresence, just like incorporeality and transcendence, provides prima facie reason for one to expect God to be hidden.

Thomas Morris rightly notes that these suggestions are provocative but fail to capture the essence of the question. The problem of divine hiddenness is

---

[10] See Morris, *Making Sense of It All*, 90.
[11] Ibid.
[12] Ibid., 91.
[13] Ibid.
[14] Ibid.

primarily an affront to the *activities* of God, not the *attributes* of God—why he acts as he does or refrains from acting when he does. Presumably God has the resources to take on a body, thus overcoming the limitations of incorporeality. Furthermore, God's transcendence does not entail his inability to communicate discernibly those features of his existence that *can* be grasped by the human mind, albeit with his assistance. And so, if God can take on a body he can also provide in that activity an image of his own existence, overcoming any limitations on our part that hinders our ability to know him.[15] Appeals to divine attributes, at least as they are construed so far, will not answer the problem of divine hiddenness.

## DIVINE CONCEALMENT

As was noted, the previous use of the divine attributes did not sufficiently answer the activities of God, and in this section I want to address one reason for this, as derived from the attributes mentioned above, that provide God ultima facie reason to hide from us. If my suggestion is correct, then the problem of divine hiddenness will take a different shape. As I will argue, God's hiddenness is better understood as divine concealment for which he has a morally sufficient reason.

Isaiah 6 records an unusual event in the life of Isaiah. As the chapter describes, Isaiah experiences heaven, the literal dwelling place of God where he sees seraphs calling out:

> Holy, holy, holy is the LORD Almighty;
> The whole earth is full of his glory. (Isa 6:3)

These angels have dwelled continually in God's presence, never separating themselves from God through disobedience, unlike other angels who were cast out from the presence of God (Jude 6). The stain of sin is not upon them, and yet even in the throne room of God "they covered their faces" as the "train of his robe filled the temple" (Isa 6:1). We cannot claim from this passage that God was hidden to them, but the fullness of his glory was concealed from them.

Scripture has numerous instances where the same theme is played out. In Exodus 33 Moses pitched a tent known as the "tent of meeting" outside of the camp at Mount Horeb. The tent served as the meeting place between people

---

[15] Ibid.

and God. In one exchange in the tent of meeting Moses asked God to show him his glory (33:18). God's response:

> "I will cause all my goodness to pass in front of you, and I will proclaim my name, the LORD, in your presence. I will have mercy on whom I will have mercy, and I will have compassion on whom I will have compassion. But," he said, "you cannot see my face, for no one may see me and live." Then the LORD said, "There is a place near me where you may stand on a rock. When my glory passes by, I will put you in a cleft in the rock and cover you with my hand until I have passed by. Then I will remove my hand and you will see my back; but my face must not be seen." (Exod 33:19–23)

The passage in Isaiah has the angels conceal themselves from God's glory, and the passage in Exodus has God conceal himself from Moses. In neither case is God hidden, at least as far as arguments from hiddenness are proposed. But these passages do provide an interesting answer to the question of the hiddenness of God, even if we allow concealment and hiddenness to be treated as the same: God conceals himself as a protective measure for the well-being of his creation. Nothing in creation can bear to see him face-to-face, for as God told Moses, "no one may see me and live." Claims from persons such as Nietzsche, Hanson, and Schellenberg that God could overcome the problem of hiddenness with a single act of full self-disclosure fail to understand that such a disclosure would come at the expense of the death penalty. Insofar as this is correct, then God's act of concealment is a loving act; it also indicates that God reveals himself to creation in other ways. As he told Moses, "I will cause my goodness to pass in front of you." Or as Romans indicates, "For since the creation of the world God's invisible qualities—his eternal power and divine nature—have been clearly seen, being understood from what has been made, so that men are without excuse" (Rom 1:20).[16]

One may wonder why these invisible attributes are not clear to everyone. Paul indicates it is because they suppress the truth that God has provided for them. A more thorough treatment of this theme is the topic of our next section, but suffice it to say at this point that a full-bore experience of God is not possible, which is no indictment on God's ability to communicate or reveal. But if a full-bore experience of God is not possible for nondivine beings, then the

---

[16] Later, in the Exodus passage, the concealment of God is evident in Moses' veiling his face after speaking with the Lord on Mount Sinai (Exod 34:29–35). As it is recorded, he was so radiant that the Israelites were afraid to be near him.

measures through which God will manifest himself will be different than what that encounter could otherwise provide.

In any event, if this suggestion is defensible, then God has a morally sufficient reason for concealing himself from creation. A self-revelation of the sort requested by proponents of DH is a foolish request and one worthy of denial for the betterment of the one requesting it. This argument does not undermine every facet of the argument from hiddenness, but it does provide a coherent rationale for God's activity of concealment.

## THE FALL AND THE NOETIC EFFECTS OF SIN

One of the more promising lines of response to DH is to take seriously the implications of the fall of Adam and Eve. Recall that DH is a subspecies of the problem of evil, so presumably if there were no evil there would be no problem of divine hiddenness, at least as it is generally construed. Proponents of DH generally do not take the noetic effects of sin seriously. For example, J. L. Schellenberg provides a mere passing swipe at the claim rather than probing its implications as he retorts of the fall, "in light of the findings of disciplines like evolutionary biology and biblical criticism, it is hard to see how such an assumption could be successfully defended."[17] On this Jonathan Kvanvig makes some important observations, one of which is that "it is far from clear that a historical doctrine of the Fall is required to resolve the difficulty Schellenberg presents."[18] The story of the fall might reveal something "endemic" to the created order in that "the Fall points to a need, both cognitive and conative, that can be addressed only by the intervention of the divine."[19] The cognitive results of the fall include a "logical and empirical gap between recognized sufficient warrant and actual belief formation very much like the fallenness of humanity displayed in cases of weakness of the will."[20] So the fall cannot be passed over with the wave of a hand but must be factored in as having tremendous explanatory power concerning the problem of hiddenness. Perhaps no one has better developed this theme in recent religious epistemology than Paul Moser, and in this section I intend to develop and build on his work.

---

[17] See Schellenberg, *Divine Hiddenness and Human Reason*, 146.
[18] Jonathan L. Kvanvig, "Divine Hiddenness: What Is the Problem?" 3. Last accessed July 26, 2012, http://www.lastseminary.com/divine-hiddenness/Divine%20Hiddenness%20-%20What%20is%20the%20problem.pdf. This does not mean the fall was not historical; it means that proving the doctrine is not needed.
[19] Ibid.
[20] Ibid.

The first course of action is to note that the problem of hiddenness is a rational problem; there is a deficiency in our experience or understanding that is purportedly best explained by the nonexistence of God. But coming to the conclusion that God does not exist from one area of inquiry does not factor in other phenomena that require explanation and for which God provides the best explanation. For example, God provides the best explanation of objective moral values, of the presence of the material world, and of the presence of free, conscious beings in that world. Divine hiddenness is only one facet of our experience, and it is not even a pervasive facet of our experience, especially if we agree that God is the Good, and participating in the Good is a means of participating in God's own way life, a theme to which I will return later. A more cautious approach recognizes that hiddenness must be taken seriously but not in isolation from other features for which theism has a more solid footing than metaphysical naturalism.

So of the proposition *God exists* there may be many instances of reasoning for which evidence is abundant, but this says nothing of a person's propositional attitude in the least. Propositional attitudes matter, for they explain the disposition with which we approach an area of inquiry. Of course, this means that we have to ask about what shapes our propositional attitudes and how that affects our expectations. This is the critical juncture at which divine hiddenness and the fall intersect and is the point at which I invite Paul Moser's contribution.

There can be no doubt that sin has affected our minds, especially if we understand sin to include the failure to have pro-attitudes toward the things God requires of us. Rather than actions being the only things worthy of blame, Scripture condemns attitudes as well. Wrongful anger, lust, covetousness, jealousy, and selfishness are all attitudes that Scripture condemns (Exod 20:17; Matt 5:22; Gal 5:20). One of the greatest commandments in Scripture is to love God with the entire mind (Mark 12:30). Failure to have a pro-attitude toward the proposition *God exists* is intellectually condemnable, at least as far as Scripture is concerned.

Since sin has affected our disposition toward God, then our discernment about God first requires a transformed disposition. Moser contends God will provide an opportunity through which the needed transformation can occur. Since the problem is moral in nature, the remedy will be moral in nature as well. So the kind of knowledge God seeks to impart to everyone is not mere propositional content primarily but a volitionally transforming knowledge; it includes a change of will or orientation rather than simply a pro-attitude toward the proposition *God exists*.[21] Since God is a person and not a proposition, we should expect such a prioritizing of relationship over abstraction. We do not advance in medicine through mere armchair speculation, nor do we exhibit excellence in a relationship through theories about what is needed for it to be healthy and complete. Instead, knowledge of God requires recognition of who God is in stature, the privileges that pertain to being God, and the obligations put on us as nondivine beings. It is this last point that is telling; for the primary problem is not our intellectual abilities but a "moral orientation" regarding God's authority and lordship over our lives.[22] Accordingly, God will provide a "cognitively robust theism" that requires commitment to God in all of our endeavors, and not a "thin theism" according to which he is merely the conclusion of an argument.[23]

Cognitively robust theism highlights the need to abandon autonomy and to rely on God to lead us morally and intellectually in this transformation. The new orientation requires that we first understand that we have no right to know God; further, he is under no obligation to disclose himself in any way to his creation. We have no standing to lay claim that God ought to reveal himself in the ways that we demand and the ways that we deem fit.[24] In fact, making such demands evidences the problem at hand: the clay is attempting to dictate to the potter rather than the other way around.

Thus, our expectations should be shaped according to God's terms and not our own, and God-seekers will place themselves in the best epistemic situation through which belief (or more appropriately, acceptance) can be cultivated. We should expect God to reveal himself in a way that requires a moral transformation in us and brings us to a filial relationship with him. We come to know God in recognizing our unworthiness of knowing him.[25] As Moser indicates, the new expectation that God will confront the core of our being also reveals the inadequacy of "signs and wonders" as means by which we know God with depth and nearness.[26] Notice that there is no shortage of such occurrences in human history, and within a breath of the event persons are providing rival explanations, as in the resurrection of Jesus. Crying out for God to do more is kicking at the goads. Furthermore, asking God to do more of the same when

---

[21] Paul Moser, "Cognitive Idolatry and Divine Hiding," in *Divine Hiddenness*, ed. Paul Moser and Daniel Howard-Snyder (Cambridge: Cambridge University Press, 2002). Accessed July 14, 2010, http://luc.edu/faculty/pmoser/idolanon/CognitiveIdolatry.html .

[22] Ibid., 10 (in the online version of the document, all other references are from this document as well).

[23] Ibid.

[24] Ibid., 11.

[25] Ibid., 12.

[26] Ibid., 15.

we have already built systems through which we may reject his work indicates a level of disingenuousness in rational inquiry. It also betrays a painful ignorance of the Bible, which has already said we have everything we need to know God.

Thin theism's focus on a theoretical knowledge of God's existence is to be juxtaposed with cognitively robust theism, according to which God will reveal himself to persons who expect a moral and relational transformation in their lives—a transformation that involves identifying and killing the idols that pervade our lives and minds. Idolatry is . . .

> Not letting God be the Lord in our lives. It is a commitment to something other than the true God as our ultimate authority and source of flourishing. It is inherently a rejection of God's authority and quest for self-definition, self-importance, and self-fulfillment on our own terms.[27]

Cognitive idolatry occurs when we see fit to determine the parameters of divine self-disclosure. Instances of cognitive idolatry include espousing a future belief in God if he were to put one million dollars in your bank account, or mounting up a stack of wood, soaking it in lighter fluid, and calling down God to light it to prove to you that he exists. In both cases a purported belief is promised, but the requisite humility is lacking. If these demands are instances of mental-attitude sins, then it is more reasonable to expect that God will *not* answer when the supposed epistemic gauntlet is thrown down—not just for nonbelievers but for believers as well. Indeed, divine hiddenness is in part derived from God's regard for himself as the Creator of every contingent being and also derived from his disregard for all things that distort the direction of proper worship from the Creator to creation, especially the self as a part of creation (Rom 1:18–25).

The demand that we have control over knowledge reveals a cognitive idol that God will not feed; and given that God is not an enabler of sin, he will not bow to our demands. This is not to say that God will hide at all times, but it does indicate how our expectations should be shaped when we are pursuing a filial relationship with him. If our mental attitudes are incorrect, then we should *expect* God to hide rather than disclose. If we expect God to hide when we bear a demanding spirit toward him, then there will be no perceived failure on his part through his nondisclosure when we know we have sought to place a cognitive idol on his throne. Strangely, epistemic integrity demands that our expectations have actually been satisfied when we see things in just

---

[27] Ibid., 17.

such a way; we come to expect hiddenness rather than disclosure. Moser's suggestion thus far is rather instructive; since God is personal, we should not be seeking primarily propositional knowledge but personal knowledge (knowledge by acquaintance), and the purported propositional knowledge will follow accordingly.

## PHENOMENAL PRESENCE

Admittedly, some instances of God's hiddenness are not the result of *personal* sin.[28] Jesus' cry of dereliction (Matt 27:45–46) on the cross is one such instance. But it must be noted that the problem *of* hiddenness from this narrative is self-defeating to the argument *from* hiddenness. Jesus was not questioning the existence of God as he cried out. What the narrative indicates is that there is hiddenness that is derived from personal sin, and there is hiddenness derived from others' sin. Sin has a personal dimension and a social dimension. Sin affects not only individuals but also the communities in which individuals exist. The cry of dereliction was not Jesus' first encounter with sin, but it was his first encounter with taking the consequences of sin on himself in a redemptive manner. The social dimension of sin involves coming to grips with the hiddenness of God as it pertains to how we might perceive, or fail to perceive God, in states of affairs. For example, we cannot see God's moral goodness in the rape and murder of Sue precisely because his moral goodness was not expressed in that action; his moral goodness was suppressed, thus concealed, in that action. The same reasoning applies to other sins as well that have social ramifications. Accordingly, trying to discern the moral goodness of God from these atrocities is a fool's errand from the start; if it is suppressed, it will not be phenomenally present. This is not to say that God's presence is wholly absent from these states of affairs, for his activity of conservation is present in each and every one; rather, God's moral nature is not always expressed through embodied beings created in his image. Even though we are created in his image, it does not mean that we always resemble him in our deliberations and actions.

Much like the problem of cognitive idolatry mentioned before, this construct helps shape our expectations in a different way. We should never expect to have a phenomenally robust awareness of God in states of affairs that do not embody his goodness. Such a phenomenal distance is not derivative of God's

---

[28] Moser makes the claim that not all hiddenness is from the problem of sin. I am making a cautious proviso to say that not all of hiddenness is a result of *personal* sin. Divine hiddenness, as the problem is normally constructed, is always a result of sin.

indifference but is predicated on our previous discussion of the ways in which God can reveal himself given that we cannot endure a direct experience of his being. Beyond the fact that nature expresses his power and creativity, humans are designed to express his moral goodness. One manner of experiencing God is through others embodying his goodness in their intentions and actions. Jesus embodied in human form everything that God originally designed for humans in the first Adam, literally imaging the Father's perfect nature in his human form. As Jesus says, "Anyone who has seen me has seen the Father" (John 14:9). Hebrews says that Jesus "is the radiance of His glory, the exact expression of His nature, and He sustains all things by His powerful word" (Heb 1:3 HCSB). Unlike Jesus, given the pervasiveness of sin in the human condition, we are not an exact expression of his nature, nor are we the radiance of his glory. Rebellion hides God not only from ourselves but cloaks his presence in creation by suppressing the benefits of participating in his goodness.

The previous point has an important application, for it is in our suffering that we want to see God all the more. We need the comfort of his presence and the council of his understanding. Yet as he has revealed in his Word, we receive these things by individually and communally participating in the good, overcoming selfishness with selflessness, and tending to the needs of others. Jesus expressed how participating in God's own being expresses itself to others:

> For I was hungry and you gave Me something to eat;
> I was thirsty and you gave Me something to drink;
> I was a stranger and you took Me in;
> I was naked and you clothed Me;
> I was sick and you took care of Me;
> I was in prison and you visited Me. . . .
> Whatever you did for one of the least of these brothers of Mine, you did for Me. (Matt 25:35–36, 40 HCSB)

Previously Jesus remarked that the Pharisees neglected the more important matters of the law, including justice, mercy, and faith; he denounced them as blind guides (Matt 23:24). Not only were they blind, but they were leading others in their blindness. Paul admonishes the Corinthian church to "comfort those who are in any kind of affliction, through the comfort we ourselves receive from God" (2 Cor 1:4 HCSB). If God's phenomenal presence is connected to manifestations of his being through creation, then we can expect a law of diminishing returns as the human condition becomes more hardened against him. Given that Scripture indicates most people do not participate in the good, then we can expect, at least phenomenally, that God's existence will not be evident from states of affairs connected to our nonparticipation.

The case of Jesus is particularly interesting, for in the cry of dereliction we have both divine hiddenness and divine revelation. The Father was hidden to the Son, but the Son was the manifestation of the invisible attributes of God through his incarnation. Moser suggests that God hid from Jesus to foster deeper trust in his "unpredictable but redeeming Father."[29] This suggestion has its place. After all, the Passion of Jesus is the fulcrum on which God's salvation story hinges—so supposing that Jesus trusted the Father in the Passion for redemptive purposes is an important point.

I wish to chart out another line of thought about this critical passage. In a previous chapter on the evidential argument from evil, I suggested that no greater horror has occurred in the history of humankind than the suffering and death of Christ on the cross. I also suggested that if this event provides a picture of the worst suffering imaginable, and if God has an end for which he permits it, then presumably he has an end for which he permits all of our suffering. If the Passion of Christ embodies purposeful suffering at its worst, then we cannot use cases such as Sue or Bambi as instances for which there is an evil that was unnecessary or unjustified, at least if the reasoning is predicated on the amount of evil. The same point has application in our current discussion. The God-man was subject to hiddenness as a way by which he understands our distance from God because of sin and because of the fragmentation sin has created not just for individuals but for the entire cosmos. In his Passion Jesus took the effects of sin on himself, which includes the hiddenness of God concomitant to sin's confrontation. Even the hiddenness of God is defeated in the cross of Christ, as he not only experiences it firsthand on our account but addresses it on our behalf. He does in his Passion what we are powerless to do; he remedies sin and all of its perversions. So even though we now see "through a looking glass dimly" Christians will one day see God as did the angels in Isaiah—truly, yet veiled. The problem of hiddenness has a tenable solution, and given that the purpose of the incarnation of Christ was to address the sin problem, it should be expected that hiddenness was addressed in the cross as well.

---

[29] Ibid., 22.

## Is There an Epistemic Problem of Divine Hiddenness?

To this point an emphasis has been placed on the problem of sin and a volitional transformation needed to overcome the problem of hiddenness, but there are other ways of confronting DH. One approach, suggested by Jonathan Kvanvig, is to draw suspicion to the idea that an epistemic problem of hiddenness even exists.[30] Epistemic hiddenness occurs when the evidence for God's existence is inadequate to ground belief in God; it is a *de dicto* (literally "of the proposition") objection to the rationality of theistic belief. As Schellenberg has argued, a loving God would provide "sufficient" evidence to produce belief.[31] So of the proposition *God exists*, God will provide every evidential measure to produce belief. God's providing sufficient evidence means the evidence is not only adequate for belief but is efficacious for belief as well.

This is a questionable requirement for several reasons. First, if evidence for the existence of God is adequate, then there is no such thing as an epistemic problem of hiddenness. Adequate evidence can be a feature of reality even if no one or at least very few believe what is produced through the evidence. Copernicus's revolution in cosmology provides an illuminating example of just such a fact. If evidence is there, then it is just there, regardless of whether or not anyone believes it or yields to it as evidence for belief in God.[32] The problem may be one of human inability to comprehend, even if the evidence were there, or as we have noted before, it could be sheer resistance to the evidence provided. In either case *the evidence* is not the problem—the inability or unwillingness to appreciate the evidence is the problem. This may seem a trifling distinction, but it does remove some of the powder from the keg.

Second, Schellenberg indicates God would provide evidence that is sufficient to produce belief. But one wonders why belief should have anything to do with evidence whatsoever. God could simply force belief on us, or God could so construct humans that we just have belief already in us—everyone could be born causally determined to believe. In either of these cases, the problem of hiddenness is solved; but it also reveals that the problem of hiddenness can be solved in nonevidential forms, which creates a divide between evidence and belief formation. Rather than being an issue of the rationality of belief, it is a volitional solution to hiddenness. Of course, Christians have long thought that the only meaningful worship is worship given freely. Such a belief about

---

[30] Kvanvig, "Divine Hiddenness: What Is the Problem?"
[31] Schellenberg, *Divine Hiddenness and Human Reason*, 33.
[32] Kvanvig, "Divine Hiddenness," 11.

worship explains why there is a distance between created persons and God—to provide the grounds for which genuine worship can occur. The objection, however, centers on the claim that there will be evidence sufficient to produce belief and drawing to light that evidence is simply not needed for belief.

Third, recall that the problem of hiddenness is a subcategory of the problem of evil. It is intended to be a part of the counterbalancing evidence against the rationality of theistic belief. Perhaps we can take arguments for the existence of God, religious experience, and the like on one side of the ledger and then place the problem of evil on the other side as counterbalancing evidence.[33] If this situation is correct, then there is no positive epistemic evidence on either side of the ledger, for every instance of evidence has a counterbalancing claim (not necessarily in the same domain).

It is hard to see how the evidence of evil can be used as a counterbalance against the existence of God when it has already been conceded that God and evil are logically compatible with one another. If there is no logical objection to the claim that God exists and evil exists, then there is "no objective epistemic connection" between the claims either.[34] This conclusion in turn shows that there is no epistemic objection to hiddenness in any important way. The objection to theistic belief from the problem of divine hiddenness, as just mentioned, is a subspecies of the problem of evil. As Kvanvig notes, "If hiddenness is an epistemic problem, it is because the inscrutability of divine existence is a bad thing that a perfectly loving God would not or could not allow. But that, of course, is simply a special case of the problem of evil, and on the picture above of how the evidence is counterbalanced between theism and atheism, no instances of evil are relevant at all to the truth or falsity of theism."[35]

Even under the strictures that there is solid evidence for the existence of God, each measure of evidence is counterbalanced in some way (rebutters, defeaters). Evil has been the go-to argument for atheists toward this end. However, if we appropriate this as a legitimate measure of counterbalancing epistemic information, then it is not clear how hiddenness provides any compelling rational grounds for disbelief in God, especially as we understand hiddenness to be just one instance of the problem of evil. We cannot *both* treat it as an instance of the problem of evil *and* as an individual argument used to show atheism has more epistemic force. Hiddenness is not a further problem by which atheism garners strength; it is a part of the already existing counterbalancing evidence; as such, it does nothing to bolster the epistemic standing of

---

[33] Ibid., 11.
[34] Ibid., 12.
[35] Ibid.

atheism. Following Kvanvig, even if the atheist treats it as a unique kind of evil adding to the effect of their case, it does nothing to offset new religious experiences to the other side of the ledger.[36] Kvanvig states:

> The theist can say, "I'll see your hiddenness problem and raise it five religious experiences." That is, if adding new evils to one side counts, certainly adding new proofs, or new grounds, or new religious experiences (I don't mean *kinds* of religious experiences, but I don't rule that out either) has to be allowed on the other side.[37]

The emphasis in this discussion must be understood. It has not been claimed in this section that the problem of hiddenness is not a problem. It is a problem of a special sort—phenomenal; that is, it is a problem about appearances (or the supposed failure to appear). What has been claimed in this section is that hiddenness does not provide any *epistemic* grounds for disbelief in God, thus undercutting the purported "evidential" strength of the argument from hiddenness. If arguments from hiddenness and evil mount up, and so do arguments for theistic belief, then one is not entitled to the claim that disbelief is more rational than belief.

## Reflective Nonbelievers

There is yet one more way to make the case from hiddenness against the existence of God that is somewhat different than the way the conversation has been shaped thus far. Even though Schellenberg recognizes that it is possible that all doubters have sinfully rejected belief in God, he still finds the claim unlikely. Given that his case only requires one doubter that has adequately investigated the arguments and is open to belief in God, surely it is the case that at least one person fits that description. Thus, Schellenberg thinks there is reason to accept premise 3: reasonable nonbelief does occur, where reasonable nonbelief concerns those persons who are in doubt about both the truth and falsity of the proposition *God exists*. Douglas Henry points out that there are two issues bearing on finding a member of the class of reasonable nonbelievers: (1) the nature and scope of adequate investigation and (2) the means of judging the adequacy of investigation.[38] In other words, it requires (1) data gathering and (2) an objective criteria to adjudicate fairness in the process of

---

[36] Ibid., 13.
[37] Ibid.
[38] Douglas Henry, "Does Reasonable Nonbelief Exist?" 7, italics mine; last accessed December 20, 2010, www.baylor.edu/~Douglas_Henry.

interpreting the data gathered. Accordingly, Henry explains, "appreciating the nature and scope of adequate investigation underscores how small the class of reflective nonbelievers is likely to be. Appreciating the difficulties of judging the adequacy of investigation highlights the difficulty of confirming *claims* of adequate investigation."[39]

The following questions should be asked about the qualities of the person investigating whether or not God exists: (1) Has he shown himself to be honest, a lover of the truth? (2) Does he resist his wants when his head tells him he ought not to give in to them? (3) Is he not self-deceived? (4) Does he desire to have the issue settled responsibly?[40] Given these traits, the person who arrives at nonbelief will do so only reluctantly. There are several things to note concerning these criteria. First:

> The presence of exemplary investigative procedure, honesty in other situations, love for truth, etc., does not render a judgment about the adequacy of investigation straightforward and uncontroversial. After all, one can give the appearance of exemplary investigative procedure without the reality of it. One can seem a generally honest person without being one. One can speak about a love for truth without being committed to the truth. In short, the presence of each of those qualities, whether individually or jointly, can be both deceptively and self-deceptively instantiated, i.e., not really instantiated at all—The problem is that the very traits which give good cause for believing in the adequacy of one's investigation—passion for truth, anxiety when in doubt, intense desire for a well-justified belief, whatever it may be—make eminently improbable a commitment to evidential parity.[41]

The second point is related to the first:

> Would a person possessing the intellectual and character virtues to which Schellenberg appeals ever judge that all alternatives are exhausted and foreclose their pursuit? The more such traits coincide, and the more clearly they are exemplified, the less tenable becomes the notion that evidential parity could appeal to such a person. As the virtues he identifies diminish in intensity, the acceptability of evidential parity becomes more likely, but the possibility of deception or self-deception also increases, problematizing claims to inculpable nonbelief.[42]

---

[39] Ibid.
[40] Schellenberg, *Divine Hiddenness and Human Reason*, 66.
[41] Henry, "Does Reasonable Nonbelief Exist," 10–11.
[42] Ibid., 11.

In other words, the virtues that constrain the proper activity of data gathering and interpreting create an "inverse" relationship between the conditions for genuine truth-seeking and the one pursuing truth being content with his unresolved epistemic stance concerning the proposition *God exists*. Perhaps the last thought is better captured by saying the parity position will be especially less appealing given the importance of the proposition *God exists*. Thus the following argument against the likelihood of reasonable nonbelief existing:

1. Reasonable nonbelief requires that the person in the state of nonbelief be honest, a lover of the truth, resist his wants when his head tells him he ought not to give in to them, not be self-deceiving, and desire to have the issue settled responsibly.
2. A person who is honest, a lover of truth, resists wants when in conflict with his head, is not self-deceived, and desires to have the issue settled responsibly will never be satisfied with an epistemic state of parity regarding the proposition *God exists*.
3. Therefore, reasonable nonbelief does not exist.

It must be remembered that it is not reasonable to accept a state of epistemic parity when the virtues governing the investigation do not permit such a conclusion, which is why the conclusion to the argument is that reasonable nonbelief does not exist. Reasonable nonbelief, if the argument is correct, is an oxymoron.

## Conclusion

Certainly this will not be the last word on the problem of divine hiddenness, but I hope it has been a suggestive one. By utilizing and developing Paul Moser's account of cognitive idolatry, one can see that the personal problem of hiddenness has a cogent solution. It has been argued that a fully-orbed experience of God will never occur given our finitude and inability to comprehend and tolerate what comes with that experience, which provides God a morally sufficient reason to conceal himself from agents (human and nonhuman) in creation. As such, our expectations should be not to experience God, *per se*, but to experience God through particular manifestations, including the incarnation of Christ. In exploring the communal effects of sin, it was noted that there will be a lack of God's phenomenal presence since the pervasiveness of sin also includes a failure to participate in the good and to provide the benefits of the good to others. By utilizing and developing Jonathan Kvanvig's contribution to counterbalancing evidence, the objection from hiddenness has a cogent response as well. Finally, attention was given to the problematic notion of reasonable nonbelief. The argument from hiddenness, though emotionally charged, is far from conclusive as evidence against the existence of God.

# CHAPTER SIX

# The Problem of Hell

Without a doubt, the most troubling belief affirmed in traditional Christian doctrine is the doctrine of hell. Most objections to the doctrine are not predicated on whether Scripture indicates hell is real. A plain-faced reading of the text indicates the reality of hell. Instead, most objections to the doctrine of hell propose a logical incompatibility between hell, as it is normally understood, and the belief that God is both loving and just. As such, the objections often leveled against hell are versions of the logical problem of evil. One may either affirm God, or hell, but not both on pain of contradiction.

Even though the straightforward reading of the Bible portrays hell as real, some theological trends have attempted to alter the traditional reading, supplanting it with other possibilities by which we may account for the language about hell found in Scripture. These are primarily hermeneutical objections rather than logical objections to the traditional view. As the argument goes, there are other, more profitable ways of treating the texts about hell that avoid the pitfalls attending the traditional view. Two options in contrast to the traditional view are annihilationism and universalism. Annihilationists believe that those persons who reject the offer of salvation in Christ are destined for an eternal separation from God. However, rather than understand this state as one of endless conscious suffering, annihilationism suggests that at the moment of judgment God destroys, or literally annihilates, the persons who have rejected Jesus. These persons' *punishment* is endless without them being subject to endless *punishing*. Since this view affirms the uniqueness of Jesus but redefines the nature of judgment, I will refer to it as Christian annihilationism (CA).

A second alternative to the traditional view is Christian universalism (CU). The basic idea here is that inevitably everyone (all fallen persons and angels) will be restored to a right relationship with God through the atoning work of Jesus on the cross. This view affirms the uniqueness of Christianity in that without the atoning work of Jesus there would remain a gap between fallen creatures and God. The obvious difference between the traditional view (TV) and CU is the extent to which the benefits of Christ's redemptive work are salvifically applied. For TV Christ's redemptive work only applies for those who accept Christ before judgment; for CU it also includes those who repent in the afterlife.

So in this chapter I have three tasks to accomplish. The first will be to develop the biblical and philosophical arguments for accepting CU, after which I will offer biblical and philosophical reasons for rejecting this view. The second project is to provide the biblical and philosophical reasons for accepting CA, subsequent to which I will provide biblical and philosophical reasons for rejecting this view as well. The third task will be to develop biblical and philosophical arguments for the traditional view (TV). I will argue that TV provides the most consistent reading of Scripture and that the traditional philosophical objections to TV concerning the alleged incompatibility between hell and the love and justice of God are not successful.

## CHRISTIAN UNIVERSALISM: BIBLICAL AND PHILOSOPHICAL ARGUMENTS

According to CU, God will eventually reconcile all things to himself through the person and work of Jesus Christ. The usual line of thought is that God cannot fail in his endeavors, and since he desires that none should perish he will eventually succeed in bringing every broken member of creation back into a right relationship with him. The emphasis in this line of reasoning is not on sin or the effects of sin but on the power of God to overcome sin and the effects of sin. Ironically, proponents of TV usually indict CU as having a naïve view concerning sin and what Scripture teaches about it, and adherents of CU charge those holding TV as having an unusually man-centered view (emphasis on human sin, human depravity) and a rather anemic view of God (his love, power, and determination to overcome evil and its effects). John Hick, Marilyn McCord Adams, Thomas Talbott, and Morton Kelsey all take this line of thought. Kelsey says, "To say that men and women after death will be able to resist the love of God forever seems to suggest that the human soul is stronger than God."[1] Thomas Talbott arrives at CU along the following lines:

---

[1] Morton Kelsey, *Afterlife: The Other Side of Dying* (New York: Paulist Press, 1979), 251.

> If you simply take the Augustinian idea of God's sovereignty in the matter of salvation—that is, the idea that the hound of heaven cannot be defeated forever—and put it with the Arminian idea that God at least wills or desires the salvation of all, then you get universalism, plain and simple.[2]

So how might the Bible support CU? Several passages are usually invoked toward this end.

> The Lord is . . . not wanting anyone to perish, but everyone to come to repentance. (2 Pet 3:9)

> [God] wants all people to be saved and to come to a knowledge of the truth. (1 Tim 2:4)

> The steadfast love of the LORD never ceases, his mercies never come to an end. . . . For the Lord will not reject forever. Although he causes grief, he will have compassion according to the abundance of his steadfast love; for he does not willingly afflict or grieve anyone. (Lam 3:22, 31–33 NRSV)

With passages such as these in mind, one might then suggest the following passages provide even more confirmation:

> I know that you [the LORD] can do all things; no purpose of yours can be thwarted. (Job 42:2)

> Therefore just as one man's trespass led to condemnation for all, so one man's act of righteousness leads to justification and life for all. (Rom 5:18 NRSV)

> God was in Christ, reconciling the world unto himself. (2 Cor 5:19 KJV)

Moreover, when we conjoin John 6:44 where Jesus says, "No one can come to Me unless the Father who sent Me draws him" (HCSB), with John 12:32 where He says, "And I, when I am lifted up from the earth, will draw *all* people to myself," we get the conclusion that no one will escape the saving grace of Jesus.

Suppose that we accept these passages as indicating an endorsement of CU. How are we then to understand the plethora of passages that speak of hell or at least indicate that such a thing exists? Rather than deny the reality of hell, proponents of CU often take the redemptive plan of God to extend into the

---

[2] Thomas Talbott, "Towards a Better Understanding of Universalism," in *Universal Salvation: The Current Debate*, ed. Robin A. Parry and Christopher H. Partridge (Grand Rapids: Eerdmans, 2004), 7. Talbott seems to be treating God willing and God desiring as the same thing, when they are not. I will give attention to this distinction when I develop TV.

afterlife. Thus, persons who have accepted Jesus' offer of salvation in the here and now participate in the benefits of being united with God in Christ both now and subsequent to their deaths. Those persons who reject Jesus in the here and now will face an indefinite separation from God in hell but ultimately will be restored to God through Christ. This is not a denial of the reality of hell but a different understanding of its extent and purpose. Whereas TV has hell as a place of unending suffering, CU suggests it is a place that will ultimately be escaped. Whereas TV views the justice of God as primarily punitive (backward looking), CU understands it as primarily rehabilitative in nature (forward looking). In structuring their view of hell in this way, CU considers their model as one that accounts for the biblical passages that speak of hell, as well as one that explains those passages previously mentioned that provide prima facie reason to accept universalism.

The biblical evidence for CU is not as compelling as its proponents suggest. According to J. P. Moreland and Gary Habermas, passages that "appear to support universalism should be understood as doing one of two things. Either they are teaching what God's desire is without affirming what will happen, or they are describing, not the ultimate reconciliation of all fallen humanity, but a restoration of divine order and rule over creation taken as a whole."[3] I. Howard Marshall writes that Jesus warns that sinners "and those who lead others into sin will suffer an unimaginable fate and be cast into Gehenna, a place of unquenchable, everlasting fire."[4] What is more, Marshall explains that there is no biblical evidence for any Jewish belief in the ultimate restoration of those condemned to Gehenna.[5] Marshall's point is suggestive, for it elicits an important point necessary for CU that has no biblical support—that there is a second chance for salvation after death. Indeed, Luke 13:22–30 indicates that final judgment is indeed final; the door to God "has been closed and nothing is said about ever reopening it."[6] If one is endorsing CU, then an *explicit* case for postmortem conversion must be made, especially if the claim is that Scripture best evidences that view. However, rather than affirm a second chance at salvation after death, Scripture indicates something different—there is death, and then there is judgment (Heb 9:27).

---

[3] J. P. Moreland and Gary Habermas, *Beyond Death: Exploring the Evidence for Immortality* (Eugene, OR: Wipf and Stock, 1998), 300.

[4] I. Howard Marshall, "The New Testament Does Not Teach Universal Salvation," in Parry and Partridge, *Universal Salvation: The Current Debate*, 57.

[5] Ibid.

[6] Ibid., 58.

How, then, are we to understand passages that express God's desire that no one perish? If God does not desire that anyone perish, then presumably no one will perish. Thomas Aquinas provides a helpful distinction between God's antecedent will and God's consequent will. He explains:

> The words of the Apostle, *God wills that all men be saved*, etc., can be understood in three ways. First, by restricted application, in which case they would mean . . . *God wills all men be saved that are saved, not because there is no man whom He does not wish to be saved, but because there is no man saved whose salvation He does not will.* Secondly, they can be understood as applying to every class of individuals, not to every individual of each class; in which case they mean that God wills some men of every class and condition to be saved—but not all of every condition. Thirdly, they are understood of the antecedent will of God; not of the consequent will. This distinction must not be taken as applying to the divine will itself, in which there is nothing antecedent or consequent, but to the things willed.[7]

Theologians have drawn on the third distinction to resolve the apparent discrepancy in Scripture in the doctrines of eschatology and soteriology. God wills, for instance, that all persons be saved and yet not all persons are saved (Matt 7:13–14; 1 Tim 2:3–4). A moral corollary may be found in the Holiness Code of the Old Testament or in the Sermon on the Mount of the New Testament where Jesus utters the imperative, "Be perfect, therefore, as your heavenly Father is perfect" (Matt 5:48). As Mark Murphy notes, "What makes this coherent is that the sense of willing in which God wills that all be saved is antecedent: prior to a consideration of all the particulars of persons' situations, God wills their salvation."[8] To use a moral example, God wills that all people be perfect prior to and independent of any action being instantiated by the agent(s). The sense in which everything that God wills obtains is grounded in God's consequent will that is posterior to and with regard to particular actions by moral agents. The upshot is that the distinction between God's antecedent and consequent will grounds a sense of willing strong enough for moral obligation to obtain, but it does not make God the author of sin. Regarding salvation, God wills *prior to and independent* of considering the free decisions of people that all of them will be saved; *after* consideration of a person's free decision he may or may not will for them to be joined with him in glory. Understanding

---

[7] Thomas Aquinas, *Summa Theologica*, vol. 1, 272.
[8] See Mark Murphy, "Theological Voluntarism," in the *Stanford Encyclopedia of Philosophy*, last accessed June 29, 2010, http://plato.stanford.edu/entries/voluntarism-theological.

God's will with the antecedent/consequent distinction allows for the sense in which God desires that none perish, while taking seriously all of the passages that speak of the reality of hell (e.g., Matt 8:12; 25:31–46; Rom 2:8–10).

The more promising passage for CU is Romans 5, where Paul indicates that all are dead in Adam, and all are made alive in Christ. Paul uses the word "all" for both sinners and the justified (5:18). The question in this passage concerns the scope of the effect of Jesus' work on the cross—it does not concern whether or not Jesus' atoning work was effective but for whom his atoning work was effective. The effects of Adam's sin were inevitable and universal.[9] However, this does not provide the rationale to say that the effects of Christ's redemptive work were universal. Instead, Paul's teaching is to be understood as "Christ's one action is the only basis for justification and life for all people but that it is made operative through faith."[10] Thus, the "all" referred to in this passage is all people (cf. Gal 3:27–28), but the "gift becomes a reality for them when they believe."[11] It is not a question as to whether or not belief is required for salvation—everyone agrees that it is. The question is *when* the person can come to faith, and as we have noted this must occur before death. Romans 5 centers on the state of persons before their death; it cannot be used to support a view of conversion after their death.[12]

Certainly more responses to Christian universalism are available, but suffice it to say that for every biblical argument for the view there is one that refutes it. The more important approach hermeneutically is to bear in mind the entirety of Scripture on this topic, which includes discussions of the necessity of premortem conversion as well as the reality of hell. These two features make the biblical case for CU extremely difficult to provide. Insofar as the doctrine of hell is derived only from special revelation, then providing the most compelling reading of what we find there is essential. CU does not measure up in this regard.

Now for the philosophical arguments that are leveraged to support CU. Generally speaking, proponents of CU argue that endless suffering is a punishment that does not fit the crime; thus TV is unjust. A second consideration is that TV is incompatible with the love of God. The arguments against TV from divine justice and divine love will be developed in the section where I defend the traditional view.

---

[9] Marshall, "The New Testament Does Not Teach Universal Salvation," 63.
[10] Ibid.
[11] Ibid.
[12] Ibid., 65.

In this section I want to consider an interesting argument for CU from Marilyn McCord Adams.[13] Adams says,

> My own view is that hell poses the principal problem of evil for Christians. Its challenge is so deep and decisive, that to spill bottles of ink defending the logical compossibility of (I) [God exists, and is essentially omnipotent, omniscient, and perfectly good] with this-worldly evils while holding a closeted belief that (III) Some created persons will be consigned to hell forever is at best incongruous and at worst disingenuous.[14]

Adams's thoughts run accordingly:

1. If God existed and were omnipotent, He would be able to avoid (III).
2. If God existed and were omniscient, He would know how to avoid (III).
3. If God existed and were perfectly good, he would want to avoid (III).
4. Therefore, if (I), not (III).[15]

Adams thinks premise 1 is true because God could simply refuse to create people or he could annihilate people. Premise 2 seems to piggy-back on the rationale behind premise 1; if God knows in advance how to annihilate people, then he could avoid III simply by blotting them out of existence. So premise 2, presumably, holds up. Premise 3 rests on a very specific understanding of divine goodness, such that God's goodness involves God guaranteeing a life to all persons that is on the whole good.[16] Hell would be a place for persons that makes their life horrendous on the whole, such that it would be better for them had they never been born; for whatever goods one participates in on this side of the ledger, it falls tragically short when compared to the endless suffering of hell. This first defense of CU rests on certain understandings about *God*.

One may object to such an emphasis on God without a fuller display of the evidence, and the second aspect of the equation regards human freedom and human responsibility. TV proposes that God created humans with significant freedom. Perhaps hell is the logical outcome of a life lived in perpetual rejection of God, and the natural consequence of such a life is hell. Adams does not have such a high view of this classical response. Her rejection of this free-will theodicy results from the following:

---

[13] Marilyn McCord Adams, "The Problem of Hell: A Problem of Evil for Christians," in *God and the Problem of Evil*, ed. William Rowe, Blackwell Readings in Philosophy (Malden, MA: Blackwell, 2001), 282–309.
[14] Ibid., 283.
[15] Ibid., 283–84.
[16] Ibid., 285.

(i) The human capacity to cause horrors unavoidably exceeds our abilities to experience them . . . for example, on the traditional doctrine of the fall, Adam experiences one individual's worth of ignorance and difficulty, but his sin brought it on his many descendants. . . .

(ii) Where suffering is concerned, conceivability follows capacity to experience, in such a way that we cannot adequately conceive of what we cannot experience. . . .

(iii) Agent responsibility is diminished in proportion to his or her unavoidable inability to conceive of the relevant dimensions of the action and its consequences, and I draw the conclusion that human agents cannot be fully responsible for the horrendous consequences of their actions.[17]

Being damned is a token instance of something that exceeds our abilities to understand; therefore we cannot appreciate the consequences of a choice such as that.

Where does this purported inability to conceive of hell come from? Several factors are in play here. The first issue concerns the noetic effects of sin—the idea that sin has so distorted our mental abilities that we are unable to discern the things of God (1 Cor 2:14; Eph 2:6). This line of thought is well attested to in Christian literature (biblical and otherwise).

Adams also has some "pragmatic implications" in mind regarding human freedom. The issue of personal sin aside, our freedom is obviously compromised from another standpoint. According to Adams, we start life ignorant and weak; we construct a world concept under the influence of nonoptimal people; we form habits in this situation that are entrenched in our personality; and these habits are acted on for years before they are ever acted against (if ever) by spiritual formation.[18] Thus, starting in a state of immaturity, "we arrive at adulthood in a state of impaired freedom."[19]

Perhaps an analogy will help. In the United States we do not traditionally execute persons that are severely mentally retarded under the auspices that (1) they do not understand what they are doing, and (2) given that they do not understand the implications of their choice, their freedom is compromised. Following Adams, everyone is spiritually and intellectually disabled and thus is not in the position to be held accountable for their choice of rejecting Jesus. It would be one thing for our condition to be self-imposed; however, according

---

[17] Ibid., 290.
[18] Ibid., 293.
[19] Ibid.

to Christian tradition, we inherit the consequences of Adam's sin not only directly but also in terms of the effects it has on the entire world into which we are born.

So, Adams's argument is not entirely without purchase. She is taking the doctrine of sin into unbroken waters and fleshing it out with common views about justice. Moreover, her appeal to divine love is rather attractive. God does not ever give up, nor does God ever accept defeat. There is no limit (time or otherwise) upon God in his pursuit of his wayward children.

Though these features of Adams's universalism are endearing, there are several concerns that must be mentioned. First, I agree with Adams that sin has cognitively impaired persons such that without divine assistance we would not be morally responsible for our actions; and if we are not morally responsible for our actions, then TV is misguided. However, it is in virtue of the fact that God has worked graciously that a substantive account of moral responsibility is to be expected. The thought runs as follows:

> $P_1$: If God has provided sufficient grace to overcome the effects of sin, then using the effects of sin (both inherited from Adam and its effects on others) as a defeater of moral responsibility does not follow through.
>
> $P_2$: God has provided sufficient grace to overcome the effects of sin.
>
> C: Therefore, using the effects of sin (both inherited from Adam and its effects on others) as a defeater of moral responsibility does not follow through.

Suppose it is true that sin has distorted the mind and broken our community such that we are not in an optimal state for mental and personal development; this says nothing of God's intervention to mitigate the full effects of sin in the life of the person. All that is needed to counter Adams's rejection of the free-will theodicy is the following:

> $P_3$: If God provides sufficient grace to all persons such that they are able (literally, *made* able) to respond decisively to his offer of reconciliation, then they are morally responsible for their choices.
>
> $P_4$: God has provided sufficient grace to all persons such that they are able (i.e., made able) to respond decisively to his offer of reconciliation.
>
> C: Therefore, persons are morally responsible for their choices.

In this argument I am simply trying to affirm what Adams has predicated her argument on, namely that God loves people and is more powerful than the sin that pervades them and their culture. The difference is that once God has provided sufficient grace to optimize humanity for moral responsibility, I argue that moral responsibility has attached. This line of thought is much akin to the character Charlie in the story *Flowers for Algernon*. Charlie has an IQ of 68 and comprehends very little, even misunderstanding people's joke-making *about him* to be joke-making *with him*. After receiving a revolutionary surgery, Charlie eventually becomes a genius, understanding things that most around him cannot. However, in the end, Charlie returns to his pregenius state. I surmise that the human scenario is much like this story. God's initiating grace overcomes the deficiencies in ourselves and our communities so that we can comprehend his offer of reconciliation in Christ. However, if we can comprehend the offer of reconciliation in Christ, then the argument from mental impairment does not follow through. Even if we return to our "pregenius" state, if this condition is due to something that we have chosen for ourselves, then the rationale behind Adams's argument from impaired freedom will not work.

There is a more telling concern to Adams's view, and it centers on an equivocation as to what is meant when she says God will provide for persons a life that is on the whole good. Good in what sense? It seems the best reading of Adams's intent is to say that the good mentioned will be subjectively good—there will be a personal sense of well-being, self-understanding, and self-worth.[20] If this reading is correct, then she has her universalism by definition. However, there is another way of understanding how hell can be a good, even subjectively, and that is to include the impenitent in the reconciliation of all things, just as 2 Cor 5:17–20 demands. How might there be reconciliation while at the same time there is separation—are these ideas not in stark contrast to one another? In one sense the answer is yes; in another sense the answer is no. Upon a divine pronouncement of guilt, the impenitent may come to the understanding that given their rejection of Jesus and God's offer of making amends through him, they have denied friendship with God as the chosen course for their life. The impenitent can also appreciate the verdict as just, even though the logical outcome of the verdict is separation from God. In this

---

[20] Even though this is never explicitly spelled out by Adams, I take it to be correct. Further, she agreed with this assessment in an exchange [April 20, 2010] with me at Southeastern Baptist Theological Seminary. There are other reasons for thinking this is her view of the good, such as her emphasis on participating in horrors such that they psychologically destroy the person—an emphasis on the psychological state of the person, how the person views his life on the whole.

sense those who are rebellious against God will, as Scripture declares, bow at the feet of Jesus (Phil 2:10), "accepting God's sentence and turning it into his praise."[21] Such an idea is not uncommon even to our experience. Criminals have been known to agree with the pronouncement of a life sentence while at the same time understanding that in the pronouncement their life in other subjective ways will be bad. By parity of reasoning, there is a sense in which we can say, even subjectively, that hell is a good for an individual. If we cry out for justice when we are the victims, can we not expect our victims to cry out for justice against us? If we believe that wrongful actions demand justice, do we not implicitly accept that our wrongful actions demand justice as well? If so, then even when justice is meted out on us we can appreciate it *as just*, regretting the consequences of the life we have chosen. Thus, distinguishing between good and bad is helpful, but these are not to be conflated with what is right and wrong. A state of affairs can be bad (in one sense) and yet right at the same time. What this line of reasoning exposes is that we cannot take an isolated feature of a state of affairs and determine even the subjective value contained within it, especially if our reactive attitudes are sincere (as the demand for justice, previously mentioned, indicates).

While Adams's argument is interesting, these concerns provide compelling reasons to question it. First, it does not account for the many biblical passages that reject CU as a viable option. Second, it does not take seriously the power of God to overcome the effects of sin *in the here and now*, thus creating an unnecessary extension of opportunities in the eschaton. Third, there is a troubling use of the word *good*. If the good is primarily contained to a psychological sense of well-being, then even the denizens of hell can have an admixture of reactions to their position—as for justice, a good is being carried out, and as for enjoying what justice demands, they live in a state of regret. While we can agree that hell is regrettable, it does not mean that it is to be considered bad in a wholesale sense, even to the persons consigned there.

## ANNIHILATIONISM: BIBLICAL AND PHILOSOPHICAL ARGUMENTS

Annihilationism (CA) is the view that those persons not redeemed by God in Christ are ultimately extinguished from existence upon judgment. What this

---

[21] Andy Saville, "Reconciliationism: A Forgotten Evangelical Doctrine of Hell," *Evangelical Quarterly* 79, no. 1 (2007): 38. One distinction I make with traditional reconciliationism is the idea that sin does not continue in hell. Some provide a line of thought such as this to avoid a continuing dualism—that good and evil are eternally propagated, as the continuing sin response declares.

means is that sentient beings do not suffer consciously forever, but those persons who have never accepted Jesus are fated to an eternal separation from God. Hence, this view is sometimes referred to as conditional immortality—immortality is predicated on accepting Jesus and being united with him in glory.[22] So, this view denies eternal *punishing*, understood as sustained conscious awareness of the punishment. Instead, it affirms an endless *punishment*—it is a punitive measure by God not to permit those who have rejected him to partake in his blessings, even if they are not aware of it.

CA has some biblical credentials in its favor, most of which hinge on a literal understanding of the Hebrew *abad* or the Greek *apollumi* to make its case. Both words have multiple instances in Scripture, especially regarding the fate of those who reject God. Consider the following instances in the Old Testament:

> When the wicked perish, there are shouts of joy. (Prov 11:10)
>
> And in your steadfast love you will cut off my enemies, and you will destroy all the adversaries of my soul. (Ps 143:12 ESV)
>
> You have rebuked the nations and destroyed the wicked; you have blotted out their name for ever and ever. (Ps 9:5)
>
> The LORD will not be willing to forgive him, but rather the anger of the LORD and his jealousy will smoke against that man, and the curses written in this book will settle upon him, and the LORD will blot out his name from under heaven. (Deut 29:20 ESV)
>
> But rebels and sinners shall be broken together, and those who forsake the LORD shall be consumed. . . . For you shall be like an oak whose leaf withers, and like a garden without water. And the strong shall become tinder, and his work a spark, and both of them shall burn together, with none to quench them. (Isa 1:28, 30–31 ESV)
>
> Let them be blotted out of the book of the living; let them not be enrolled among the righteous. (Ps 69:28 ESV)
>
> For the evildoers shall be cut off, but those who wait for the LORD shall inherit the land. In just a little while, the wicked will be no more; though

---

[22] There is a difference between annihilationism and conditional immortality. Conditional immortality begins with the assumption that persons are not inherently immortal but have immortality conferred on them by God. For those who do not believe in Jesus, God simply does not confer immortality on them. However, CA begins with the belief that persons are inherently immortal, and for those who deny Jesus, God destroys them at the moment of judgment. This point is more thoroughly developed by Millard Erickson, "Is Hell Forever?" *Bibliotheca Sacra* 152 (1995): 259–72.

> you look carefully at his place, he will not be there. . . . But the wicked will perish; the enemies of the LORD are like the glory of the pastures; they vanish—like smoke they vanish away. (Ps 37:9–10, 20 ESV)
>
> When the tempest passes, the wicked is no more, but the righteous is established forever. (Prov 10:25 ESV)
>
> The wicked are overthrown and are no more, but the house of the righteous stands firm. (Prov 12:7)
>
> For the evil man has no future; the lamp of the wicked will be put out (Prov 24:20 ESV)

Passages such as these give Clark Pinnock the confidence that the Old Testament "undeniably" teaches annihilationism because it gives us a "clear picture of the end of the wicked in terms of destruction and supplies the basic imagery of divine judgment for the New Testament to use."[23]

So do we find similar themes in the New Testament as Pinnock indicates? Admittedly there are some:

> For God so loved the world that he gave his one and only only Son, that whoever believes in him shall not perish but have eternal life. (John 3:16)
>
> Enter by the narrow gate. For the gate is wide and the way is easy that leads to destruction, and those who enter by it are many. (Matt 7:13 ESV)
>
> Do not be afraid of those who kill the body but cannot kill the soul. Rather, be afraid of the One who can destroy both soul and body in hell. (Matt 10:28)
>
> For we are the aroma of Christ to God among those who are being saved and among those who are perishing, to one a fragrance from death to death, to the other a fragrance from life to life. (2 Cor 2:15–16 ESV)

The biblical evidence for CA is much more compelling than what is provided for universalism. Furthermore, CA accounts for the plethora of passages that speak of separation from God in a much more satisfying way than does universalism. Also, given that the finally impenitent are subject to a literal death penalty, the worries of endless suffering for no remedial purpose are no longer an issue.[24] Since the philosophical arguments typically deployed in favor of CA are mirror-images to those of CU, I will delay that conversation

---

[23] Clark H. Pinnock, "The Conditional View," in *Four Views on Hell*, ed. William Crockett, Counterpoints (Grand Rapids: Zondervan, 1996), 145.

[24] This point might be reason to accept TV as opposed to CA, depending on one's attitudes toward the death penalty.

for my defense of the traditional view. In this next section I want to critique the biblical arguments proposed in favor of CA.

## A Critique of Christian Annihilationism

The primary biblical problem with the doctrine of annihilation is that it does not accommodate the full scope of evidence from Scripture. There are numerous biblical passages that indicate the endurance of *conscious* punishment is endless:

> Then he will say to those on his left, "Depart from me, you who are cursed, into the eternal fire prepared for the devil and his angels." . . . Then they will go away to eternal punishment, but the righteous to eternal life. (Matt 25:41, 46)

> And if your eye causes you to stumble, pluck it out. It is better for you to enter the kingdom of God with one eye than to have two eyes and be thrown into hell, where "the worms that eat them do not die, and the fire is not quenched." (Mark 9:47–48)

> "If anyone worships the beast and its image and receives a mark on his forehead or on his hand, he will also drink the wine of God's wrath, poured full strength into the cup of his anger, and he will be *tormented* with fire and sulfur in the presence of the holy angels and in the presence of the Lamb. And the smoke of their torment goes up forever and ever, and they have no rest, day or night." (Rev 14:9–11 ESV, italics mine)

> And the devil who had deceived them was thrown into the lake of fire and sulfur where the beast and the false prophet were, and they will be *tormented* day and night forever and ever. (Rev 20:10 ESV, italics mine)

More passages could be mentioned, but these will suffice for our purposes. Matthew's passage mentions that the punishment will be everlasting (*aiōnios*) which could mean either eternal (1 Tim 1:17) or for an age (Luke 1:70). So why is the better reading one for endless conscious suffering? Alan Gomes provides a helpful note—this passage forms a parallel with the duration of life for the righteous.[25] Thus:

> It would do violence to the parallel to give it an unlimited signification in the case of eternal life, but a limited one when applied to the punishment

---

[25] Alan Gomes, "Evangelicals and the Annihilation of Hell, Part One," *Christian Research Journal* (Spring 1991), last accessed June 17, 2010, http://bible-researcher.com/hell4.html.

of the wicked without at the same time limiting the duration of eternal life for the redeemed.[26]

Perhaps the passage in Revelation 14 makes things even more clear, for there it indicates the nature of punishment is torture. Gomes notes that "torture" (*basanizō*) indicates "grievous pains of body or mind," which suggests conscious misery either psychologically or physically.[27] In any event, the underlying assumption is that without consciousness there cannot be either psychological or physical torment.

Admittedly, the strongest argument for CA is that Scripture itself indicates that the impenitent will be destroyed, which can mean the utter blotting out of existence (see the passages quoted earlier). However, there are other ways of construing the meaning of *abad* or *apollumi*. The primary contrasting meaning is that these words connote utter ruin.[28] Moreover, there are other passages where the word for "perish" occurs that clearly rule out the possibility of CA, such as Jer 48:28 where it refers to being enslaved. Also, as Jeff Spencer explains:

> New Testament words translated into a form of the word "perish" mean anything from a grain of wheat which "dies" (John 12:24), to things which are "corrupted" by moth and rust (Matt 6:19–20), to a "corrupt" mind (2 Tim. 3:8). In the New Testament as well as the Old Testament, like the words translated into a form of "destroy," none of these words translated into a form of the word "perish" in context mean annihilation.[29]

The same problem attends other word studies intending to provide clear denotations of annihilationism, including words such as *consume* (Rev 14:9–11) and *devour* (Ps 78:45)—other meanings are not only available but profitable in their context.

A more telling biblical criticism against CA is an inference drawn about the doctrine of hell from other doctrines that Scripture uses to describe hell. More specifically, there is strong biblical support for the idea of degrees of suffering in hell; that is, for the idea that Hitler and Gandhi, assuming both end up in hell, would not be in the same vicinity of one another in hell. The most prominent passages indicating degreed suffering include:

---

[26] Ibid.
[27] Ibid.
[28] See John Broadus, *Commentary of Matthew* (Grand Rapids: Kregel, 1990), 230.
[29] Jeff Spencer, "The Destruction of Hell: Annihilationism Examined," *Christian Apologetics Journal* 1, no. 1 (Spring 1998): 13.

> Truly, I say to you, it will be more bearable on the day of judgment for the land of Sodom and Gomorrah than for that town. (Matt 10:15 ESV)
>
> Woe to you, Chorazin! Woe to you, Bethsaida! For if the miracles that were performed in you had been performed in Tyre and Sidon, they would have repented long ago in sackcloth and ashes. But I tell you, it will be more bearable for Tyre and Sidon on the day of judgment than for you. (Matt 11:21–22)
>
> And that servant who knew his master's will but did not get ready or act according to his will, will receive a severe beating. But the one who did not know, and did what deserved a beating, will receive a light beating. Everyone to whom much was given, of him much will be required, and from him to whom they entrusted much, they will demand the more. (Luke 12:47–48 ESV)
>
> How much more severely do you think someone deserves to be punished who has trampled the Son of God underfoot, who has treated as an unholy thing the blood of the covenant that sanctified him, and who has insulted the Spirit of grace? (Heb 10:29).
>
> Behold I am coming soon, bringing my recompense with me, to repay each one for what he has done. (Rev 22:12 ESV)

Holding to TV does not require one to hold that everyone consigned to hell has the same experience. The telling criticism of CA from this teaching about hell is that it logically precludes CA as a viable contender of explaining Scripture's description of hell. Persons who do not exist do not suffer, nor can they suffer in distinguishable ways (more or less).

Is TV a viable hermeneutical option to explain the doctrine of hell as opposed to its alternatives? I think so for several reasons. First, TV can accommodate the passages it typically uses as support for its view (e.g., passages that indicate conscious suffering) *as well as* passages CA uses to support its view (e.g., destruction passages). In other words, TV is more comprehensive in explanatory scope. Second, TV can accommodate other passages, such as those indicating degreed suffering in hell, while CA cannot.

In this final section I want to offer a word of caution to proponents of CA. The problem of hell is derivative of the problem of sin. If there is no sin, there is no hell. If we recall, in Gen 3:1–6 Satan enticed Eve with the forbidden fruit by avoiding any explicit mention of the fact that God had forbidden her to partake of it and instead focused on the positive features of the fruit. Satan said the fruit would open her eyes and that she would "be like God," knowing good and evil (3:5). Moreover, Eve saw the fruit was good for food (v. 6). The problem is not entirely with Eve's perceptions about the fruit. The narrative indicates it was good for these things. The problem is that in eating the fruit Eve defied a divine command and pitted her dominion over God's for her own life. Adam followed accordingly. On this Hugh McCann makes an important point:

> God had ordered them not to eat of the tree, and they knowingly did so, thereby putting themselves in rebellion against God. Not that rebellion was the point of their decision; the point was to achieve a certain kind of standing. But for the sake of that standing the two were willing to rebel, to set aside a life in which their wills would be subordinate to God's edict, and instead to *strike out on their own* (italics mine).[30]

And here is the backdrop to my word of caution for annihilationism:

> They [Adam and Eve] sought, in short, the very thing that we noted a moment ago has a suspicious ring to it: an independent destiny, founded upon their own autonomy, and aimed at becoming like God.[31]

Because sin is primarily an attempt (albeit futile) to usurp the dominion of God as our own, there is no better way to facilitate such an attempt than through relegating the eternal status of the impenitent to a place where they most want to be—in a position where the affairs of God are of no discernible concern to them. As such, in a strange twist of events, annihilationists have given atheists a theological premise upon which their eschatology is justified and have provided grounds for the hope that persistence in their rebellion ultimately fulfills the *aims* of their rebellion—a destiny independent of God altogether, a status finally fulfilled by none other than God himself when he annihilates them from existence. Upon the assumption that God is not an enabler of sin and that the strivings of the atheist is to have such a status, it seems suspicious to think that God might work so that the hopes of *both* the Christian and the atheist will be fulfilled, especially in matters attendant to which the results of our decisions are brought to fruition. As a brief way of defending the traditional view: in this regard it makes more sense to think that hell is a place that is a consistent reminder for the wicked that their rebellion was a misplaced one and that the strivings for a destiny independent of God were ones of utter futility. Is this a definitive argument against annihilationism? It is doubtful. However, the ideas expressed here are counterintuitive at best.

---

[30] Hugh McCann, "The Author of Sin?" *Faith and Philosophy* 22 (2005): 150.
[31] Ibid., 151.

## Responding to Objections to the Traditional View: The Argument from the Injustice of Hell

I've attempted to give some of the biblical data that justifies belief in the traditional view, and as we've noted TV has a solid biblical foundation. However, at the beginning of the chapter I mentioned that most objections to TV are not derived from speculations on the biblical data. Instead, there is a purported incompatibility between TV and the love and justice of God. Concerning divine justice, hell seems to be a penalty that does not fit the crime—an objection often called the proportionality problem, based on the premise that justice must be proportionate to the crime committed. For example, we do not (or should not) chop off a man's hands for stealing a loaf of bread, nor do we flog a man for jaywalking. Hell, as the argument goes, is a disproportionate punishment for the crime committed. What is more, if persons are consigned to hell for rejecting God, then why persist in torturing them if they are willing to repent and believe? Charles Seymour schematizes the proportionality problem:

1. All human sin is finite in seriousness.
2. It is unjust to punish sins disproportionately to their seriousness.
3. To punish sins finite in seriousness with infinite punishment is to punish sins disproportionately to their seriousness.
4. Therefore, it is unjust to punish sins finite in seriousness with infinite punishment.
5. Therefore, it is unjust to punish human sin with infinite punishment.
6. Hell is infinite punishment.
7. Therefore, it is unjust to punish human sin with hell.
8. God does nothing unjust.
9. Therefore, God does not punish human sin with hell.[32]

Several responses to this objection are in order. Before turning to these, we must remember that just like the logical problem of evil, the claim here is that there is a contradiction in claiming TV is compatible with divine justice. So the lines of reasoning I will deploy here are admittedly more of a defense than a theodicy. If my responses are *possibly* true, then the argument against TV does not succeed.

With that proviso in mind, a first line of response to the argument from justice is to avoid the philosophical objection altogether and "let the nature of eternal punishment be determined by exegetical considerations of the relevant

---

[32] Charles Seymour, "Hell, Justice, and Freedom," *International Journal for Philosophy of Religion* 43 (1998): 69.

passages."[33] I doubt this maneuver is going to satisfy anyone except for the naïve defender of TV. I do not deny the authority of Scripture, but here I simply point out that if the argument is that the doctrines affirmed in Scripture contain a contradiction, then simply appealing to Scripture as a resolution is begging the question. We are better off proving that the doctrines may be mysterious but not a contradiction; and proving that the ideas in Scripture do not contain a contradiction requires us to deploy some principled reasons for the claim. I will chart out and defend two such responses.

## CONTINUING SIN RESPONSE

As a first line of defense for TV, it is claimed that the impenitent continue to sin even after judgment and sentencing, thus warranting further punishment. By way of analogy, if a murderer is judiciously convicted and imprisoned, then commits another murder while behind bars, then he has committed a crime that deserves more punishment. The crimes committed in hell go on forever; therefore, the guilt that accrues from these actions merits continued separation from God. Sometimes referred to as the continuing sin response, it provides a direct affront to the idea that persons have committed only a finite number of sins, for in this case the continuing sin includes the continued rejection of submission to God.

Admittedly, there is not much support for this view biblically, at least from the vantage point of how agents are deliberating and choosing once they are in hell. However, there may be some evidence for this view biblically about how agents will deliberate and choose in hell *before* they get there. In this section I am going to assume libertarian free will is true. According to libertarianism, moral responsibility belongs to a person in virtue of the fact that it was within her power to choose or refrain from choosing a certain action. As the argument from the continuing sin problem goes, if a person really is endowed with this ability, then presumably a person in hell might repent, thus mitigating the need for continued punishment. But the idea of repentance in hell is far from clear. And as I will attempt to show, there are agent-causal reasons for rejecting the idea that a person in hell will repent and submit to God.[34]

---

[33] Shawn Buwalski, "Annihilationism, Traditionalism, and the Problem of Hell," *Philosophia Christi* 12, no. 1 (2011): 61–79.

[34] There are numerous forms of agent causation. My reference here is to indicate that the cause of the choice to reject God is the agent (or person) and not some factors independent of the person that causes them to reject God.

My defense of the continuing sin problem in hell consists in making a distinction between sin (generally construed), transgression, and perversion. Scripture distinguishes these terms, and their implications in Scripture are far-reaching about the nature of our choices and the effects these choices have on our character formation. I'm assuming a libertarian construct because it best explains the grounds upon which we are morally responsible. If it was not within my ability to choose God or reject God, then the foundation for moral responsibility collapses. However, I do not assume or agree with a common libertarian assumption that contra-causal freedom always requires the ability to do otherwise. As I will mention, contra-causal freedom is lost when the agent becomes perverse. Moreover, this distinction helps avoid the common assumption in arguments for justice that God is punishing persons for discrete sins they have committed, as Seymour's argument reveals. Instead, the real problem attending the denizens of hell is that they have a disposition that is bent against God.

There are many instances where Scripture speaks of the unwillingness of a person to submit to God. Jesus weeps over wayward Jerusalem, speaking of her unwillingness to repent (Matt 23:37). The infamous rich young man loved his possessions more than Jesus and left his encounter with Christ in great despair because he could not have both what prohibited his entering the kingdom and the kingdom itself (Mark 10:17–25). Biblical language describing sin varies, but the emphasis on those sins for which we are accountable do not include the sins of inadvertence (Ps 58:3; Ezek 44:10); instead, there is a focus on conscious and intentional inner corruption (Isa 21:3). Language often juxtaposed against righteousness includes wickedness, uncleanness, guilty, godlessness, or badness (e.g., 1 Kgs 21:10; Ps 1:4; Isa 57:20). It is to be noted that these terms refer to an inner state of being and are not just token adjectives that describe specific actions a person commits. When we sin, something in our character is shaped; what Scripture is indicating is that sin deforms our character.

To be more precise, the sins that distort our character are those that we knowingly and intentionally choose as acts against God, very likely as an attempt to establish an independent status, as mentioned before. Sins that involve knowledge and intentionality are called transgressions.[35] Thus, actions that are those of a transgressor include intentional defiance against God. David referred to his sin with Bathsheba as a transgression (Ps 51:1, 3). Isaiah declares:

---

[35] There are transgressions against the law that are unintentional, but my focus here is on sinful acts that are understood as sinful by the person and are, in spite of this knowledge, still chosen.

> Our transgressions are multiplied before you,
> and our sins testify against us;
> for our transgressions are with us,
> and we know our iniquities:
> transgressing, and denying the LORD,
> and turning back from following our God,
> speaking oppression and revolt,
> conceiving and uttering from the heart lying words. (Isa 59:12–13 ESV)

We knowingly violate the law of God, as Romans explains, because he has written it on our hearts (Rom 1:21–32; 2:15–16).[36] It is not the case that an individual transgression yields a heart that is utterly bent against God; rather, it is persistence in transgressions that ultimately yields a heart hardened against God. David repented of his transgression, as the Psalms indicate; the Pharaoh did not repent of his transgressions, as the book of Exodus indicates. The same point can be made when comparing the betrayal of Jesus by Judas and the denials of Christ by Peter. Judas did not repent, while Peter did.

Thus, the focus in Scripture is often on the will. As Jeremiah says, "the heart is deceitful above all things, and desperately sick" (Jer 17:9 ESV). I contend that what Scripture indicates about the effects of transgression on the person is that as we persist in these choices we forge a character toward a particular destiny, the culmination of which (in the negative sense) is a completely hardened heart against God. There is a twofold dimension to the hardening of heart. The first is the active sense of hardening, which is done by perpetual transgression, as I have mentioned before. The second sense of hardening is a passive sense, which is the permissive act of God for the full effects of deliberate rebellion to be meted out on the reprobate. This contention is not without purchase in Scripture. For example, numerous times the Bible describes Pharaoh as hardening his own heart by persisting in disobedience to God's messenger Moses (Exod 7:14; 8:15, 32; 9:7, 34), only after which do we find the Lord hardening Pharaoh's heart (9:12; 10:1, 20, 27). Notice the active verb indicates an effect on Pharaoh's character from the very choices Pharaoh made himself, consequent to which God hardens (passive mood) Pharaoh's heart.[37] Likewise, in Romans "God gave them up to dishonorable passions" and "God gave them up to a debased mind to do what ought not be done" (Rom 1:26, 28 ESV). There are ontological consequences to the decisions that we make, but

---

[36] Even if this passage is not limited to persons who knowingly violate the law, it certainly includes those who do.

[37] Admittedly, this point is debatable. The Hebrew utilizes a Niphil stem, which can have either an active sense or a passive sense. The passive reading is both cogent and fair to the context.

Scripture is clear that (1) we make these decisions for ourselves, and (2) there is a point after which God will not pursue us for fellowship with him. As it were, God will not cast pearls before swine (Matt 7:6).

Concerning this second point, I need to make a few notes of clarification. First, the passive sense in which God brings about hardness may be likened to when a cement mixer stops churning cement to keep it from hardening; the only thing that kept the cement from hardening on its own was the intervention of the cement mixer. Thus, when the cement mixer stops churning cement, it is not the cement mixer that brings about the hardness. Accordingly, Scripture indicates that God gives us every opportunity to respond to his gracious initiative, after which he has no obligations whatsoever to continue his pursuit of a wayward child. Indeed, God may well realize that such pursuits will be ineffective. Second, hardening connotes a state of being, and as such is more revealing of the *nature of a person* rather than the *nature of a person's actions*. More germane to our current discussion, instances such as Pharaoh's indicate that hardening is a process that comes to fruition *before* a person goes to hell. Hell is not what hardens a person; instead, hell is a place for hardened persons.

In regard to the continuing sin response, the implications are quite clear. Even though there is no explicit reference to people continuing to sin in hell, there is solid evidence to ground the claim that the denizens of hell persist in their rejection of God. But what is more, this construal of the continuing sin response shifts the emphasis from discrete sins to their cumulative effect on the character and disposition of the person, which certainly gels more with the biblical problem of hell than how many times a person uttered their favorite curse word. Thus, with this version of the continuing sin problem there is no obligation to provide an account where the reprobate could complete their punishment but in fact never do; the objection is predicated on the assumption that libertarian freedom always requires contra-causal freedom.

One possible objection to this version of the continuing sin response is that after persons experience the horrors of hell they most certainly would not want to be there. Even the most perverse persons, it might be claimed, would seek escape. On this Paul Copan rightly notes that the question is inadequately structured; instead, the probing question is "are you willing to submit to God and his claim on your life?"[38] There are many things that we know are harmful and detrimental, but we still select those things for ourselves rather than what is right. Likewise, simply because people are suffering in hell does not mean

---

[38] Paul Copan, *Loving Wisdom: Christian Philosophy of Religion* (St. Louis, MO: Chalice Press, 2007), 150.

that they would rather submit to God. So even on the *logical* possibility that people in hell could repent and turn to God, it might be the case that they never exercise that option due to the metaphysical damage brought about by sin. But what is more, given the severe nature of the ontological implications of sin and the nature of perversity, the objection may be missing the point entirely. The objection assumes that for an agent to be free there must be contra-causal freedom *in every instance* of a person's life. Along with Robert Kane, I contend that so long as the irreparable damage to people's character is derived from decisions that were previously within their control, then they are ultimately responsible both for the current decision that they make as well as for the current state in which they find themselves.[39] As such, the continuing sin problem provides at least a tenable biblical and philosophical defense of TV.[40]

## Corporate Justice

As a second line of response, it is worth considering the tension between justice as it pertains to individuals and justice as it pertains to communities. Hell is only one dimension of eschatology; heaven is the other. If our eschatology is derived from token acts from an individual, from which the injustice of hell is derived, then we must also agree by parity of reasoning that heaven is a reward that awaits no one. No one, given the limitations in time, has committed an infinite number of goods such as to merit heaven, even under the assumption that merit is an aspect of one's salvation, which it is not. The idea of meriting heaven has some strange consequences, including the bizarre possibility that our beliefs about God really don't matter, only our personal behavior.

That issue aside, Scripture describes heaven as a restored creation (Rom 8:19–23), where all of the negative features of the present age are brought under Christ and are reconciled through him (Rev 7:15–17). Moreover, heaven is a place of unbroken fellowship with Jesus due to the glorification of all believers (Rom 8:11). Thus, the strife that attends this life will be defeated in the eschaton for those sheep that follow the Shepherd who

---

[39] Robert Kane, *The Significance of Free Will* (Oxford: Oxford University Press, 1998). See also Robert Kane, "Some Neglected Pathways in the Free Will Labyrinth," in *The Oxford Handbook of Free Will*, ed. Robert Kane (Oxford: Oxford University Press, 2002), 407–9.

[40] For other resources that address the concerns I am dealing with in this line of argument, see Kenneth Einar Himma, "Eternally Incorrigible: The Continuing Sin Response to the Proportionality Problem of Hell," *Religious Studies* 39 (2003): 61–78. See also Andrei Buckareff and Allen Plug, "Escaping Hell: Divine Motivation and the Problem of Hell," *Religious Studies* 41 (2005): 39–54; Charles Seymour, "On Choosing Hell," *Religious Studies* 33 (1997): 249–66; James Cain, "On the Problem of Hell," *Religious Studies* 38 (2002): 355–62.

provides for our every need (Psalm 23). Instead of strife, there is peace (Psalm 23); instead of suffering, there is physical and psychological integrity (Matt 11:29); instead of corrupt governance, there will be perfect governance (Isaiah 65–66); instead of fragmented relationships between people, there will be fellowship (Matt 8:11); there will be no sin in heaven (Rev 21:8; 22:15).[41] In other words, Scripture describes heaven as a place where there is unity between the intellect and the will which is directed at the good of submission and service to God (Revelation 5).

With these features in mind, we can understand why hell is sometimes viewed as a place of quarantine. If the denizens of hell have a perverse disposition, then the outcome of God's permitting them into his presence is that he also permits them into the presence of the heavenly community, thus permitting the same problems that attend this age to infect the next. My view presents an eschatological answer to the well-worn question, "Why does God let the wicked prosper and the righteous suffer?" Ultimately, the wicked do not prosper, and the suffering of the righteous is abated; but protecting the righteous from suffering means that God will, in the restoration of creation, protect them from persons that produce the suffering. As Richard Swinburne notes, heaven is a place fit for a certain type of people, and those who do not fit have a bad will and wrong beliefs about God.[42]

Rather than wonder how principles of justice are only meted out on the individual, perhaps we should consider whether God also has the heavenly community in mind when he separates those who have freely rejected him as a measure of justice to those who have accepted his offer of reconciliation. The wicked prosper because they are parasites on the good. When God quarantines them in hell, they are prohibited from being a parasite on others anymore. It is imaginable that such a view helps explain the hellishness of hell—a person with a distorted will still aims at fulfilling the features attendant to their vices, and yet even this is frustrated in hell because what they aim for can never be achieved or participated in again (Eccl 9:3–6). So when the community of heaven is considered, God has good reasons to separate those

---

[41] Presumably the model of agency I described before can account for this feature of heaven. The objection to libertarian views of freedom from the ability to sin in heaven *assume* libertarians must always affirm contra-causal freedom; this assumption can be denied. The main distinction between this type of libertarianism and compatibilistic views of freedom is that compatibilism affirms that there are causes beyond our direct control that bring about specific desires, consequent to which we choose according to those desires. The ability to do otherwise is only hypothetical. However, libertarians affirm that God provides initiating grace to overcome sin but also affirm the agent's ability to reject God's offer of salvation even after receiving this initial grace. Again, so long as the current state of the agent is derived *from the choices of the agent, and not some external cause*, a libertarian model of freedom is affirmed.

[42] Richard Swinburne, *Faith and Reason* (Oxford: Clarendon Press, 1981), 143–72.

who do not want reconciliation with him from those who are reconciled with him. God's sentencing the impenitent is partly derived from his regard of the condition of the one sentenced and is partly derived from his regard for the protection and well-being of his children and community.

One other note deserves mention here. I contend that one reason we recoil from the doctrine of hell is that we have not taken seriously the biblical concept of church discipline. In both Matthew 18 and Luke 17 we are provided with a charge to seek reconciliation with others when there is a fractured relationship. If one-on-one reconciliation fails, then we are to seek help from others to bring about reconciliation. If this fails, the matter is to be brought before the church with the aim of restoration. Finally, if a person continues to reject reconciliation, he is to be cast out from among the church. One such instance in Scripture is when Paul questioned the Corinthian church for failing to practice diligence in protecting God's house and his community by tolerating incest between a young man and his step-mother (1 Corinthians 5).

God works for reconciliation in the same way that he has commanded the church. He sought out those who despise him by coming down from glory seeking to make amends. He has appealed for reconciliation through the disciples of his church. We can trust that he has given every measure needed for reconciliation, and the ultimate consequence for denying it is being cast out from among the fellowship. Given these attempts at reconciliation, God cannot be charged with indifference in his actions.

A final theological word is in order—our practices in the church are intended to mirror God's practices and principles in Scripture. The house of God and his honor are to be protected. The malaise in the church about such a feature in Scripture provides grounds for those inside and outside of the church to question the seriousness with which we take God at his Word in this domain. My suspicions are that if the progressive discipline outlined in Matthew and Luke were more carefully implemented, objections from the principle of justice would diminish.[43] Furthermore, the more we neglect this charge as God's church, the more we can expect evil to persist in our midst and the effectiveness of the church in service to diminish.

## THE ARGUMENT FROM DIVINE LOVE

Is it unloving for God to send a person to hell? Perhaps one might argue that although it is not unjust for God to send anyone to hell because he has no

---

[43] This theme is developed in the first chapter of Jerry Walls, *Hell: The Logic of Damnation* (South Bend, IN: University of Notre Dame Press, 1992).

obligations to permit them into heaven, given his undying devotion to his creation he will in the end allow everyone into heaven.[44] In the last section it was argued that divine justice is compatible with TV, and as such we can expect God's justice to "set limits on the exercise of divine love."[45] God's actions will be both loving *and* just; a loving motive does not override his interests in justice. The two attributes will complement one another.

In a provocative work, Thomas Talbott argues that understanding heaven as a place of perfect peace and happiness entails the nonexistence of hell.[46] The sanctified in heaven are perfectly loving and compassionate to all living beings. But if the sanctified are truly loving and compassionate, then they will be unhappy with the ruined state of those in hell. This unhappy state is incompatible with any description of the blessings of heaven; thus, if one affirms the existence of heaven as a perfect place and state of being, he must also deny the reality of hell.

While this argument is interesting, it is ultimately unsuccessful. Thomas Aquinas considered this argument well before Talbott and responded by distinguishing two types of pity.[47] The first type of pity does not take into account the moral dimension of a person's suffering. As Seymour notes, Aquinas refers to this type of pity as the pity of passion.[48] As Aquinas understands it, the passions of a person are derived from things that they desire and do not have. The blessed in heaven do not have passions because they are perfectly happy—there is nothing lacking in them such that they would desire anything else. The extension of Aquinas's thought is that in some sense this must mean that the persons in heaven are not considering the people in hell as in some way depriving them of their experience.

There is a second kind of pity that Aquinas calls the pity of reason.[49] The pity of reason expresses itself in the desire not to see another person suffer, except that those in heaven cannot "rationally desire that the suffering of the damned come to an end."[50] If the damned deserve their punishment, then even the citizens of heaven will consider that punishment just and right. Biblically there is some merit to this view, for love "does not delight in evil but rejoices

---

[44] This is the line of reasoning from both Marilyn McCord Adams and Thomas Talbott. See her "The Problem of Hell: A Problem of Evil for Christians"; and his "Providence, Freedom, and Human Destiny," *Religious Studies* 26 (1990): 239–41.

[45] Charles Seymour, *A Theodicy of Hell* (Dordrecht: Kluwer Academic, 2000), 95.

[46] See Talbott, "Providence, Freedom, and Human Destiny."

[47] As quoted in Seymour, *Theodicy of Hell*, 122. See also Aquinas, *Summa Theologica*, Q. 94. A.2.

[48] Seymour, *Theodicy of Hell*, 123.

[49] Referenced in Seymour, ibid. See also Aquinas, *Summa Theologica*, Q. 94. A 3.

[50] Seymour, *Theodicy of Hell*, 123.

with the truth" (1 Cor 13:6). Those in heaven can rejoice in justice even if that means a person's being sent to hell is relegated to a life of suffering; there is, as Corinthians indicates, a greater love for God than for those who have rejected him.

But what is more, Talbott's argument conflates suffering with evil. As we have seen, there are instances of suffering that are not evil. Evil, if we recall, is the privation of a good—it contains a normative element and not just a descriptive element. If justice is a good, then it would be evil for the world to be deprived of it. What is more, desiring that the world be deprived of justice is an evil as well. Talbott is assuming that heaven *lacking* everyone is the same thing as heaven being *deprived* of everyone. We can agree that being deprived of something is evil, for deprivation involves not having something that *should be*. However, lacking is not the same thing as being deprived. We consider privation an inherently evil notion because something is being taken away from the well-being of a thing's essence. However, there can be a *lack* of something such that it does not involve a privation in any way. A snake *lacks* arms, but we would not say it is *deprived* of arms (as mentioned before). Likewise, heaven *lacks* certain people, but we would not necessarily claim that it is *deprived* of those people. We can lack something and still be perfectly content because lackings are derived from wants (which Aquinas suggests do not exist in heaven). However, we cannot be deprived of something and have the same contentment, because privations include states of affairs that threaten a thing's needs, and heaven has no such states of affairs. That being said, several distinctions are needed at this point. First, people in heaven are not rejoicing at the suffering of those in hell—they are rejoicing in the justice that has been meted out. Scripture is filled with affirmations of just such a view (Pss 58:10–11; 63:11; 68:1–3; 94:16–23). The rightful pity to have is one where a real evil has befallen another rather than simply when suffering has befallen another; when evil has come down on those who do not deserve it, not when suffering has come down on those who do.

Second, "we must be careful not to think of the damned as the unfortunate victims of God's arbitrary will, or as earnestly repentant sinners who do wish for reunion with God."[51] The blessed in heaven, in virtue of their sanctification, accept the divine will over and above all else. What Talbott has assumed is that the blessed would be wrong for not feeling badly for those in hell, which is simply not true. Even if persons in heaven are aware of people suffering in hell, it does not mean that they are less virtuous for not feeling pity on their

---

[51] Ibid., 124.

behalf. Charles Seymour rightly notes that pity on earth is meant to prod us to action.[52] However, since there is nothing to be done in the eschaton such that the impenitent can be saved, pity would be a worthless affection.[53]

The more tenuous problem about divine love concerns God's foreknowledge. As it is argued, God's omniscience entails that he knows in advance whether or not a person will go to hell. So why doesn't God simply *not* create the people he knows would go to hell were he to create them? Would this not be the most loving thing for him to do?[54]

This is an interesting question, but its implications cannot be limited only to the doctrine of hell. It seems that the implications of this question point back to a more basic problem attending this issue, namely the problem of sin. Presumably, God knows that a fall goes before destruction. So the charge cannot be "why does God create persons whom he knows will go to hell," for the answer is going to be that he also knew in advance that they would freely reject him and ultimately seal that fate on their own accord. The question must be "why does God create persons whom he knows are going to reject him, the consequence of which will be that they go to hell?" In other words, why doesn't God only create people who will freely accept him, not creating anyone who would freely reject him were he to create them? This question should sound familiar, for it was the same question that J. L. Mackie proposed and that we addressed in our discussion of the logical problem of evil. So, for a perfectly acceptable, logical answer to this question I recur to Plantinga's free will defense and his notion of transworld damnation.[55]

This is not the end of the matter, though. In the discussion on the problem of justice, the questions were posed "to whom is justice owed, and what is meant by justice?" Regarding the problem of love, the same questions are viable: "What do we mean by love, and to whom is God loving?" It is not loving for God to be indifferent about the choices that we make, nor is it loving for him to regard those who have given their lives over to his service as equivalent in disposition to those who have not. God's love is more comprehensive than

---

[52] Ibid., 129.
[53] I am working under the auspices that the previous biblical arguments confirm TV.
[54] See Adams, "The Problem of Hell: A Problem of Evil for Christians," 316.
[55] One might object that the notion of transworld damnation hinges too tightly on Middle Knowledge, and that this model of divine providence is at best questionable. Indeed, I agree and do not hold to Middle Knowledge. This objection is beside the point, though. Middle Knowledge need not be true, only possibly true. Likewise, transworld damnation need not be true, only possibly true. To my knowledge, no argument has been made that solidifies the defeat of Middle Knowledge or transworld damnation—only appeals that undercut the system.

what he might do in the interests of an *individual* but will include consideration of others, especially himself.

God's love is expressed through his advocacy of making amends and honoring the dignity with which he created human beings—a dignity that is derived from being made in his image. One manner of recognizing the inherent dignity of persons is to permit their choices to go through *and* to expect an account of those choices. As for love, we are to love God and others, *as well as ourselves* (Matt 22:39). Failing to love God and others is a failure to love oneself, which is an ironic turn for the problem of hell. It is not that hell is God's failure to love us; it is the failure of the impenitent to love others, especially God, but also themselves.

True love, as Paul says, is patient, kind, and avoids envy; it is not arrogant or rude, insisting on its own way; it is not resentful, nor does it rejoice in what is wrong, but rejoices in what is true (1 Cor 13:4–6). These are the markers not only of what it means to love others but to love oneself. Love of oneself consists in knowing who we are and who we are not. Given that sin is an attempt to usurp God's position as one's own, it is not only a failure to avoid envy as well as rejoicing in what is wrong; it is self-deception of the highest order. What is more, the fragmented world reveals that the effects of this deception reach beyond individuals and infect the world around them, which is a failure to love others for their own sake. Is this not what is portrayed in Genesis 3 as Eve not only ate the fruit but brought it to Adam for his participation in the same mistake? Presumably, one may infer the same principle from Satan's participation in the Genesis narrative as he approached Eve.

As for God's love, he loves himself as well as others. God's love for himself means that he will not share his glory with anyone else, for that would indicate a self-deception on his part that there is another worthy of sharing his glory (Isa 48:11). People who have rejected him have his status as their aim, a teleology God will not accept as a matter of loving himself and rejoicing in the truth of his uniqueness as God over all.

His love is extended to the righteous in honoring their choice of servitude to him; to the impenitent, his love is expressed through his honoring their choice as their own and in following his word that these choices have consequences, albeit dire consequences. Let us remember that the problem of hell is the problem of *unrequited* love—a love offered and a love rejected. It is not a problem of love never being offered. Those sympathetic to this line of reasoning may hear Alfred Lord Tennyson in the background, for in his famous work *In Memoriam* he expressed that:

> I hold it true, whate'er befall;
> I feel it, when I sorrow most;
> 'Tis better to have loved and lost
> Than never to have loved at all.

Closer inspection of the objection reveals how bizarre a claim is being made. In essence, we are asked what a loving God would do to *possible* people, not actual people. Love is essentially relational, not in the abstract but in the concrete. But as the objector opines, God is more loving through an act of preemptive annihilation than in his act of creating would-be ultimate rebels. Even if we leave this concern to the realm of *abstracta*, it is not at all clear that preemptive annihilation is the more loving thing to do. In essence, the concerns attending annihilationism previously rear their ugly head once again, just in a different place. As I mentioned, annihilationism suggests a dualistic eschatology—a Christian eschatology for those who accept Christ and an atheistic eschatology for those who reject him, thus providing for the impenitent a destiny that is without God and devoid from the affairs of God altogether. Preemptive annihilation simply moves the process back one step but provides the same conclusion. Those who *would* finally reject Christ are somehow precluded from ever existing, which amounts to an act of noncreative annihilationism.

So, what God does in his act of judgment on those who would be finally impenitent is to provide the destiny that, *had they been born and allowed to live*, would have befallen them anyway, given that this view is logically correlative to annihilationism. Even more interesting, God does all of this and the person never knows about it because they were never created in the first place.

So this view (preemptive annihilation) still requires several things to be the case. First is that the persons not only would sin but would ultimately persist in their sin if they were created. Second, it still requires God to make the judgment that if the persons are created they will not be fitting citizens of heaven. Third, the traditional view of hell is deemed unloving, so a different model must be proposed. Fourth, that different model is preemptive annihilation whereby the would-be-finally-impenitent is destroyed through God's act of noncreation. It is a literal death sentence, except before there was actual life. Thus, fifth, there is still a separation of believers and unbelievers, but it occurs prior to creation. These descriptions have all of the concomitant elements attending the actual world in an annihilationist view except for the actual existence of the person. But it must be remembered that human attempts to forge a destiny independent of God is the problem, not the answer. The proposed solution from the objector is logically equivalent to Christian annihilationism rejected before, with the assumption of epistemic backward causation thoroughly at work. Given that the future reality that awaits the impenitent is hell, God—prior to creation—simply refuses to create such persons. If annihilationism is not a viable model for the actual world, then relocating it will not provide it anymore explanatory power. The objection that God could refrain from creating those who would be finally impenitent will not work.[56]

## Conclusion

In this chapter I have detailed the arguments for Christian annihilationism (CA), Christian universalism (CU), and the traditional view (TV) of hell. After these considerations I think it is fair to conclude that the evidence from Scripture supports TV. Moreover, charges against TV from the love and justice of God were brought to light and rejected as viable defeaters of TV. The most telling observation is that the typical objections to TV are first cousins of the logical argument from evil, and as such establish a tremendously high burden of proof for the rejecter of TV. Moreover, when it came to responding to these objections, I structured my line of response more as a defense than as a theodicy—the burden of proof established in these arguments have not been met; therefore, they cannot be considered viable contenders to defeat TV.

That being said, if this is a victory for endorsing TV, it is not one in which proponents of TV can revel. The doctrine of hell is emotionally charged and troubling. Christians are well advised to avoid the pitfall of claiming to believe a doctrine like this and then following up such a claim with indifference about the fate of those who do not know Jesus. Such indifference could reasonably lead a person to believe that while you accept the doctrine of hell, you have not appropriated its significance. Along those lines I offer the following admonition:

> Remember that you were at that time separated from Christ, alienated from the commonwealth of Israel and strangers to the covenants of

---

[56] One objection to the idea of annihilating possible people is that possible people cannot be annihilated since they do not yet exist. In the strict sense of the term that is correct. My point here was to emphasize the noncreative act of God concerning persons who would freely reject him is still an act of judgment on those persons, namely their eternal nonparticipation in the presence of God. In other words, the model provided here is a heuristic device deployed to make this point.

promise, having no hope and without God in the world. But now in Christ Jesus you who once were far off have been brought near by the blood of Christ. . . . So then you are no longer strangers and aliens, but you are fellow citizens with the saints and members of the household of God. (Eph 2:12–13, 19 ESV)

CHAPTER SEVEN

## Natural Evil: Comparing Theism and Naturalism

It seems that the lion's share of literature on the problem of evil is directed at what we have called the problem of moral evil: evil that is connected to a person in such a way that they are blameworthy for what they have done. The typical line of address for the problem of moral evil is that human freedom, perhaps along with some other attendant goods, provides God a morally sufficient reason for his permission of the evil we find in our world. If God creates us significantly free, then for the most part he will not impede the exercise of our freedom, and the resulting evil that is derived from evil intentions can rightly be expected to obtain.

But one wonders whether the same type of story can be told regarding the problem of natural evil. The received wisdom suggests that natural evil is evil that results from natural processes such that no humans can be accountable or blameworthy for the suffering that results from that evil. The paradigm examples of natural evil include natural disasters such as hurricanes, earthquakes, or debilitating diseases such as blindness or Alzheimer's. If the received wisdom is correct, then it seems that free will has no place in resolving this dilemma, for these are evils that are not connected to the exercise of free will. Theism is therefore confronted with a different problem of evil. In this chapter I will develop and address the problem of natural evil. I will give attention to some other features of this discussion, largely based on work by Stephen Layman.[1] Before turning to that task, some preliminary comments are in order.

---

[1] C. Stephen Layman, "Natural Evil: The Comparative Response," *International Journal for Philosophy of Religion* 54 (2003): 1–31.

## Preliminary Comments

The concept of natural evil is not as clearly delineated as that of the problem of moral evil. For instance, in what sense can we say that natural events are *evil*? In this work we have taken the efforts to indicate that not all suffering is evil. So it is no trifling matter to point out that even if there is suffering that results from natural events, this does nothing to provide an argument from *evil* based on the suffering that persons undergo as a result of, for example, a hurricane. No one denies that suffering is involved in such an experience, but there is still the question of whether objections raised against the term natural evil are judiciously considered. Natural suffering—no problem; natural evil—more work is needed. In order for an argument to be labeled appropriately as an argument from natural evil, the necessary premises will include an account of how hurricanes, earthquakes, and the like are intrusions on the way the world *ought* to function; and by "world" I am referring to the physical structure of the earth and the balances in nature contained therein.

Why is this proviso important? First, it is generally agreed that the regularities in nature provide a great good to the overall well-being and daily functions of creatures in the world. Our basic activities work under the assumption that the present and the future will resemble the past; the force of gravity, for example, will not alter to such an extent that we are either unable to move due to its overbearing power, or float away if its strength were lessened. The regularity of these laws that govern our daily activities are a great good to us, and revoking them in every instance where a problem may arise provides a world that is less predictable for our ordinary life experiences and provides prima facie reason for these regularities to persist.[2]

A second point about using the term *natural evil* is in order. A fantastic amount of what is called natural evil is brought about by the misuse of free will. For example, consider the person we will call "Old Smokey" who has a cigarette habit of one pack per day. To call the lung cancer that results from this habit a "natural evil" is an inappropriate use of the terms, for clearly this is a moral evil that has direct bearing on Old Smokey's health. Suppose further that you are raised by Old Smokey and are subject to the secondhand smoke from his pack-a-day habit for the eighteen years you live in the house with him. You find out at age twenty-five that you have lung cancer. Insofar as the cancer is connected to eighteen years of secondhand smoke, this too does not count as an instance of natural evil. The same type of reasoning may be applied to other test cases, including the loss of life that results "from irresponsible city

---

[2] I gave attention to these argument types in the introductory chapter.

planners locating their creations on faults that will ultimately heave and split; and some droughts and floods may have been prevented if not for the careless way we have treated our planet."[3] What is more, if a person has antecedent knowledge of the likelihood that living in a certain region brings with it a greater threat of danger from natural disasters, this too is more of an issue of choice than of suffering born from purely natural causes. For example, several months after Hurricane Katrina, my wife and I moved to New Orleans from College Station, Texas. We knew that making such a move incorporated some risks to our well-being, especially as the hurricane season began the next year and the levees were hardly in a position to protect the city if another hurricane passed over. If such an event occurred, and the city became prey to yet another trauma, it would be right to conceive of our suffering as bad but not right to infer that we were the victims of natural evil.

The same principle holds with the story of Job. The narrator tells us that Satan used natural forces to inflict suffering on Job:

> He was still speaking when another [messenger] came and reported: "A lightning storm struck from heaven. It burned up the sheep and the servants, and devoured them, and I alone have escaped to tell you!" . . . He was still speaking when another [messenger] came and reported: "Your sons and daughters were eating and drinking wine in their oldest brother's house. Suddenly a powerful wind swept in from the desert and struck the four corners of the house. It collapsed on the young people so that they died, and I alone have escaped to tell you!" (Job 1:16, 18–19 HCSB)

So the principle under review must allow for the exercise of free will in rational agents, which includes the activities of demonic agents. That being said, Scripture gives no indication that every atrocity that results from the natural order is caused by the misuse of free will by either humans or demons. The point here is to suggest that some unknown quantity of suffering that is usually described as resulting from natural causes may have a non-natural explanation for its coming about, and these instances are more evidence of the moral problem, rather than a natural problem, of evil. Even though the quantity of events independent of free will is unknown, a case can be made that many of the purported natural evils in the world are really manifestations of a causal nexus of events generated from the misuse of freedom. So even if there is no

---

[3] Nick Trakakis, "Is Theism Capable of Accounting for Any Natural Evil at All?" *International Journal for Philosophy of Religion* 57 (2005): 36.

explanation for how free will is involved in a hurricane, sin is an explanation for every calamity that is an affront to human well-being.

Given these considerations, a better definition must be provided for what is meant by natural evil. Consider the following definition:

> Natural evil is evil resulting solely or chiefly from the operation of the laws of nature. Alternatively, and perhaps more precisely, an evil will be deemed a natural evil only if no non-divine agent can be held morally responsible for its occurrence. Thus, a flood caused by human pollution of the environment will be categorized a natural evil as long as the agents involved could not be held morally responsible for the resultant evil, which would be the case if, for instance, they could not reasonably be expected to have foreseen the consequences of their behavior.[4]

Is this definition anymore satisfying than the previous ones considered? Even though it does factor in human and angelic free will and the implications thereof, it conflates moral responsibility with other types of responsibility for human conduct. For example, suppose there is a drug that, when ingested by a pregnant woman, produces mental and physical defects in her baby. All of the studies done on the drug before its release indicated no danger to the short- or long-term well-being of the baby. Only after the birth were any defects discovered, and the resulting studies indicate that the use of the approved drug caused the defects. It is doubtful that anyone would describe the action of the mother in taking the drug as morally reprehensible, nor would anyone charge the medical industry with failure to practice due diligence. It is not a *moral* failure on anyone's part, thus there is no moral accountability attached. However, it is also not clear that we are then permitted to call this an instance of natural evil; perhaps suffering resultant from natural causes is a better representation. It is a bad state of affairs, but given that no clear case of intentional neglect is provided, the moral claims pertaining to what occurred is an inappropriate label. It is simply not true that every regrettable state of affairs is therefore relegated to a moral category.

To better see the intention behind these distinctions, consider what is needed for successful medical research. We need an understanding of (1) the origins of diseases, (2) chemistry as it pertains to the production of a drug that addresses either the symptoms or the disease, and (3) *consistency* in the chemistry so that there will be continuity of results from person to person.[5] We need the chemistry to be consistent; otherwise, the enterprise of medical research is a

---

[4] See ibid., 37.
[5] Obviously this is not a comprehensive list.

fool's errand. There would be no way to know, without such consistency, how the advances in research were going to be of medical value. In other words, a promising avenue for knowledge as it pertains to a worthy vocation such as medical research is largely based on trial and error.

The only account for which I can conceive of the appropriate use of the term natural evil is after the following exceptions to what is often called natural evil are ruled out:

1. *Not connected to the free choices of any nondivine agent.* At least from the Christian vantage point, this rules out diseases and other natural disasters such as those found in the book of Job. Nondivine agents include humans and demons.
2. *Not connected to the necessary balance of nature.* As Paul Copan notes, "Planetary scientists have observed that certain natural processes—though they can be deadly—bring an overall benefit to humankind. They help the earth to maintain its delicate atmospheric balance and other environmental conditions necessary for our survival. Tornadoes and hurricanes help equalize global temperatures. Tectonic plate-shifting, which produces earthquakes, actually helps replenish the soil so that it isn't all washed away."[6] This does not rule out the possibility of double effect, whereby one action yields two results in nonmoral value (for example, the good of a balanced global temperature with the bad of high damaging winds).
3. *Not connected to divine judgment.* Divine judgment is not evil; it is judgment. We have evidence of divine judgment manifesting itself through natural events in the flood narrative (Genesis 7), the ground swallowing up Korah (Numbers 16), and the sulfur and fire from the sky in the Sodom and Gomorrah narrative (Genesis 19). These are divinely caused events whereby the natural order is the means through which God exacts judgment. It is a complete misuse of the term evil in cases such as this, for these are stories expressing a judgment against evil, not the perpetration of it. Admittedly, not every natural event is a divinely caused instance of judgment, but if it is then the moniker of "evil" must be removed.
4. *Not conflating bad states of affairs with wrong states of affairs.* It is bad for the zebra to be eaten by a lioness, but it is good for the hungry lioness to eat the zebra. Simply because something is bad does not mean it is

---

[6] Paul Copan, *Loving Wisdom: Christian Philosophy of Religion* (St. Louis, MO: Chalice Press, 2007), 131.

immoral; otherwise, we need to develop a judicial system for hungry lions that satisfy their hunger on zebras. Again, evil is a deviation from how things *ought* to be, and it is doubtful that anyone will argue that lions should not eat zebras, or that zebras should make themselves easy prey for hungry lions. Moral categories do not pertain to these states of affairs, for these animals are not morally comparable to human beings. I do not mean to say that the suffering is not real, but that the zebra does not attempt to answer the question as to whether the suffering it endures is too great for any God-justifying reason, or even thinks in such graded categories at all; it simply has the phenomenal experience of pain. Moreover, there is biblical evidence that suggests predation, and thus animal death, occurred before humans ever existed, and thus before the fall of Adam (Job 41:1, 14; Ps 104:21, 29). While the fall of Adam did have the natural consequence of God's pronouncement of death for humans, this does not necessarily extend to the death of animals.[7]

With these distinctions in mind, it becomes clear that what is often described as natural evil more appropriately refers to events that produce suffering from natural causes, but that in and of themselves are not evil.

## C. Stephen Layman: Comparing Theism and Naturalism

C. Stephen Layman provides an interesting approach to the problem of natural evil.[8] Insofar as natural evil is intended to provide probative reasons to reject theism, Layman explains that theists can respond in one of four ways: theodicy, skeptical theism, the overrider response, or a comparative response. We have already treated the notions of theodicy and theistic skepticism, and there is nothing in what Layman argues that requires dismissing these as significant contributions to the discussion. The overrider response, as Layman explains, involves the claim that some reason or warranting factor overrides the evidence evil provides against theism. I have alluded to this approach as well when arguing that a person is perfectly rational to believe in God in light of having a religious experience or due to an argument for the resurrection of Jesus. The comparative response involves juxtaposing theistic explanations of evil with nontheistic worldviews such as metaphysical naturalism to see which has more explanatory power. Consequent to the investigation one may

---

[7] Paul Copan, *That's Just Your Interpretation* (Grand Rapids, MI: Baker, 2001), 150–51.
[8] Layman, "Natural Evil: The Comparative Response."

conclude that theism has more explanatory power, is equivalent in explanatory power, or has less explanatory power. The only conclusion that is troubling for theism is the third. If theism has greater explanatory power than its metaphysical rivals, then it is the more rationally compelling view to hold. If theism is equal in explanatory power, then one is not entitled to the claim that the argument purportedly against theism succeeds; for it has no more explanatory power than theism in the same area of inquiry. As Layman notes, theism may not explain all evils well, but on the whole theism explains the presence of *natural* evil at least as well as naturalism does.[9]

In order to determine when a hypothesis provides a better explanation of a phenomenon than its rival, two questions must be asked and answered:

> A. Does the hypothesis lead us to expect the phenomenon in question?
>
> B. How probable is the hypothesis independently of the phenomenon in question?[10]

The first question leads us to ask which worldview hypothesis makes the phenomenon in question less *surprising* given what that worldview affirms to be true. The second question attempts to address the likelihood of a worldview independent of the phenomenon under consideration. This is known as the *prior probability* of a hypothesis.[11] Prior probability is determined by several factors, including (1) the fitness of the worldview with background knowledge and (2) its simplicity. Background knowledge contains information that may be taken for granted such as necessary truths, well-confirmed scientific results, and common sense claims. The simplicity of the worldview contains four aspects:

1. The first facet of simplicity is just a matter of the number of things postulated. To borrow an example of [Richard] Swinburne's, Leverrier postulated one planet to explain irregularities in the orbit of Uranus, not two planets, or three, and so on.
2. The second facet of simplicity is the number of kinds of things postulated. For example, a theory that postulates three kinds of subatomic particles is simpler than a theory that postulates, say, eight kinds.
3. The third facet of simplicity may be called the simplicity of the terms, and concerns whether a term used to state a hypothesis can be

---

[9] Ibid.
[10] Ibid., 3.
[11] I will be using the terms *hypothesis* and *worldview* interchangeably in this chapter even though their designations are not literally the same. Since we are dealing with worldviews as the hypotheses, namely theism and naturalism, I will generally refer to worldviews but may allude to hypotheses as a replacement term.

understood only by someone who understands some other term. To illustrate (again, borrowing from Swinburne), "All emeralds are green" is simpler than "all emeralds are grue" because one must understand "green" in order to understand "grue" but not vice versa. This facet of simplicity will lead us to select terms that stand for objects or properties more readily accessible to our cognitive faculties. And thus it will lead us to avoid a more theoretical term unless we need it to obtain a hypothesis that yields the data.
4. The fourth facet of simplicity is the number of theses within a hypothesis that receive little or no probabilistic support from other theses belonging to that hypothesis—This rule ensures that the more one says, the more likely one is to say something that is false.[12]

Beyond these factors two more distinctions regarding the *type* of explanations involved are important for our discussion. Naturalism proposes inanimate explanations for all of the features of the world, where inanimate explanations are "given in terms of natural laws and conditions."[13] Theism, by contrast, may utilize personal explanations for the features of the world, where personal explanations involve the "beliefs, purposes, and powers of personal agents, including the power to make choices" (as well as inanimate explanations).[14] In fact, the formulations of what theism and naturalism propose help make the comparison more crisp. Theism holds that (1) exactly one nonphysical entity exists who (2) is perfectly morally good, (3) almighty, (4) and exists necessarily; and that (5) every ultimate, complete explanation is personal. Naturalism, by contrast, proposes (1) there exists a physical reality; (2) it is self-organizing, i.e., it has an inherent structure as opposed to a structure imposed by a god or some other agent; (3) it exists either necessarily, eternally, or by chance; (4) all property bearers (leaving aside properties, sets, and numbers) are physical; and (5) every ultimate, complete explanation is inanimate.[15]

With this information in mind, let us ask the question, "Does theism lead us to expect the presence of natural evil?" Layman provides two reasons to think so. First, if God exists, then he has strong reasons to create humans

---

[12] Layman, "Natural Evil: The Comparative Response," 3–4.

[13] Ibid., 4.

[14] Ibid., 5. The use of inanimate explanations in a theistic structure is my use and not Layman's. I suggest this point as a matter of theological commitment. The natural laws that govern the universe are created by God, and as such are fair game for theists to use in their model. Given that naturalists begin without a conscious being, they are bound to explain the phenomena in the world through purely inanimate explanations.

[15] Ibid., 7.

and animals.[16] Humans, given their intelligence, have the ability to ponder the wonder of creation and given their volition can invest in relationships of great significance. Second, nothing counts as physical unless it is governed by natural laws.[17] As was noted in the introduction to the book, natural laws also are a necessary condition for physical beings to experience suffering in the natural order. Or as Layman explains it, "as best as we can tell, in any universe containing forms of life similar to those known to us, many natural evils are bound to occur in the absence of supernatural intervention (i.e., miracles) on a wide scale."[18] The regularities that govern our everyday life make various types of decisions possible, for they provide a world that is consistent in its functions and discernible for our everyday decision making. In other words, the everyday benefits that persons receive from the ordering of nature and God's having created us the *kind* of beings we are makes the existence of what is normally called natural evil unsurprising.

Well and good for humans, but what of Rowe's fictitious account of the suffering of Bambi? It must be admitted that Bambi also benefits from the facts about the regularities of the world, though it is unlikely Bambi has any appreciation of such facts. Nevertheless, the argument from Rowe concerning this instance of natural "evil" is suspicious. If Scripture really evinces the idea that animal death and suffering is not pursuant to the fall of Adam, then it is questionable, at least doctrinally, to suppose that God's original created plan for animals was for their endless existence. In fact, such a claim is not only demonstrably false but makes the phenomenon of animal suffering in the world, even large amounts of it and in a variety of ways, unsurprising. The deeper issue to press again concerns the use of the word *evil*. Natural suffering is not the same thing as natural evil; a bad state of affairs is not the same thing as a wrong state of affairs. In other words, the argument has no moral premise and thus makes no moral argument from natural suffering at all. The suffering that occurs in the animal kingdom may be, as I indicated before, so that the higher forms of life are nourished. Layman makes the point more explicit:

> While there is little doubt that higher animals, such as birds and mammals, can suffer, there is good reason to doubt that lower forms of animals, such as insects and mollusks, can suffer. Consider: (a) Damage to body parts does not necessarily cause pain even in humans. And a nervous response such as withdrawal from a stimulus that causes damage is

---

[16] Ibid., 12.
[17] Ibid.
[18] Ibid.

> not by itself good evidence that pain or suffering has occurred. Even in humans an automatic nervous response can occur in the absence of pain.[19]

While Layman's claim is certainly true, it is predicated on a number of necessary conditions obtaining such that without them suffering is not logically or ontologically possible, and for which naturalism provides the thinnest of explanations, if any at all. Again, consider Layman:

> (b) Generally speaking, the more limited the behavioral repertoire of the animal, the less reason there is to suppose it has conscious mental states. On this ground there is much less reason to suppose that a jellyfish is conscious than to suppose that, say, a raccoon is.
>
> (c) The differences in the central nervous systems of animals must also be taken into account. For example, a nervous system composed of ganglia linked by nerve fibers (as in a worm) is vastly different from a nervous system involving a spinal column and a large brain of 40% of which (by weight) is composed of highly developed cerebral cortex.
>
> (d) As we have seen, suffering involves an *awareness* of the nonsatisfaction (or apparent nonsatisfaction) of a desire or instinctual drive—To sum up, while we can claim with confidence that higher animals can suffer, there is good reason to doubt that animals below the evolutionary level of fish possess centers of consciousness of the sort required to suffer.[20]

As a final point on the matter, while consciousness is a necessary condition for suffering, it is not a sufficient condition for evoking every painful conscious state as evil.

The issue of consciousness evinces an important principle: when comparing theism and naturalism with regard to their explanatory power, one must ask (a) what the necessary conditions are for the phenomenon in question, and (b) which position provides a better explanation of the necessary conditions for the phenomenon in question. To see why naturalism does not satisfy, recall its basic metaphysical commitments as provided above in (1) to (5). What is more, several other inferences attend each of the five propositions delineated:

*Proposition 1*: Physical reality is the composition of simple physical structures that evolve into complex structures. The process that yields these complex structures is not goal directed (i.e., nonteleological), that is, they do "not involve the power to act with a purpose or to make choices" as mentioned before.

---

[19] Ibid., 16.
[20] Ibid., 17.

*Proposition 2*: Physical entities have inborn tendencies to act, and these tendencies are not given by God—it's just the "nature" of physical reality to organize itself given the laws of nature and time enough for the process to come to fruition. In other words, take elementary evolutionary biology and insert it here.

*Proposition 3: Chance*: suggesting that something comes from nothing is substituting a bad explanation for a good argument. Chance, if it has any place at all in discussions about life, is better situated in evolutionary theory than as an account of life's origins. Evolution does not explain the origin of life but purportedly explains how already existing entities evolved through time. Admittedly evolution is a random process, which is why I concede chance better fits evolution than physics. *Eternal*: If the universe had a beginning in time, then an explanation for the universe's beginning is needed. If no such account can be provided, then one might be interested in postulating that the universe is eternal. The eternality of the universe does not comport with modern physics, which agrees that our universe had a definite beginning in time. *Necessary*: a necessary being is, like the traditional understanding of God, a self-existent being. Self-existent beings do not derive their existence from other beings, nor are they caused in any way. Since metaphysical naturalism postulates that all entities are physical, the self-existent entity must also be physical. What is more, the self-existent physical entity is what produces the universe(s) in a random way.

*Proposition 4*: Given that ultimate reality is physical, then there are no such things as God, angels, or souls.

*Proposition 5*: Understanding this proposition requires thinking more deliberately about what was affirmed in proposition 1. In proposition 1 it was noted that there is no mind directing the events of the world. Accordingly, there is no "personal" explanation for the features found in the world, for personal explanations involve the desires, intentions, and decisions of an agent. Personal explanations may be used to explain other facets of our world, but not the existence of the world itself or the features contained within it. Moreover, propositions 1 and 2 are married to one another, for once you concede 1, you get either 2 or something strikingly like it—the presence of life is explicable by evolutionary theory, an inanimate explanation for the features of the world.

What does this have to do with the problem of natural evil? Codifying the entailments of a worldview such as metaphysical naturalism helps us to answer an important question about the problem of suffering resultant from natural causes. If metaphysical naturalism fails to explain the features of the world, then it also fails to explain the experiences of the creatures that exist and persist in that world.

So the theist rightly asks, "Given these explanatory theses of naturalism, what is the likelihood that such a view can explain the presence of consciousness and the presence of objective moral values?" I have already addressed the issue of objective moral values in a previous chapter, and after articulating the necessary and sufficient conditions for objective moral values, defended the claim that theism has much more explanatory power than naturalism as pertains to the presence of such values. In the rest of this chapter, I am going to give attention to which view better explains the presence of (1) the fine-tuning features of the universe and (2) the presence conscious life. I will offer reasons to think theism has the upper hand in this story as well, even though the upper hand is not what is needed to respond sufficiently to the naturalist regarding natural evil. If theism explains the presence of natural evil as well as naturalism on the whole, then the naturalist cannot claim to have the upper hand regarding the problem of natural evil.

## FINE TUNING: A COMPARATIVE APPROACH

It is hardly a contribution to modern scholarship to suggest that the universe appears fine-tuned for life. The *appearance* of fine-tuning is not a debated point. The postulate that there is a fine-*tuner* is a debated point. Even though the fine-tuning features of the universe do not logically necessitate God as their cause, the God hypothesis certainly accords well with the features necessary for a life-supporting universe. In essence, the fine-tuning features are such that if they are altered even slightly, life would not be possible. In his treatment of the fine-tuning argument, scientist and theologian Alister McGrath distills six "constants" of the universe to demonstrate the precision with which the universe operates:

1. *The ratio of the electromagnetic force to the force of gravity*, which can also be expressed in terms of the electrical (coulomb) force between two protons divided by the gravitational force between them. This measures the strength of the electrical forces that hold atoms together, divided by the force of gravity between them. If this were slightly smaller than its observed value, "only a short-lived universe could exist: no creatures could grow larger than insects, and there would be no time for biological evolution."
2. *The strong nuclear force*, which defines how many atomic nuclei bind together. This force, which has a value of .007, "controls the power from the Sun and, more sensitively, how stars transmute hydrogen into all the atoms of the periodic table." Once more, the value of this

constant turns out to be of critical importance. If it were ".006 or .008, we could not exist."

3. *The amount of matter in the universe.* The cosmic number Ω (omega) is a measure of the amount of material in our universe—such as galaxies, diffuse gas, and so-called "dark matter" and "dark energy." Thus, Ω tells us the relative importance of gravity and expansion energy in the universe. "If this ratio were too high, relative to a particular 'critical' value, the universe would have collapsed long ago; had it been too low, no galaxies or stars would have formed. The initial expansion speed seems finely-tuned."

4. *Cosmic repulsion.* In 1998, cosmologists became aware of the importance of cosmic antigravity in controlling the expansion of the universe, and in particular its increasing importance as our universe becomes even darker and emptier. "Fortunately for us (and very surprisingly to theorists), $\lambda$ is very small. Otherwise its effect would have stopped galaxies and stars from forming, and cosmic evolution would have been stifled before it could even begin."

5. *The ratio of the gravitational binding force to rest-mass energy*, Q, is of fundamental importance in determining the "texture" of the universe. "If Q were even smaller, the universe would be inert and structureless; if Q were much larger, it would be a violent place, in which no stars or solar systems could survive, dominated by vast black holes."

6. *The number of spatial dimensions*, D, which is three. String theory argues that, of the 10 or 11 original dimensions at the origin of the universe, all but three were compactified. Time, of course, is to be treated as a fourth dimension. "Life," [Martin] Rees comments, "couldn't exist if D were in two or four."[21]

Again, God unquestionably provides a compelling plausible explanation of these features. The comparative approach ponders whether or not God is the best explanation for such features. "Some argue," writes Alister McGrath, "that the apparent cosmic fine-tuning is nothing more than an interesting happenstance. The fundamental constants in question had to have some value—so why not these ones?"[22] In order to capture the essence of the claim, McGrath provides the following analogy:

---

[21] Alister McGrath, *A Fine-Tuned Universe: The Quest for God in Science and Theology* (Louisville, KY: Westminster John Knox, 2009), 120–21. See also Martin Rees, *Just Six Numbers: The Deep Forces that Shape the Universe* (London: Phoenix, 2000), 2–4.

[22] Ibid., 121.

> The population of the United States of America is over 300 million. There is only one president. The odds of any one American becoming president are thus 1 in 300 million. But so what? Someone has to be president. It might be highly improbable that any given individual should be president, but it is a certainty that someone will be.[23]

There are several analogy-disrupting differences to observe. First, each of the constants that are mentioned for the universe to have life can be present without life being present. The analogy has two important features to distinguish. The first distinction is about the *conditions* under which one person becomes president. The probabilities about the constants do not change whether we are talking about theism or naturalism. What does change is the type of explanation to deploy concerning how those probabilities become actualities. Theism has a personal explanation; naturalism has an impersonal explanation. This difference draws forward a second distinction worthy of notice: having life-supporting conditions does not entail that life will then come about; it only offers that the conditions are present for life. The presidential analogy has *both* the conditions under which a person may become president as well as the guarantee that at least one person will hold that office. There is no such guarantee about the obtaining of life in a life-supporting universe. The idea that the life-supporting universe is an amazing happenstance is an admission of the inability of a hypothesis (in this case naturalism 1–5 above) to explain what it purports to explain. As McGrath points out, "It is clearly inadequate to account for the actualization of a highly improbable scenario: the emergence of a universe adapted for life."[24] In this case, the happenstance proponents are treating a necessary condition for life as the cause for life, which is simply mistaken. Moreover, the appeal in the argument has rather troubling extensions for those naturalists who do not like theistic skepticism regarding the question *why* God permits so much evil. If we recall, theistic skepticism says that our cognitive abilities, when compared to God's, make it unlikely that in some circumstances we could comprehend any greater good for which he permits evil. God's ways are higher than our ways, thus inscrutable (unable to be examined). Naturalists who suggest that there are both the conditions for life *and* the presence of life, and thus there must be *some* way of reconciling the two, are equally making an appeal to inscrutability—the only difference is where they situate the claim. Accordingly, naturalists who make such an appeal have two options available to them. First, admit inscrutability as a

---

[23] Ibid.
[24] Ibid.

viable suggestion. If the naturalist concedes that inscrutability is acceptable then it must be permitted to both theist and naturalist alike. The obvious consequence of such an admission is that it makes theistic skepticism regarding some horrific evils fair game. Another possibility is to deny inscrutability and admit the obvious inability of naturalism (1–5) coupled with a "happenstance" claim to explain anything at all concerning the features of the actual world.

A second possibility, and supposedly a more promising approach, is to endorse a multiverse theory (multiple universes). To quote McGrath:

> On this view, there exists a multiplicity of universes, so that the one we inhabit is an inevitability—On this model, the observable universe is therefore to be conceived of as a miniscule region or "bubble" within this vast spatial structure, consisting of multiple universes. This multiverse consists of a vast ensemble of existent universes, in different spatial domains of varying sizes and structures. Within each domain, the constants of nature could take on distinct values as a consequence of the different ways that inflation begins and ends in that cosmic region. Current interpretations of string theory suggest that the multiverse may consist of as many as $10^{500}$ sets of constants. In most of these domains, the set of values inherited would be expected to be biophobic.[25] However, on probabilistic grounds, there will be some region on which the set of values are biophilic.[26] We *happen* to live in one such universe.[27]

In other words, in order to explain the features of our universe, multiverse theorists postulate many distinct physical universes (the physical parameters are different from one universe to the next). Most universes do not have life, nor are they life sustainable; our universe happens to be one of the fortunate few that are life friendly. As the reasoning goes, if we are given a mind-bogglingly large number of universes, at least one of them is bound to be life supporting.

However, as McGrath notes, "it is important to appreciate that at present the multiverse hypothesis remains little more than a fascinating yet highly speculative mathematical exercise. It has, perhaps unwisely, been adopted by atheists anxious to undermine the potential theological significance of fine-tuning in the universe."[28] Indeed, it is troubling to postulate perhaps an infinite number of other, nonobserved universes to explain the presence of our

---

[25] Meaning unfriendly to the possibility of life.
[26] Meaning friendly to the possibility of life.
[27] Ibid., 124, italics mine.
[28] Ibid. John Polkinghorne provides the insight that even if the multiverse were proven correct, it does nothing to undermine the idea of God's existence. See *Belief in God in an Age of Science* (New Haven, CT: Yale University Press, 1998), 1–24.

biophilic universe, especially if the hypothesis admits these other universes bear no necessary resemblance to our own. The theist rightly wonders what the multiverse has to do with the price of tea in China.

A more troubling issue with the multiverse is that it trades in naturalism's supposed advantage over theism, the comparative simplicity of naturalism, in order for naturalism to have any explanatory power concerning the apparent fine-tuning of our universe. Layman captures this point well:

> In adding MU [multiple universe hypothesis] to naturalism we greatly complicate it. For we are now saying not merely that physical reality is self-organized, but that this self-organization takes the form of an underlying mechanism that generates universes at random. Moreover, the number of universes generated at random is very large—millions, or perhaps even infinite—In postulating millions (or even infinitely many) universes, the naturalist surely loses any advantage connected to the first facet of simplicity (i.e. number of objects postulated)—Moreover, the many universes postulated by the naturalist fall under an important new kind, namely they are unobserved and not subject to empirical tests—for there is no way to observe these other universes or to run tests to verify their existence.[29]

Accordingly, the benefits the multiverse theory provides for the naturalist cannot include a simpler explanation for the universe than theism. Moreover, it also postulates universes that we cannot observe, making an assumption for which there is no evidence. Given that the multiverse theory is based on mathematical possibilities, and that we have no empirical way of offering its confirmation, we are not privileged to call this a scientific theory in any strong sense. Yet, the multiverse theory is the primary rival to theism as an explanation of the fine-tuning features of the universe. Given its speculative nature, empirical inadequacy, and lack of simplicity, it is not to be considered a better explanation than theism for the existence of the universe. Thus, if naturalism does not provide a better explanation for the existence and features of the universe than theism, then it also does not account for the events that occur in the universe as well as theism, including events described as evil born from natural causes.

## Consciousness: A Comparative Approach

A great deal of ink is being spilled over the problem of consciousness, and for good reason. If naturalism fails to explain the presence of sentient beings, that is,

---

[29] Layman, "Natural Evil," 20–21.

beings that are able to suffer, then naturalism fails to provide an account of the feature of the world we are currently discussing. Even if we grant that naturalism leads us to expect the presence of life, such an admission does not invite the further agreement that naturalism leads us to expect the presence of *conscious* life. Consciousness is a different property of existing beings that requires an explanation.

Given its inability to account for the origin of life from these precepts, the following addition is needed:

7. Living things were brought into existence by non-living, physical causes.[30]

If we grant the proposition as representative of naturalism, the problem of consciousness becomes very clear. Simply because a universe is life-supporting does not mean that the life it supports will possess consciousness. In fact, given that starting point it is perfectly tenable to suggest that our world could have possessed nothing other than living, nonsentient creatures (e.g., plants, viruses, simpler forms of animal life). So, does naturalism explain the presence of sentient beings in the world? Not yet. The additional postulate needed for that is something like this:

8. Conscious living things were caused to exist by entirely natural factors.[31]

Stephen Layman rightly notes that Darwinian theory can explain why conscious creatures remain once they appear, but it doesn't predict or have the explanatory mechanism to tell how they came to be. Stephen Jay Gould concurs, arguing:

> Four controlling biases of Western thought—progressivism, determinism, gradualism, and adaptationism—have combined to construct a view of human evolution congenial to our hopes and expectations. Since we evolved late and, by our consciousness, now seem well in control (for better or for worse), the four biases embody a view that we rule by right because evolution moves gradually and predictably toward progress, always working for the best. These four biases have long stood as the greatest impediments to a general understanding and appreciation of the Darwinian vision, with its explicit denial of inherent progress and optimality in the products of evolution. Yet Darwinism does not confute all our hopes. It still smuggles the idea of progress back into empirical expectation, not by the explicit workings of its basic mechanism, but by an accumulation of superior designs

---

[30] Ibid., 22.
[31] Ibid., 24.

> through successive local adaptations. All the great modern Darwinians have come to terms with (and supported) the notion of evolutionary progress, even though they recognized that the basic mechanism of natural selection contains no explicit statement about it. Moreover, in viewing selection as a deterministic process, Darwinism supports our hope that the directions of change have their good reasons. In this Darwinian climate, we may still view the evolution of human consciousness as the predictable end of a long history of increasing mentality. Yet our new ideas about the importance of randomness in evolutionary change—particularly at the highest level of mass extinction—seriously upset this comforting and traditional notion and strongly suggest that we must view the evolution of human consciousness as a lucky accident that occurred only by the fortunate (for us) concatenation of numerous improbabilities.[32]

The objection mentioned is derived from a simple observation: how consciousness emerges from unconscious living entities and is detailed only through inanimate explanations is left as a complete mystery. Mysteries are not the foundation from which good explanations are derived. And if the naturalist persists in telling such a story, honesty requires an admission that their starting point makes the prospects for spinning a good yarn very unlikely; it is, perhaps, an inscrutable suggestion.

However, the theist has no reason to constrain himself to explaining consciousness through material causes and inanimate explanations. God has good reason to create conscious life—namely so that those things created with consciousness as one of their properties can lovingly relate to him. The prospects for theism's account of the origin of consciousness is forthright, for we can expect that if a loving God created life, then he will create at least some of that life with properties enough like his so that reciprocity in relationships can obtain. As such, theism has at least as much explanatory power, if not more than naturalism, regarding the problem of natural evil.

## Conclusion

The project in this chapter was to offer a more coherent concept of the idea of natural evil, for many things often called natural evil do not rightly fit into that category. Subsequent to that project I set out to compare and contrast theism and naturalism with regard to which worldview best explains the presence of natural

---

[32] Stephen Jay Gould, "Challenges to Neo-Darwinism and Their Meaning for a Revised View of Human Consciousness," delivered as the Tanner Lectures on Human Values at Cambridge University on April 30 and May 1, 1984. File may be accessed at: http://www.tannerlectures.utah.edu/lectures/documents/gould85.pdf, 64.

evil. Three questions were given attention: which worldview best explains the origin of the universe, the presence of fine-tuning in the universe, and the presence of consciousness in the universe. The rationale behind this endeavor is to investigate which view better explains the presence of the universe and its features that provide the conditions under which creatures *can* suffer. For the reasons articulated here, naturalism simply lacks explanatory power and scope. Regarding these matters, Paul Copan provides a nice synopsis of this line of thinking[33]:

| STAGES TO CONSIDER | CALCULATED ODDS |
|---|---|
| 1. A Universe (Or, Producing Something from Nothing in the Big Bang): | **Exactly 0**. (Something cannot come into existence from literally nothing; there isn't even the *potentiality* to produce anything.) |
| 2. A Life-*Permitting* Universe | Roger Penrose (non-theistic physicist/mathematician) notes that the odds of a life-permitting universe: "the 'Creator's aim must have been [precise] to an accuracy of one part in $10^{10(123)}$." What number are we talking about? It "would be 1 followed by 10/123 successive '0's! Even if we were to write a '0' on each separate proton and on each separate neutron in the entire universe—and we could throw in all the other particles as well for good measure—we should fall far short of writing down the figure needed. [This is] the precision needed to set the universe on its course." Astronomer Donald Page (a theist) calculates the odds of the formation of our universe at **1 in 10,000,000,000**[124]. |
| 3. A Life-*Producing* Universe (Life from Non-Life) | Stephen Meyer (a theistic philosopher of science) calculates the odds for the necessary 250 proteins to sustain life coming about by change as being **1 in $10^{41,000}$**. |
| 4. A Life-*Sustaining* Universe (Moving from the Bacterium to Homo Sapiens) | Frank Tipler and John Barrow (astrophysicists, the latter accepting the Gaia hypothesis) calculated that the chances of moving from a bacterium to *homo sapiens* in 10 billion years or less is $10^{-24,000,000}$ (a decimal with 24 million zeroes). Francisco Ayala (naturalistic evolutionary biologist) independently calculated the odds of humans arising just once in the universe to be $10^{-1,000,000}$. |

If a worldview cannot provide answers to these questions (origin of life, consciousness, etc.), then it cannot answer the other questions that are derived from them (natural evil, creatures capable of suffering). As a result, the problem of natural evil is not to be seen as a solid argument against the existence of God but is a compelling argument *for* the existence of God.

---

[33] Paul Copan, "Keeping the Main Thing the Main Thing." Last accessed December 2011, http://www.reclaimingthemind.org/blog/2011/12/creation-and-evolution-keeping-the-main-thing-the-main-thing.

CHAPTER EIGHT

# Prolegomena to the Deontological Problem of Evil

The first part of the book was devoted to what I deem the more traditional issues attending the problem of evil. In the next several chapters I address some issues that have arisen in more contemporary analytic philosophy.[1] As such, these chapters will have a decidedly more analytic tone than those written in the first section.

The deontological problem of evil has several dimensions. First, a distinction must be made between axiological and deontological arguments from evil. Axiological arguments debate the merits of the goodness or badness, the desirability or undesirability, of *states of affairs*.[2] Deontological formulations, such as that found in Michael Tooley's work, focus on the rightness or wrongness of *actions* instead of "concepts that focus on the value or disvalue of states of affairs."[3] It is also claimed that in order for God to be morally perfect, or moral in any meaningful sense of the term, God must fulfill certain obligations to his creation.

Regarding the problem of evil, the deontological argument claims that there are states of affairs such that, if an agent allows them to be performed, the agent has performed an action that is morally culpable. For example, if God knows that Hitler is going to build Dachau for the purpose of annihilating the Jews, then God has a moral obligation to keep Dachau from being built if the wrong-making character of permitting it to be built outweighs the

---

[1] See Michael Tooley, "Does God Exist?" in *Knowledge of God*, ed. Michael Tooley and Alvin Plantinga (Malden, MA: Blackwell, 2008), 70–147. See also Alvin Plantinga, "Naturalism, Theism, Obligation, and Supervenience," *Faith and Philosophy* 27 (2010): 247–72.

[2] Tooley, "Does God Exist?" in Tooley and Plantinga, *Knowledge of God*, 105. Axiology is the philosophical term for the study of value theory. Deontology is the ethical term deployed to describe actions that we are obligated to perform, that is, actions that ought to be done.

[3] Ibid., 106.

right-making character of permitting its construction. This argument is decidedly different than any we have discussed before, for it is not about balancing goods with permitted evils but is about the nature of moral obligation and how the evils in our world demonstrate that God's permission of them violates a divine moral obligation. So the discussion is not just about actions that humans perform but also analyzes the moral status of the actions God performs, even if the action he performs is the permission of evil. Thus, the deontological argument presupposes that it is logically possible that divine actions can, in principle, be morally wrong. Since God is morally perfect, then he must have a moral duty not to perform actions that are morally wrong.

The interesting part of the discussion is that in order for the argument to succeed there must be some account of moral value that is independent from God and some source of authority that morally obligates God to perform the actions that he does. Consider the Lisbon earthquake of 1755 in which more than 60,000 people died. Tooley argues:

> (12) The property of choosing not to prevent an event that will cause the death of more than 50,000 ordinary people is a wrongmaking property of actions, and a very serious one.
>
> (13) The Lisbon earthquake killed approximately 60,000 people. Therefore, from (12) and (13),
>
> (14) Any action of choosing not to prevent the Lisbon earthquake has a very serious wrongmaking property.
>
> (15) No rightmaking properties that we know of are such that we are justified in believing both that an action of choosing not to prevent the Lisbon earthquake would have had those rightmaking properties, and that those properties are sufficiently serious to counterbalance the relevant wrongmaking property.[4]

There are several possible lines of response, one of which I will quickly make here, and the others will be developed in great detail in the chapters to follow. Premise (15) is as subject to the criticism levied by Wykstra and Alston (see chap. 3), as the axiological argument mentioned before; just because we do not know of the right-making properties of an action does not mean an omniscient God does not know of its right-making properties. In other words, theistic skepticism is just as applicable here as before. Even if we grant that the permission of the Lisbon earthquake was prima facie wrong, this does not

---

[4] Ibid., 122.

entitle us to the conclusion that it was ultima facie wrong. In other words, simply because God permitted the Lisbon earthquake does not mean that his permission of it is a right-making property of the earthquake.[5]

I think there is a better way to address the concerns in the deontological argument from evil, and that is to make the case that God has no moral obligations whatsoever, and yet his essential moral goodness remains as one of his perfect-making properties. Several lines of thought attend such a claim, each of which deserves its own attention. In the following chapters I will be making this argument:

- The existence of God provides the best explanation for objective moral values.
- Moral obligations are imposed through commands from a person with a title or position that gives the person the right standing to obligate others morally.
- No person has a proper title or position to obligate God morally to any action whatsoever.
- Therefore, God has no moral obligations from anyone other than, perhaps, himself.
- The idea that God can obligate himself is logically absurd, given that the command obligating God to perform an action can come only from himself.
- First person commands (I command myself to) make no sense at all.
- Therefore, God has no moral obligations to perform any action.
- If God has no moral obligation to perform any action, then God cannot possibly violate a moral obligation to a specific action (e.g., regarding the Lisbon earthquake).
- God has no obligation to perform any action.
- Therefore, God has not violated any duty in his actions (which include his permissive acts).

A great deal of my reasoning in this section is derived from Plantinga's essay "Naturalism, Theism, Obligation, and Supervenience." In this essay he argues:

> Theists typically think ethical properties are intimately related to what God approves or values or commands. Thus they will often think of moral obligation as a matter of what God commands. What is obligatory are those actions God commands or wills; what is wrong are those

---

[5] This idea was originally suggested by Alvin Plantinga in *Knowledge of God*, 122.

actions God prohibits; what is permissible are those actions God does not prohibit.[6]

The reference to a divine command theory of ethics is important, for what the divine command theory engenders is precisely the idea that God's unique position and subsequent issuance of a command make obedience to the command a right-making property of the action, contrary to premises (12) and (15) above. Recognizing that a defense of the divine command theory does provide a response to his approach, Tooley offers reasons to think the divine command theory is untrue—namely what philosophers refer to as the Euthyphro objection. This objection argues that the theistic view of God and goodness results in a dilemma: is something good because God loves it, or does God love something because it is good? I will address the concerns related to either perspective in a later chapter.

Accordingly, the next several chapters develop and defend a divine command theory of ethics as a defeater of the deontological problem of evil. Admittedly, it will read more like a treatise in ethics than in the problem of evil traditionally construed, but that is because the contemporary deontological arguments are ethical objections in nature. With this in mind I will argue that God is the best grounds for objective moral values, after which an account will be given for a divine command theory of ethics. More specifically, I will be addressing the relationship between God's will and his commands and arguing that moral obligations are derived from the commands of God. After making this case, I will turn to address the Euthyphro dilemma, as it is the main objection to any divine command approach, and the one usually deployed for thinking any divine command theory is untrue. It has been suggested that if God does not fulfill certain moral obligations, then God cannot be understood to be "moral" in any meaningful sense of the term. If God is not a moral agent, then one rightly questions whether or not he is worthy of worship. What is more, the argument goes, the traditional Christian view of God's essential perfection draws suspicion to the idea that he is free, thus implying that he is not worthy of worship. In the final chapter I will address these concerns.

---

[6] See Alvin Plantinga, "Naturalism, Theism, Obligation, and Supervenience," 268.

CHAPTER NINE

# Moral Evil: Comparing Theism and Naturalism

There is an ongoing debate as to whether morality is dependent on religion. There is also a question, if such a relationship exists, as to how it should be characterized. Some argue that morality is normatively dependent on God—often on the basis of a "laws entail a lawgiver" premise. Another line of thought has it that morality is logically dependent on religion.[1] Here the discussion turns on whether ethical notions are defined explicitly by, or at least deduced from, theological concepts. A third line of inquiry examines whether a person could be motivated toward moral actions if God does not exist.[2]

Historically, after the publication of G. E. Moore's *Principia Ethica*, the conversation focused on metaethics proper: how we define the ethical term *good*.[3] The reason Moore's work is influential is that it focuses ethics on its foundations—without which all of our ethical inquiries are a waste of time. Moore's purpose is to articulate an argument proving that any account according to which moral properties may be reduced to nonmoral terms must fail; this is famously known as the open-question argument. Moore invites us to answer the question "what is good?" By this Moore means not that we are to offer an account of what things are good, or exhibit goodness, but rather that we are to explicate the property (or properties) of goodness. Moore argues that only three options are possible for answering such a question:

---

[1] William Frankena, "Is Morality Logically Dependent on Religion?" in *Divine Commands and Morality*, ed. Paul Helm (Oxford: Oxford University Press, 1981), 14–33.

[2] Michael Martin takes up such a concern in *Atheism, Morality, and Meaning* (Amherst, NY: Prometheus Books, 2002).

[3] G. E. Moore, *Principia Ethica* (Cambridge: Cambridge University Press, 1903).

1. Goodness is a complex property that can be broken down by analysis into its parts, in which case one can offer an illuminating definition of the property that works by identifying the various parts that combine to constitute goodness (in the same way that, for instance, one might define the property of being a bachelor as being a male human over a certain age who is unmarried) or
2. Goodness is a simple property that itself cannot be broken down by analysis into parts, in which case the only accurate definitions are those that trade in synonyms and so shed no real light on the nature of the property (there must be at least some simple properties, Moore argued, since they are needed as the building blocks out of which all more complex properties would have been built) or
3. Goodness is no property at all and the word "good" is meaningless, in which case, of course, no definition can be offered.[4]

Answering this question takes us to the very foundation of ethics—the account of our value term "good" in its objective existence.[5] More specifically we want to consider who it is who has the best answer to the question of the source of objective values, our concentration being on moral values. Are objective moral values inextricably tied to a divine origin, or can naturalism proffer an account that is validated through the conditions of objectivity? Or are moral properties "emergent properties, supervening upon natural processes and social configurations"?[6] It is the project of this chapter to argue that objective moral values are best grounded in a theistic construct. Second, we will turn our attention to the possibility of naturalistic accounts of objectivity, only to conclude that such accounts fail. In this second part of the project, we will consider an evolutionary account of objectivity and ask whether under such an account there can be proper moral motivation for human actions. What we will find, if my argument is correct, is that the motivation for human actions will ultimately fail if the foundation upon which those actions are based is flawed.

---

[4] This account is found in Geoffrey Sayre-McCord, "Moral Realism," in *The Oxford Handbook of Ethical Theory*, ed. David Copp (Oxford: Oxford University Press, 2006), 6.

[5] Admittedly, some are not concerned with objective value and postulate other types of value, both moral and otherwise. Our primary concern is to consider what makes values objective, rather than give substantial attention to the postulate that values, both moral and otherwise, are subjective.

[6] Paul Copan, "God, Naturalism, and the Foundations of Morality," in *The Future of Atheism: Alister McGrath and Daniel Dennett in Dialogue*, ed. Robert B. Stewart (Minneapolis: Fortress Press, 2008), 141. In fact, the organization of this chapter follows that of Copan's chapter, at least in terms of the ordering of naturalistic attempts to provide an objective foundation to ethics. While remaining in agreement with Copan, I have made a number of points that differ from his.

## Perspectives on the Objectivity of Values

It is interesting to note that when Moore provided his tripartite analysis of the possibilities of defining the good he did not consider a fourth option, namely a supernatural entity that is goodness itself. We want to consider this possibility but only after we have made clear what it means for a value to be objective. After all, if there is one aspect of ethics upon which both theists and atheists converge, it is that objective moral values are a basic part of human moral evaluation. For example, Kai Nielsen writes:

> It is more reasonable to believe such elemental things [as wife beating and child abuse] to be evil than to believe any skeptical theory that tells us we cannot know or reasonably believe any of these things to be evil. I firmly believe that this is bedrock and right and that anyone who does not believe it cannot have probed deeply enough into the grounds of his moral beliefs.[7]

If we assume objectivity as a basic moral starting point, then we need to offer an account of objectivity to arbitrate among the competing views of its source. And so the discussion begins with defining the necessary and sufficient conditions of objective value. William Wainwright provides an excellent account:

> First, value claims are either true or false. Second, values are universal. If something is good or right or beautiful, it is good or right or beautiful at all times and all places. Third, values aren't products of our desires. The goodness of truthfulness or friendship, for example, can't be reduced to the fact that we desire them or would desire them if we were fully informed. But while these conditions are necessary they are not sufficient. To be objective in the intended sense, values must also be part of the "furniture of the universe."[8]

I think the first condition is mostly uncontroversial, at least in the parlance of moral realism.[9] What is to be emphasized under this first condition is that the values spoken of are not merely *perceived* to be true or false; rather, the commitment is that for any action the perceived value intended in the action

---

[7] Kai Nielsen, *Ethics Without God* (Buffalo, NY: Prometheus Books, 1990), 10–11. Moral realism simply indicates that the values we are speaking of are real values, and that we did not simply make them up.

[8] William Wainwright, *Morality and Religion*, Ashgate Philosophy of Religion Series (Burlington, VT: Ashgate, 2005), 49.

[9] One might, however, be a moral antirealist and question this first condition. One proponent of moral antirealism is J. L. Mackie, *Ethics: Inventing Right and Wrong* (London: Penguin Books, 1977).

is either objectively present or not. In other words, our perceptions of value in an action perhaps motivate the action but do not ground the value of the action. It is interesting to note how this principle vies with some naïve forms of utilitarianism. The truth or falsity of a value claim is settled *before* any action ever takes place. Of course, we may only find out after the action whether or not there was any good in performing the action. But what this entails is that even if we endorse teleological ethics of some sort, the ends do not justify the means. The ends only reveal whether or not our *perceptions* of the value in the action were correct.

The second condition requires some clarification, for it seems to confuse what is objective with what is absolute. For something to be absolute means that it admits of no exceptions, such as the claim that murder is wrong at all times and in all places. Objective value, per condition three, means that these values are not constructs of value *preference*, nor do we (or I) ground the truth value of the proposition per condition one. What this leaves as the ground of objective value is that these values exist independent of human minds and constructions.

The third condition of objectivity counters the notion that objective values are grounded in desires.[10] We can agree that persons have a tendency to pursue the fulfillment of their desires, but we must not claim that desire fulfillment yields objective value. If we recall, Moore argued against such a claim in the *Principia*, highlighting the fact that reducing goodness to a set of properties, such as pleasure or happiness, will not work. There is an asymmetrical dependency relationship between goodness and the descriptive properties of what is good. As we know, to postulate that "pleasure is good" does nothing to answer the question "is the good pleasure?" The implication of this objection carries over to other complex properties such as preference and happiness. If we replace the variable $x$ with any property or set of properties in the proposition "$x$ is good," the question will always remain whether or not "the good is $x$." Moore's response to the problem is that the good is unanalyzable: "Good is good, and that is the end of the matter."[11] I will soon be arguing that the good is a person who is intentional, causal, and so forth, much like the God of traditional theism.

I think the sufficient condition of objectivity—that values are part of the furniture of the universe—is certainly correct. If the discussion at hand is not

---

[10] We could also speak of preferences because it seems to me that desires and preferences are not the same thing. One may desire something but not prefer it to another course of action, say a greater desire. Preference is connected to the settled intent of desire satisfaction.

[11] See Moore, *Principia Ethica*, 6.

a matter of ontological fact, then the previous three conditions do not have any footing. Without value being part of the furniture of the universe, value statements may be true but only as a matter of subjective or conventional definition (contra condition one).[12] We have good reason not to accept this as a condition of objectivity, for if I am the truth maker of a moral proposition then two things (at least) follow.

First, I can never enjoy any moral progress. To say that a person is progressing morally means that he is advancing toward a value independent of himself. It is a value onto which he is "mapping." On the other hand, if I ground the truth of values, then I can never be wrong. Even if my mind changes and the content of the moral proposition is its logical complement, no absurdity follows. Why? It goes back to who grounds truth—in this case the truth is always contingent on me. More can be said, but I think this suffices.

The second issue is that there is an odd relationship under this scheme between the moral values derived from my edict and their import on a wider community. Does my having the property of truth maker in any sense obligate other persons to the values I define? There is no reason to think so. Consider the fact that under this rubric *all* moral values are determined by the individual—including competing claims on value between persons. Not only is it the case that contradictory propositions can both be true; it also follows that no imposition of obligation can occur from one agent to the other. My reasoning hinges on the first aspect of our discussion, namely that under this construction no one makes any moral progress. Obligation, in virtue of the very concept, entails both moral progress and moral lapse (when one strays from obligation). But if we cannot make any moral progress, then we have no reason to think that we have any obligations of any kind. It seems the subjectivist paradigm is found wanting.

Perhaps we are on better footing to hold a *conventionalist* account of values whereby values are a matter of social adoption. There is the obvious question of what it is that makes these values true. More pointedly, what is it about a society that provides a suitable source of objective values? The motivation for asking this question is straightforward—at least under the subjectivist account of value we have a definite ontology, in which the self governs value. It is not clear what it is about a society that gives it such a clear function.

---

[12] Some noncognitivists argue that there are no truth values ranging over moral propositions, and moral statements are merely a matter of preference. For example, see C. L. Stevenson, "The Emotive Meaning of Ethical Terms," *Mind* 46 (1939): 14–31.

It has also been argued that what grounds moral values or truth (and there are moral truths) is a matter of rational deliberation and choice.[13] If one adopts this stance, which is traditionally called *constructivism*, a sufficient account of rationality must be provided. Specifically, how there can be convergence on a rational principle within a culture to determine what maximizes rights and liberties. Whether or not these rational choices are aimed at some value is not the real question; instead the question is, "how can it be the case that rationality is merely a matter of cooperatively rubbing our heads together?" To point out the obvious, combining a thousand leaky buckets does not mean that we have one that is functioning properly. But supposing constructivism is possible, and I doubt that it is, then all we have done is beg the question. If we are trying to ascertain the objective source of human value, which is an explicitly ontological category, we do not determine its essence simply by thinking it—an explicitly epistemic operation. What the epistemic project does is ground what is *perceived* to be true about values but in no way entails that these values are intrinsic.

But even if we grant that the truth-making condition is met, such an account will not likely get through the other conditions of objectivity. I think the real concern here is how it can be said, apart from theism, that morality is a part of the furniture of the universe—our sufficient condition for objectivity. If constructivism defaults into a view like Christine Korsgaard's, such that values are "grounded in the structure of rational consciousness" and "projected onto the world," then there *is* no sufficient grounding for objectivity.[14] Further, I do not see a clear reason for thinking these "projections" could satisfy the necessary condition of objective values being independent of our desires and preferences. In fact, if what we have is that through tacit consent we arrive at what we desire as a community, there still remains the problem of whether or not our collective perspective on human needs and desires is correct. I agree with the constructivist that our worldview is largely a matter of where we stand and how we see things—hence our perspective on the resolution. But all this reveals is how important it is to be standing in the right place so that our perspective is, to borrow from the normative notion, as it *should* be. I think there is another serious concern, similar to the one that affected the subjectivist account of values—namely that objectivity requires the "possibility of error."[15] Suppose we take the following:

---

[13] For example John Rawls, *A Theory of Justice* (Cambridge, MA: Harvard University Press, 1971).

[14] Christine Korsgaard, *The Sources of Normativity* (Cambridge, UK: Cambridge University Press, 1996), 116. This point is more developed by Wainwright in *Religion and Morality*, 53.

[15] See Wainwright, *Religion and Morality*, 53–54.

(P1) Murder is wrong at all times and in all places.
(P2) Torturing innocent children for fun is morally wrong.

What we have in these two propositions is an appeal to universal moral principles that admit of no exception. But what is implicit in their content is that they are not grounded in our judgment regarding them. Rather, these propositions have a truth value independent of our perceptions and beliefs about them. They are not to be likened to collective preference claims, nor to mere matters of judgment—such as on which side of the plate to organize our dinnerware—which highlights my concern very nicely. If moral values (or even other values) are mind-dependent in the sense that constructivism has charged, then it is entirely unclear what it would mean for someone to err in judgment. The ontological implications of such a view deny moral realism and ground the objective nature of value in rationality. So long as this is the standard, then there is nothing to arbitrate between competing claims about a moral proposition *when identical standards of rationality are employed*. At best, the constructivist may claim that in such cases bivalence does not hold, which undermines the original assertion about the truth value of moral propositions. It is not that moral propositions do not have any truth values. The problem is that they can have mutually exclusive truth values in the same time and in the same way—which is counterintuitive.

If we do not endorse either of these subjectivist stripes, then what is left for nontheistic accounts of objective value? We could postulate that ethical statements such as (P1) and (P2) are true even if God does not exist and in order to avoid the snafus of our previous discussion assert that these truths are "brute facts" about reality. The strengths of such a view are obvious. In saying that these statements are true, we have grounded value independent of any human minds or constructions—thus the truth condition is met. Further, it seems that the brute fact view postulates moral values as real values; in some sense they are ontologically a part of the furniture of the universe. And from this our sufficient condition of objectivity is met as well. Also, given that their ontology is not contingent upon our perceptions of their value, these values would exist even if it were to be the case that no human existed—thus they are independent of our preferences and mere judgments. But there is a lingering concern, having to do with the principle of what philosophers call "queerness" (meaning a quality of strangeness or incongruity with our perception of reality). Even if the necessary and sufficient conditions of objectivity have been met, one may still inquire about the "oughtness" of the principles that get articulated.[16] Consider Michael Martin's account of the Argument from Queerness:

1. If there were moral facts, they would have an intrinsic prescriptive quality.
2. If moral facts have an intrinsic prescriptive quality, then naturalism is not true.
3. Naturalism is true.
4. Hence, there are no moral facts.
4a. Therefore, objective morality is impossible.[17]

Martin finds premise 1 of the argument problematic, and in fact denies that moral facts have an intrinsic prescriptive quality—the prescriptive quality follows from "what the moral fact is" and the "psychological state of the agent."[18] But I find this attack on premise 1 seriously flawed. Its most obvious weakness is that the psychological state of the agent has nothing to do with the prescriptive force behind the moral fact. Whether or not I *accept* the force of the statement's content is not the same as whether or not I *should* accept the force and content of the statement. It is unclear what Martin means in stating that the prescriptive quality comes from moral facts and psychological states, but it seems the best reading is that these two conditions are conjunctive properties. It is the case that (1) if it is a moral fact, and (2) the psychological state of the agent understands and accepts the content of the moral fact (e.g., an ideal observer), then the agent is bound by its content. But here it seems (2) falls prey to some of our earlier concerns, namely that a condition of objectivity must be that obligation be independent of our desires and beliefs.

An analogy will help here. If we take the statement "Racial discrimination is morally wrong" and apply Martin's critique, we can see his error. What we have in this statement is that the representative force follows from the fact that there is a negative value term ranging over a specific action; if the statement were "Racial discrimination is morally permissible," the prescriptive nature changes. In this second version there are two possibilities open to the agent, and these possibilities follow from the concepts of the statement. If an action is morally permissible, then the agent is free either to perform or not to perform that action. Thus, I do not see how the conjunction of moral facts and psychological states refutes in any way what Mackie proposed in

---

[16] This is a concern of Mackie in *Ethics: Inventing Right and Wrong*.
[17] See Michael Martin, *Atheism, Morality, and Meaning* (Amherst, NY: Prometheus Books, 2002), 37.
[18] Ibid.

the "queerness" objection. At best, Martin's critique arrives at something like a Kantian Hypothetical Imperative. Concerning racial discrimination, if we deny it as a means to human flourishing we have good reason not to practice it. The contingency of its moral reprehensibility is obvious—if discrimination does promote human flourishing, then there are rational, if not pragmatic, grounds to endorse it.

Obviously, the Categorical Imperative will not arrive at this conclusion. The Categorical Imperative has the universalizability principle as its maxim; we act according to that rule whereby we could at the same time will that it (discrimination) become a universal law. The practice of discrimination cannot be morally permissible in this system. Discrimination succeeds only when a select group benefits from its practice, which is a violation of the universalizability criterion. Further, the Categorical Imperative systemically includes treating persons as ends-in-themselves and not as a means to an end. But this is just what we mean by (1). (2) holds that *if* the agent *both* understands and accepts the moral fact, then the agent is bound by its content. Given that Kant holds that reason binds the will, the agent is bound to the content through intellection, whether or not he or she accepts it. Thus, it appears this possibility will not work.

## IDEAL OBSERVER THEORY

Martin's own proposal, which will be our final candidate for a naturalist account of objectivity, is to make an epistemic argument from an ideal observer theory (henceforth IOT).[19] According to this theory, the meaning of ethical expressions is "analyzed in terms of the ethically significant reactions of an observer who has certain ideal properties such as being fully informed and completely impartial."[20] Once we define the term in this way, the normative construct follows. Martin's view holds:

> 1. X is morally wrong = If there were an Ideal Observer, it would contemplate X with a feeling of disapproval.[21]

According to Martin, the strength of IOT is that it postulates an agent, whether hypothetical or real, whose properties of being fully informed and completely impartial are "reducible to empirical properties and are not ethical ideals on a par with being completely just or fully benevolent."[22] IOT is a

---

[19] Ibid., 49–73.
[20] Ibid., 50.
[21] Ibid.
[22] Ibid.

cognitivist model; hence, ethical propositions have truth values that are not relativistic. Contrary to subjectivist views, the analysis of ethical expressions does not contain egocentric terms; thus, its content does not vary "systematically with the speaker."[23] In fact, ideal observers, being fully informed and unbiased, will agree upon the content of each ethical expression. Thus, objectivity is garnered at least in two senses. First, there are moral facts. Second, IOT is compatible with nonsubjective values. Martin explains:

> Instead of moral values being based on psychological states such as pain, pleasure, and desires, moral value is based on non-subjective states. These would include character traits, the exercise of certain capacities, the development of certain relations with others and the world.[24]

Concerning the exercise of certain capacities, an IOT holds that moral properties are properties such that the content of ethical statements have (either relationally or nonrelationally) characteristics of human experience (such as apparent rightness).[25] This overcomes, at least prima facie, the "queerness" objection to moral propositions. The moral wrongness of rape, for example, has the phenomenological property of "appearing to one" as being morally wrong—just as under proper conditions the grass will appear to me as green when I say that the grass is green. I'm afraid this last statement falls prey to a major theistic point but more on that in a moment. Central to this thesis is that it is a view about the *reactions* of an impartial observer to a moral proposition or purported moral facts. Under most accounts, the impartial observer need not be omniscient about nonmoral facts but rather have awareness of relevant data in relation of one agent to another.

I think the IOT is ultimately doomed to fail. First, contrary to the claim cited above, IOT does not provide a good response to the "queerness" objection. There are several lines of response here, beginning with the fact that an IOT is merely an account of the factual content of moral and nonmoral properties; it does not locate any being who could plausibly impose moral "requiredness" on any agent. Granted, one might hold a relational account of obligation where phenomenologically moral "oughtness" simply *appears* in either our experience or in the content of a moral proposition; and then maintain that the moral judgments of an ideal observer count as properly basic beliefs. For instance, J. Budziszewski argues that there are moral truths "we can't not know" unless

---

[23] Ibid., 52.
[24] Ibid.
[25] Ibid.

we engage in self-deception or, as the apostle Paul explains, suppress the truth in our conscience.[26] I think the point here is significant, for even if we endorse IOT, it presumes a second level of obligation, namely that of epistemic obligation.[27] If it is the case that our perceptions determine the content of our deliberation on matters moral, then it becomes all the more important, and indeed obligatory, that we be looking in the right direction in order to perceive things "rightly."

Another concern reverts to our rubric for objectivity. Even if I granted a cognitivist approach to IOT and the dispassionate nature of its scope (per necessary condition (3)), IOT fails to address the sufficient condition of objectivity—that is, it does not explain how values are a part of the furniture of the universe. If the IOT argues that they are brute facts, then our previous concerns arise and we have good reason to reject them. In a similar vein, the IOT might postulate a Moorean hypothesis that value features are simple and unanalyzable. But even so, we still have the problem of efficient causality as to their obtaining in the actual world. Recall that IOT postulates a hypothetical entity, not an actual one, and this entity has a psychological response to the content of moral propositions and actions. Hypothetical entities do not have the potency to obligate, nor evaluate, nor have any reaction (emotive or otherwise) to ethical concerns. There are other objections, such as the Euthyphro problems faced by IOT, but these objections suffice for our purposes.

## A THEISTIC CONSTRUCTION

In order to avoid the pitfalls of the previous views, let us consider how a theist might ground objective values in God. By objective I mean that there is a moral order that exists independent of human convention. In making this assertion, I am grounding the metaethical term *good* in God's nature rather than identifying it with, for example, nonevaluative natural properties. Robert Adams has recently defended this position, utilizing a realist conception of ethics, according to which comparative predication as to value entails relational properties consisting in resemblance to something that is maximally excellent.[28] By resemblance Adams means that "moral excellence" is an aspect of axiological excellence, where axiological excellence is to be understood as "resembling God in a way that could serve God as a reason for loving the

---

[26] J. Budziszewski, *What We Can't Not Know: A Guide* (Dallas: Spence Publishing, 2003), 29–53.

[27] Perhaps the epistemic supervenes on the moral.

[28] Robert M. Adams, *Finite and Infinite Goods: A Framework for Ethics* (Oxford: Oxford University Press, 1999), 13–130.

thing."[29] The particular strength of Adams's position is that the good becomes personal; but more pointedly, the personal agency typified by God entails that moral goodness is grounded in something that is the paradigm of goodness. Adams explains:

> Theists have sometimes tried to infer the personality of the supreme Good from the premise that persons, as such, are the most excellent things we know, from which it is claimed to follow that the supremely excellent being must be of that sort. A more cautious line of argument begins with the premise, harder to deny, that most of the excellences that are most important to us, and of whose value we are most confident, are excellences of persons or qualities or actions or works or lives or stories of persons. So if excellence consists in resembling or imaging a being that is the Good itself, nothing is more important to the role of the Good itself than that persons and their properties should be able to resemble or image it. That is obviously likelier to be possible if the Good itself is a person or importantly like a person.[30]

Once again, if we are willing to accept that moral goodness is implicitly relational, where the relata are agents and a paradigm of moral goodness, then a prima facie case is made by Adams such that goodness is personal, unlike Platonic archetypes, and more like the traditional God of theism.[31]

It is a central tenet of Christian thought that God has created persons in his image, and it is in virtue of this fact that our value is ontologically grounded in the conjunction of how God views himself and how, per the *Imago Dei*, he views us. God is the ultimate efficient cause of all that in any way has being. The implications of this supposition are twofold. First, this postulate is contrary to the "brute fact" thesis discussed in the previous section. If values exist as a matter of brute fact, then these values are beyond the creative will and control of God. If we postulate moral values as abstract objects, then God is at best a craftsman, molding the moral order from preexisting essences into creation. And second, this view rejects theistic views that hold necessary truths are beyond God's control.[32] What are some principles that lead one to think theism has more explanatory power in grounding objective values than its naturalistic counterpart? Paul Copan provides an excellent list:

---

[29] Ibid., 36.
[30] Ibid., 42.
[31] See Michael Murray, "Do Objective Ethical Norms Need Theistic Grounding?" currently unpublished. https://edisk.fandm.edu/michael.murray/Ethical_Murray.pdf. Permission to use this article has been obtained from the author.
[32] See Richard Swinburne, *The Coherence of Theism* (Oxford: Oxford University Press, 1977), 204.

a. *Simplicity:* Theism offers a much simpler alternative to naturalism: humans have been made in the image of God, whose character is the source of objective moral values; by contrast, naturalistic moral realists assume a pre-existent independent moral realm and the eventual evolution of valuable human beings who find themselves subject to comply with this moral realm. Theism offers a ready moral connection between a good God and humans.

b. *Asymmetrical Necessity:* Even if "murder is wrong" is a necessary truth, it need not be analytic (cp. "water is $H_2O$"); also, a necessary truth may still require some kind of explanation (e.g., "water is necessarily $H_2O$" still requires an explanation for water's existence and structure). Furthermore, certain necessary truths are logically prior to/more metaphysically basic than others: "Addition is possible" is necessarily true because "numbers exist" is necessarily true and numbers have certain essential properties. The necessity of moral truths does not diminish their need for grounding in the character of a personal God. God, who necessarily exists in all possible worlds, is the source of all necessary moral (and logical) truths that stand in asymmetrical relation to God's necessity. The necessarily existing good God is explanatorily prior to any necessary truths, whether moral or logical.

c. *Cosmic Coincidence:* Even if we grant that moral facts are just brute givens and necessarily true, a problem remains—namely the huge cosmic coincidence between the existence of these moral facts and the eventual emergence of morally responsible agents who are obligated to them. That this moral realm appears to be anticipating our emergence is a staggering cosmic coincidence that begs for an explanation.

d. *Accounting for Human Value:* Even if this Platonic realm of moral forms exists, there is no good reason to think that valuable, morally responsible human beings should emerge from valueless processes. Theism offers a far more plausible explanation for human value, as it does a better job than nontheistic accounts of explaining human dignity.[33]

I dealt with (c) in the previous section, so my intention here is to offer an argument for the necessity of a personal agent to ground objective values. I agree, generally, with the approach taken by Robert Adams—that the property of goodness requires a paradigmatic standard of goodness by which it is being gauged. Given that in the previous section the problem of the "queerness" of

---

[33] Copan, "God, Naturalism, and the Foundations of Morality," 148–49.

objectivity was such a concern, I will argue that grounding objective values in an agent who embodies those features provides a sufficient account of moral obligation.

## Divine Command Theory

Robert Adams writes that God's commands provide the best cumulative case connecting the entailment of the expression "moral obligation" to what is "semantically indicated" in that expression.[34] To be more specific, he writes of four features that are "constraints" on the nature of moral obligation—features that set the parameters of what is semantically indicated but are seldom jointly articulated sufficiently to provide an account of moral obligation. First, moral obligations are "things that we should care about complying with." Second, it follows that certain emotive responses are appropriate when a wrong is done, and these responses (perhaps including guilt) are both within the individual toward herself and from the community. Third, moral obligations are something "that one can be motivated to comply with," and as such should be "grounds for reasons to comply." From these suppositions, Adams provides a fourth feature, "it is part of the roles of moral obligation and wrongness that fulfillment of obligation and opposition to wrong actions should be publicly inculcated."[35]

According to Adams, morality is inherently social, even if one were to confine the "social" implications strictly to the agent in her relationship to God. The last condition is an explicit statement of the social element in moral evaluation. More importantly, according to social theories, "having an obligation to do something consists in being required (in a certain way, under certain circumstances or conditions), by another person or group of persons, to do it."[36] To reveal why the secular dimension alone is not satisfactory, Adams elucidates several conditions, each of which is necessary for moral obligation to obtain from "social bonds." First, the social bonds must be grounded in something good, not merely perceived to be good. The difference stipulated here is ontological rather than phenomenological. Right value (communally) comes from that which is grounded in something good.[37] Another salient feature may be summed up in the adage "consider the source," for Adams writes that the

---

[34] See Adams, *Finite and Infinite Goods*, 235–36.
[35] These four features are drawn from ibid., 235–36. A more thorough treatment of these features may be found in Wainwright, *Religion and Morality*, 84–92.
[36] See Adams, *Finite and Infinite Goods*, 238–39.
[37] This entire discussion is obtained from ibid., 244–45.

"personal characteristics" of those imposing social requirements are "relevant to the possibility of social requirements constituting moral obligation." We have more reason to follow the mandates of that which is "knowledgeable, wise, or saintly" than those of one who does not exhibit such features. Finally, the restriction on compliance follows from the gradation of good obtaining between the good demanded and the degree to which "making the demand" affects the relationship in a quantifiably better way. Though these conditions are necessary, the list may be modified to include other social standards that "approximate" the moral requirements for obligation.

Adams's contention is that the objectivity of moral obligations, which he views as requisite for social theories, cannot be accounted for on any secular model. If conventionalism is right, then "society would be able to eliminate obligations by just not making certain demands," where conventionalism is defined as the truth of moral propositions being determined by a particular social setting. The supposed objection against divine command ethics as being uniquely silent on social issues such as slavery serves as a perfect analogue. The Bible, it is argued, seems to make slavery morally permissible given that there is no explicit prohibition in either the Old or New Testament. However, Adams notes that secular moral theories are in no better shape, for "moral reformers have taught us that there have been situations in which none of the existing human communities demanded as much as they should have."[38] The moral rightness or wrongness of an action may reduce to the specific needs of a given community, but this does not account for the objectivity of, say, the intrinsic value of a human life. Adams concludes:

> These are all reasons for thinking, as most moralists have, that actual human social requirements are simply not good enough to constitute the basis of moral obligation. . . . A divine command theory of the nature of moral obligation can be seen as an idealized version of the social requirement theory. Our relationship with God is in a broad sense an interpersonal and hence a social relationship. And talk about divine commands plainly applies to God an analogy drawn from human institutions.[39]

The purported force behind Adams's statement is that divine commands provide the objectivity independent of our beliefs and motivations. And since God is, at least in perfect being theology, morally perfect, then God fills the role "semantically indicated" of the good.

---

[38] Ibid., 247.
[39] Ibid., 248–49.

Second, divine command theory offers an account of the emotions (such as guilt) brought about from wrong actions, for God is a person against which these actions are done. Granted, divine command theory is particularly theistic, and the concern may arise that atheists have no cognitive access to what is morally required. Adams contends, however, that this may be resolved in that the content of commands may come to us through the design of our mental faculties so that we are aware through conscience of what is socially required.[40] One may honor *most* social obligations through Adams's cognitive thesis. We have ideas of social good and progress because God designed us to understand how we are to function as a social entity. For example, one may come to understand that it is in his or her better interest to have regard for others. When we fail in this assignment, the requisite negative emotions such as guilt occur for those who are functioning properly cognitively. This aspect of Adams's theory does not require belief in God, since "the order of knowing is not the same as the order of being," as the Scholastics say. Thus Adams may differentiate between adherence to right conduct between human persons and right conduct between humans and God. It is this latter aspect that motivated my previous comment that one may honor *most* social obligations; God is a member of every social system, and wrongs done against him are equivalent in type to the wrongs done against humans. So, the theory has compatible notions with secular ethics; it just views them as incomplete.

I now turn my attention to Adams's argument from necessary moral truths. Suppose that we are obligated not to harm innocent children for the fun of it. According to Adams, obligation arises from the prohibitions of God. But if one were to ask whether this obligation obtains without God, either ontologically or per his command, Adams is committed to the view that no such obligation holds. This follows, he thinks, from the discussion of the nature of necessary moral truths. Michael Murray explains, "A number of theists have argued that moral claims are necessary truths and as such require some non-natural entities as their truth-makers."[41] According to Adams and in the tradition of Anselm, God is the suitable candidate to fill such a role. However, as Adams notes in chap. 4 of his book, if God does not exist or if God is quantifiably morally different (for the worse) than we believed him to be, then Adams's theory of value does not hold. For the purpose of theoretical evaluation, Adams proposes we assume God exists and morally fits the category of candidate as the good, thus "excellence is the property of faithfully imaging such a God, or of resem-

---

[40] Ibid., 257.
[41] See Murray, "Do Objective Ethical Norms Need Theistic Grounding?"

bling such a God in such a way as to give God a reason for loving."[42] More appropriate, I think, is Adams's later contention that:

> Another possibility, perhaps no more satisfying, would be to say that we evaluate possibilities from our standpoint in the actual world and that excellence in any possible world is measured by conformity to the standard of excellence as it is in the actual world—so that, on my theory, what God is like in the actual world will determine the nature of excellence in all possible worlds.[43]

What Adams is striving for is a noncontingent account of what is excellent; for to him the standard of excellence should have a definitive ontology such that persons may know and connect with it. A contingent account of excellence provides no such ontology and reduces, in Adams's estimation, to conventionalism. Thus, the best explanation is that God necessarily exists and his ontology is such that in every possible world "in which creatures like us exist, he commands them not to lie, to protect the innocent, and so on."[44] The force behind such an argument is that it seems implausible, given the nature of God, that there would be some world in which torturing children for the fun of it would be morally permissible. And, with each state of affairs, there is a triad of theological value judgments (morally forbidden, morally required, and morally neutral) such that God has an expressed will that he necessarily issues under relevant circumstances. Supposedly, this avoids God commanding that which seems to be abhorrently evil, for the content of his character is one of the relevant conditions for what is commanded. Adams explains:

> We should be clear about some things that are not claimed in the divine command theory that I espouse. Two restrictions, in particular, will be noted here. One is that when I say that an action's being morally obligatory consists in its being commanded by God, and that an action's being wrong consists in its being contrary to a divine command, I assume that the character and commands of God satisfy certain conditions. More precisely, I assume they are consistent with the divine nature having properties that make God an ideal candidate, and the salient candidate, for the sematically indicated role of the supreme and definitive Good. It is only the commands of a definitively good God, who, for example, is not

---

[42] Adams, *Finite and Infinite Goods*, 46.
[43] Ibid., 46.
[44] See Wainwright, *Religion and Morality*, 96.

cruel but loving, that are a good candidate for the role of defining moral values.[45]

We have noted that Adams's view is a "Platonic" account of the good, and this may bring up some problems. But Adams's view is not a traditional Platonic view, and for the most part I think the lingering objections can be assuaged.

## POLISHING AND AMENDING THE TRANSFINITE VIEW

I think the first objection one may lob at Adams is that if we accept his "Platonic" archetype model of goodness, then God merely exemplifies goodness rather than *being* goodness. But I think this is to misconstrue his model. What Adams means by his "Platonic" model is to offer an account such that the phrase "*x* is good" implies that it is intrinsically good to value *x*, and this even of divine agency. But one can certainly value good that is intrinsic to oneself with no necessary external referent by which that good is being measured. What I have in mind here is a Trinitarian model; the co-instantiation of perfect-making properties across the three persons of the Trinity. More importantly, though, there is nothing incoherent in the idea that one can be both an exemplar and the paradigm of an attribute, in this case goodness.

What is the upshot of this response? First, God is not good via resemblance to any external standard, nor is he good through his resemblance to his essential properties. Rather, God's goodness is an essential attribute of his existence; hence, he is necessarily good and recognizes this about himself. Thus we may adopt a Platonic "shift" whereby instances of the good "are likenesses or imitations of the Forms under which they are classed."[46] In other words, things are excellent insofar as they resemble or imitate God (rather than ideas). God, whose existence grounds the possibility of comparative predication, empowers the argument originated by Aquinas that if creatures are good insofar as they image God, then goodness may be predicated of both God and all of the elements of the created order (hence the attribution of the social element mentioned above).

I think other objections might arise. For example, in postulating that God knows his own goodness and loves himself for it, one might claim that God is narcissistic. But this hardly follows. Narcissism has to do with a deluded self-concept or the magnification of attributes not possessed by the agent. Under

---

[45] Adams, *Finite and Infinite Goods*, 250.
[46] Ibid., 28.

this construction, God's recognition of his perfect-making properties does not merit the charge of narcissism—it is recognition of an ontological truth.[47] Just as persons can introspect and find attributes that are desirable and good, all the more for the One who embodies the fullness of being. So I do not think this objection has any merit.

Does Adams's theory satisfy our criteria presented above? I think it does. Given that God's goodness supervenes on his actions, we have a solid account of these values being a part of the furniture of the universe. Further, given that these properties are objectively grounded in God's essential nature, and that persons are made in the image of God, we have a promising account of the necessary conditions of universality and truth being met. It is not that God merely exemplifies these properties; it is that God both exemplifies goodness and is the standard by which actions are measured. As we argued, it does not make sense to postulate something as a standard that does not exemplify the properties of which it is the standard. There is the lingering concern that if this argument goes through, then one becomes subject to belief in God; it would be incoherent to hold such a view without belief in God. But as we noted, given that God's goodness supervenes on creation, the epistemic question of belief becomes unnecessary. God is the best semantic indicator of these values, and the epistemic pathway to moral knowledge is not entailed through this theory. If we agree with Richard Taylor, though, then one might want to reconsider the plausibility of naturalism in light of theism's more promising account of moral values and personal duties. Richard Taylor writes:

> A duty is something that is owed. But something can be owed only to some person or persons. Similarly, the idea of an obligation higher than this, and referred to as moral obligation, is clear enough, provided reference to some lawmaker higher than those of the state is understood. In other words, moral obligations are more binding upon us than our political obligations. But what if this higher-than-human lawgiver is no longer taken into account? Does the concept of moral obligation still make sense? The concept of moral obligation is unintelligible apart from the idea of God. The words remain, but their meaning is gone.[48]

---

[47] For a more detailed account of this discussion, and one to which I am greatly indebted, see Paul Copan, "Divine Narcissism? A Further Defense of God's Humility," *Philosophia Christi* 8 (2006): 313–25. Copan gives a much more detailed account in this article than is necessary for my work here.

[48] Richard Taylor, *Ethics, Faith, and Reason* (Englewood Cliffs, NJ: Prentice-Hall, 1985), 83–84 (text emended for context).

## Conclusion

What must remain clear is that this has been a project in grounding the good; it has not been a project in grounding moral obligation—the topic of Taylor's quote. But I bring this up to highlight a very important feature of our discussion. God offers the best account of moral values as well as offering the best account of moral obligations, especially when compared to rival naturalistic theories.

Why is this nuanced discussion important for a book on the problem of evil? The title of the chapter indicates the significance of this topic, for if one's worldview cannot establish the moral foundation by which we may indict obviously heinous human behavior, then that worldview fails to launch a meaningful discussion on a phenomenon of our experience that requires explanation. Given the pervasiveness of evil in our experience, and the failure of naturalism to provide the ontological grounds for moral values attendant to the issue, one rightly questions the rationality of naturalism—at least regarding the problem of evil. This observation brings about a startling turn of events, for evil is traditionally considered to be the weightiest objection against the existence of God. How might one turn the table on the atheist objector and suggest that evil is actually an argument *for* the existence of God? William Lane Craig pares it down nicely:

1. If God does not exist, objective moral values do not exist.
2. Evil exists.
3. Therefore, objective moral values exist—namely, some things are evil!
4. Therefore, God exists.[49]

A person may be fully committed to this line of reasoning without any indication as to what God is up to in permitting atrocities, for example, in Darfur. But at least the theist has the metaphysical grounds to claim that the atrocities in Darfur *really are* atrocities. As such, even the atheist must concede that theism has great explanatory power. The claims to the demise of theistic belief as derived from the existence of evil are too quick, especially when those proclaiming its demise are borrowing from its principles to reject it.

---

[49] See William Lane Craig and Walter Sinnott-Armstrong, *God? A Debate between a Christian and an Atheist*, Point/Counterpoint series, ed. James Sterba (Oxford: Oxford University Press, 2004), 126.

CHAPTER TEN

# The Relationship between God's Will and God's Commands

To be a theological voluntarist," writes Mark Murphy, "is to hold that entities of some kind have at least some of their moral statuses in virtue of certain acts of divine will."[1] It may be the case that the status of actions described as obligatory are so in virtue of a "single supreme obligation," namely, to obey God.[2] The traditional version of divine command ethics (henceforth DC) is built upon such a framework, such that "all of the more workaday obligations that we are under . . . bind us as a result of the exercise of God's supreme practical authority."[3] Hence, the traditional DC theory is a normative metaethical thesis, and "it is a version of theological voluntarism because it holds that all other normative states of affairs, at least those involving obligation, obtain in virtue of God's commanding activity."[4]

Granted, the traditional DC view dominated the literature of the Medieval Scholastics and perhaps developed even sharper teeth in the contemporary works of Robert Adams. The current trend is to give an account of what it is in DC ethics that makes it an "interesting thesis" and an "informative account" of normative concepts, properties, and states of affairs.[5] Thus the emphasis shifts from a normative metaethical view to a descriptive project in which a version of DC is fashioned in terms of some acts of divine will. In either case, proponents of DC are in agreement regarding one thing, namely that what God wills is relevant to how moral obligation obtains.

---

[1] Mark Murphy, "Theological Voluntarism," *The Stanford Encyclopedia of Philosophy*, ed. Edward Zalta (Winter 2006), http://plato.stanford.edu/entries/voluntarism-theological.
[2] Ibid.
[3] Ibid.
[4] Ibid.
[5] Ibid.

In this chapter I will be defending a traditional DC theory of ethics whereby moral obligation arises from the commands of God. In order to succeed in my task, I will first challenge Mark Murphy's thesis that DC ethics is best articulated in a will formulation. I will offer a sketch of Murphy's thesis and give criticisms as to why such a construal will not work. Next, I will turn my attention to the development of my own theory regarding DC ethics. Here I will discuss (1) how God's will is integrated into a meaningful DC ethic, (2) how a DC theorist can ground God's authority in a meaningful way such that he has "practical" authority with regard to the content of his commands, and (3) what moral obligation entails and why moral obligation is only binding on defective moral agents.

## Mark Murphy's Divine Will Formulation

"Assume," writes Mark Murphy, "that theological voluntarism is an account of obligation-type properties. A second issue concerning the proper formulation of the view concerns the relevant act of divine will."[6] According to Murphy, there are three options that exhaust our possibilities:

1. That it is obligatory for A to $\phi$ depends on God's commanding A to $\phi$.
2. That it is obligatory for A to $\phi$ depends on God's willing that A $\phi$.
3. That it is obligatory for A to $\phi$ depends on God's willing that it be obligatory for A to $\phi$.[7]

I will save discussion of (1) for later, given that I will defend it in my own theory. Murphy thinks that the dispute is between (1) and (2), for (3) "is, understood in one way, no competitor with (1) or (2); and understood differently, it has little argumentative support."[8] Let us consider why (3) should be rejected and orient the rest of our discussion on the debate between (1) and (2).

What we have in (2) is that some person be bound by moral requirement to perform a certain action. God's commanding Abraham to sacrifice Isaac was God's willing that Abraham be morally obligated to sacrifice Isaac. Murphy notes that this view can be given either a metaethical or normative version. According to the normative version, all humans are required to do what God wills that they be morally required to do. Thus, "particular actions that God wills that we be morally obligated to perform become actual moral

---

[6] Ibid. In what follows, I am using Murphy's Greek letters to represent any action that we are obligated to perform.
[7] Ibid.
[8] Ibid.

requirements."[9] Every human, as such, is morally required to obey God's will, and all of the particular moral obligations are specifications of this general moral requirement. However, the metaethical version of (3) "does not appeal to a general moral requirement that is particularized under the content of God's will."[10] Contrariwise, the metaethical thesis is that God creates moral obligations *ex nihilo*, that is, "out of normative nothingness."[11]

What becomes clear is that the normative and metaethical versions of (3) differ in their explanation of moral obligation and in the implications of what obligations there are. The metaethical thesis explains the existence of particular moral obligations in terms of God's power to "actualize normative states of affairs; no normative states of affairs obtain prior to God's willing."[12] Given that the normative thesis explains moral obligation in terms of the normative state of affairs that persons are morally required to obey God, "it follows trivially that humans are under a moral obligation to obey God."[13] We have already noted that the metaethical view does not have this implication. Thus, our first objection is that the normative and metaethical versions of (3) are distinct theses; neither view entails the other.

One of the reasons for accepting (3) is that it best supports the doctrine of divine sovereignty. The doctrine of divine sovereignty over creation is "that nothing distinct from God is independent of God."[14] The dependence referenced here is an ontological dependence; thus, one state of affairs contributes to the obtaining of the other state of affairs. Philip Quinn, for example, argues that this dependence relationship can be understood in one of two ways. There is the stronger thesis which holds that all states of affairs, even those involving or entailing God's existence, are metaphysically dependent on God's willing them. The weaker dependence holds that only contingent states of affairs are metaphysically dependent on God's will.[15] It is this second dependence relationship that Quinn endorses. The problem with Quinn's view is that in morality most states of affairs are wholly distinct from God's existing. Murder's being morally forbidden and love's being morally required are "obviously distinct from God's existing, and so if God is sovereign over creation in this moderate sense then the obtaining of those normative states of affairs is dependent

---

[9] Mark Murphy, "Divine Command, Divine Will, and Moral Obligation," *Faith and Philosophy* 10 (1998): 11.
[10] Ibid.
[11] Ibid.
[12] Ibid.
[13] Ibid.
[14] Ibid.
[15] Ibid., 12.

on God's willing that they obtain."[16] God's sovereignty, thus construed, does not support the claim that any normative states of affairs obtain, nor "does it show that the moral requirements that we are under are a result of a prior moral requirement to obey God. Rather, the appeal to sovereignty shows only that God's will must enter into any complete explanation of why a normative state of affairs obtains."[17] This argument shows that we might get a metaethical version of (3) from Quinn's argument, but we do not get the normative version. Consider an example. From the supposition that promise-keeping is a morally obligatory state of affairs that obtains, we do not derive the normative principle from its dependence on God's existence. Murphy writes:

> This state of affairs is, I think, wholly distinct from the existence of promises: one can conceive of its being morally obligatory to keep promises yet no one has made any; and one can accept that promise-keeping is obligatory while not accepting that there are any promises to keep. One can, *pace* Anselm, conceive of God's non-existence while conceiving that it is morally obligatory to obey God, and one can accept the view that obedience to God is morally required while denying God exists.[18]

Thus, the preferred conclusion to the sovereignty thesis is not that the moral requirement to obey God implies God's existence. Even if one finds a way to make the relationship between the normative and metaethical versions of (3) symmetrical, what we have through the argument from divine sovereignty is not what (3) argues. In fact, if moral requirement does not imply God's existence, then the obligation to obey God is distinct from his existence. If moral obligation is distinct from his existence, then the only other option for (3) is that obligation depends (metaphysically) on God's will; but this is the claim of (2), not (3). For these reasons, we will not consider (3) a live option for our discussion.

I will now articulate what the dispute is between (1) and (2), first giving priority to the development of (2). We will find that there is much common ground here, but a central disagreement will center on the relationship of speech-acts and their informative and obligating power. What I hope to provide is a solid defense of DC in terms of the illocutionary and perlocutionary force of God's commands. It will be on these points that Murphy and I will disagree—for I agree in large part, with one proviso, with his views on the content of God's will. So after I offer Murphy's will construct, I do not have much interesting to

---

[16] Ibid.
[17] Ibid.
[18] Ibid., 13.

say against it merely in terms of what God wills. I do have a bone to pick with his thesis about divine will (DW) as normative, so it will be there that he and I part company. For purposes of clarity, from this point forward I will refer to (1) as DC and (2) as DW respectively to keep the contrast between the command formulation and will formulation clear.

## Mark Murphy's Argument from DW

What DW asserts about morality is that the act of will "that is relevant is God's will that some persons be bound by moral requirement to perform a certain action."[19] Indeed, one of the strengths of such a view is that it is common currency among theists to claim that they performed a certain action because it was God's will. The goal of this view is to articulate a thesis of God's activity that specifies a sense of willing that lies between two extremes. The first of these extremes is that one may specify a sense of willing that is "too strong."[20] If a picture of God's sovereignty is drawn such that his will is efficacious in all human actions, then no one could possibly violate a moral requirement.[21] Second, if one specifies a sense of willing that is too weak, then it "does not seem appropriate to connect that sense to moral obligation."[22] Let us first consider the strong sense of God's willing.

The strong sense of God wills that X is "that in which God intends that X."[23] What is needed for DW is a weaker sense of willing that does not entail intending, for God's intentions guarantee a state of affairs obtaining because it follows from God being omniscient and rational.[24] As the argument goes, if God is omniscient with regard to human actions, then God knows whether or not a certain state of affairs, say Abraham's sacrificing Isaac, obtains. As Murphy notes, if we suppose that God intends that Abraham sacrifice Isaac and God knows that Abraham will not sacrifice Isaac, then God is irrational, for "it is irrational to intend a state of affairs that one knows will not obtain."[25]

---

[19] In personal correspondence Hugh McCann points out that this sounds more like (3) than (2). My rejection of (3) is largely due to the problem within speech-act theory, which I will address in a moment. I think the other concerns we provided before are sufficient for a rejection of (3) as a viable hypothesis. This may just be an instance of inconsistency for Murphy. Rather than say that the act of will that is relevant is God's will that some persons "be bound by moral requirement to perform a certain action," he can say the relevant act of will is God's [antecedent] will for an agent to perform an action.
[20] Murphy, "Divine Command," 16.
[21] Ibid.
[22] Ibid.
[23] Ibid.
[24] Ibid.
[25] Ibid.

The problem is obvious—it must be the case that if God intends this state of affairs, then it is not true that God knows that Abraham will not sacrifice Isaac. If God intends the sacrifice to obtain, then God knows that the relevant act of sacrificing will obtain. To state the strong sense of will otherwise, "what God wants God gets."[26] Such a result is counterintuitive, for the very problem that we are dealing with is the narrative of human moral failure, not success. We need an account of willing that avoids this counterintuitive approach, one that is strong enough to account for moral obligation but is not so strong as to preclude moral violation.

At this juncture Murphy considers a promising resolution proposed by Thomas Aquinas in the *Summa Theologica*. There we find a discussion of how it can be the case that God's will is necessarily fulfilled, in a sense, while circumventing the negative effects of the earlier postulates. Aquinas writes:

> The words of the Apostle, *God will have all men to be saved*, etc., can be understood in three ways. First, by a restricted application, in which case they would mean . . . *God wills all men to be saved that are saved, not because there is no man whom He does not wish saved, but because there is no man saved whose salvation He does not will.* Secondly, they can be understood as applying to every class of individuals, not to every individual of each class; in which case they mean that God wills some men of every class and condition to be saved . . . but not all of every condition. Thirdly . . . they are understood of the antecedent will of God; not of the consequent will. This distinction must not be taken as applying to the divine will itself, in which there is nothing antecedent nor consequent, but to the things willed.[27]

The third construal is what theologians have drawn on to resolve the apparent discrepancy in Scripture on doctrines of eschatology and soteriology. God wills, for instance, that all persons be saved and yet not all persons are saved (Matt 7:13–14; 1 Tim 2:3–4). A moral corollary may be found in the Holiness Code of the Old Testament (Leviticus 19) or in the Sermon on the Mount of the New Testament where Jesus utters the imperative, "Be perfect, therefore, as your heavenly Father is perfect" (Matt 5:48). As Mark Murphy notes, "What makes this coherent is that the sense of willing in which God wills that all be [saved] is antecedent: prior to a consideration of all the particulars of a person's situation."[28] To make the moral point, God wills that all people be perfect

---

[26] Ibid. Murphy also uses this as an argument against thesis (3) above.
[27] Aquinas, *Summa Theologica*, Q.1, a.19, ad 6.
[28] Murphy, "Theological Voluntarism."

prior to and independent of any action being instantiated by the agent(s). The sense in which everything that God wills obtains is grounded in God's consequent will that is posterior to and with regard to particular actions by moral agents. The upshot is that the distinction between God's antecedent and consequent will grounds a sense of willing strong enough for moral obligation to obtain, but it is not as strong as the intention thesis that effectually makes God the author of sin (for nothing, under this rubric, occurs independent of God's intentions). Murphy explains:

> There remains the possibility that moral obligations can be held to depend on God's antecedent intentions. These might be thought to have the requisite strength to be associated with moral requirements, and since not all of God's antecedent intentions need be fulfilled, this association would not have the unwelcome implication that necessarily no moral obligations are violated—This is possible, because God's antecedently willing that S $\Phi$ does not entail that it is the case that S will $\Phi$.[29]

If we recall, Murphy is a proponent of the DW formulation, whereby morality is primarily a matter of God's will. I think he has given sufficient defense for the cogency of how God can will a state of affairs and yet that state of affairs not obtain. He contends, however, that such a distinction only makes sense under a DW formulation; for under the DW formulation "God's capacity to impose moral obligations is not objectionably contingent, depending on a very special set of institutional facts. Rather, what is relevant in a command is that God is expressing his antecedent intentions regarding human action."[30] The "institutional facts" Murphy references must be DC's analogue of human speech-acts to that of divine speech-acts; God's speech-acts impose moral obligation in the same way that human speech-acts do. He writes:

> For it to be possible for one to give another a command to $\Phi$, there must be a linguistic practice available to the addressee in terms of which the speaker can formulate a command. This is not just for the sake of having the means to communicate a command; rather; commands are essentially linguistic items, and cannot be defined except in such terms. Imagine, though, that a certain created rational being, Mary, inhabits a linguistic community in which there is no practice of commanding. One can successfully make assertions to Mary—but one cannot successfully command Mary to do anything. Here is the question: so long as Mary's

---

[29] See Murphy, "Divine Command," 18–19.
[30] Ibid., 19.

linguistic resources are confined to those afforded by this practice, can God impose obligations on her?[31]

Murphy's emphasis here is that there is an asymmetrical dependence relationship between what God wills and what God commands. For, as Murphy argues, "It is far from clear that it is a real option for God to command that A Φ while not intending that A Φ."[32] The dependence of the commands on the will hinges on a "sincerity condition," for if God commands what he does not intend, then God is "insincere" in uttering the injunction. Contrariwise, God might intend for humans to act in a certain way while not commanding them to do so.[33] The reasoning is forthright. Proponents of DC are bound to answer this question in the negative, while proponents of DW answer in the affirmative.

I have provided the contrast between DW and DC to facilitate our own argument for DC, for it is in response to these issues raised by Murphy that we are writing. Before I turn to our own DC construction, there is one more element of Murphy's argument to be considered. Murphy argues that the DW approach is superior to the DC approach for another reason: DW is "capable of providing defenses of several commonly held deontic theses that [DC] cannot."[34] Thus, we consider the following three theses:

1. If one is morally obligated to Φ, and Ψ-ing is a necessary means to Φ-ing, then one is morally obligated to Ψ.
2. If one is morally obligated to Φ, then it is possible for one to Φ ("ought implies can").
3. If one is morally obligated to Φ and is morally obligated to Ψ, then one is morally obligated to Φ and to Ψ.[35]

The claim that God's intentions regarding human actions determine our moral obligations provides an apologetic for DW on all three of these claims. For if God intends the ends, then God intends the means. "So, if God intends that S Φ, and S's Ψ-ing is necessary if S is to Φ, then God (being rational) intends that S Ψ."[36] Second, God does not intend what God believes to be

---

[31] See Murphy, "Theological Voluntarism."
[32] Ibid.
[33] Ibid.
[34] Murphy, "Divine Command," 20. Another way of reading Murphy is as follows: "If God believes it is impossible for Wendy (symbolized as S) to take care of the poor (symbolized as Φ), then God does not intend for Wendy (S) to take care of the poor (Φ)."
[35] Ibid. An easier way to understand Murphy is as follows: "If Wendy is morally obligated to take care of the poor (represented as Φ), and buying groceries (represented as Ψ) is a necessary means to taking care of the poor (represented as Φ-ing), then Wendy is obligated to buy groceries (represented as Ψ)."
[36] Ibid.

impossible. Therefore, "If God believes that it is impossible for S to $\Phi$, then it is impossible for S to $\Phi$, and God (being rational) does not intend that S $\Phi$."[37] Finally, it is a tenet of "rational intending" that one's "separate intentions" should be joined to an "overarching plan." From this we may derive, argues Murphy, that "if God intends that S $\Phi$ and God intends that S $\Psi$, then God intends that S both $\Phi$ and $\Psi$ (and is morally obligated to both $\Phi$ and $\Psi$)."[38]

There are other factors Murphy provides as defense, but what we have so far suffices for our purposes—at least as a rubric for DW and the concerns for DC. So what is the task for the DC view? I think our project, in order to be successful, must give response to three questions:

- How might the DC proponent respond to the claim that God's commands are only a byproduct of his will (and hence the preeminence of the divine will)?
- How might the DC proponent respond to the linguistic analogue of the "non-imperative community" (see the problem of Mary above)?
- How might the DC proponent respond to the claim that only through a DW approach may one endorse all three claims regarding rational intending?

## DIVINE COMMAND FORMULATION AND THE WILL OF GOD

It should be noted that proponents of DC are not saying that God's will is irrelevant to his commands. Rather, they emphasize that God's commands bring about moral obligation, and without the requisite act of commanding no moral obligation obtains. Let us now consider a DC argument.

First, I agree with Murphy that a distinction must be made between God's antecedent will and God's consequent will. But contrary to Murphy, I find the distinction problematic for the DW proponent. Robert Adams explains, "The most obvious problem for the divine will theories of obligation is that according to most theologies, not everything wrong or forbidden by God is in every way contrary to God's will."[39] Adams's contention is that the ground of moral obligation is "not to be found" in God's permissive will (understood as either his consequent or even antecedent will); rather, moral obligation obtains under God's *revealed will*.[40] By revealed will Adams means that which

---

[37] Ibid., 21.
[38] Ibid.
[39] See Robert M. Adams, *Finite and Infinite Goods: A Framework for Ethics* (Oxford: Oxford University Press, 1999), 259.
[40] Ibid.

is "substantially" the same as God's commands.[41] Thus, the bridge that covers the gap between a strictly metaethical project (descriptive) and a normative thesis is to be grounded in God's revealed will. I will treat the revealed will of God with more rigor in my section on speech-acts.

But first, what of Murphy's account of rational being Mary who inhabits a community with no concept of imperatives? Under the DW rubric we can account for how God brings about actions in that community, namely that God expresses his preferences regarding their actions in given circumstances. For example, if my wife tells me that she would like for me to wash the dishes, then there is enough content in the expression of her wishes for me to understand, as a rational agent, what state of affairs she desires to see obtain. Further, there may be enough inflection in her voice and sternness in her eyes to relay grades of intensity in her preferences. Though she cannot command me, her will can be known.

I will concede that merely from the perspective of the "nonimperatival" community an expression of will accomplishes what the DW proponent wants and the DC proponent cannot provide. However, I think that in constructing the community as such, Murphy has sacrificed his previous assertion about the sovereignty of God. Moral obligation does not obtain when God merely "prefers" or "wishes for" or even *merely wills* an agent to perform an action but in fact *antecedently wills and commands* that action to be done. Previously we noted that Murphy rejected a preferential model of DW, for it was not strong enough to account for moral obligation. So I think the sovereignty concern is warranted. Further, in creating the "nonimperatival" community it seems that Murphy cannot account for God's rationality. Consider Robert Adams:

> It leaves us faced, however, with the question of why God would ever leave the obligatory uncommanded—why would God ever want something to be obligatory but not command it? Perhaps, of course, in view of a mix of advantages and disadvantages, God would have an antecedent but not a consequent volition that the action be obligatory, and would not command it; but in that case the action would presumably not be obligatory, since what God wills antecedently but not consequently does not happen—certainly insofar as it depends on God. So it seems implausible to think of divine volitions regarding obligations as grounding obligations without issuing the relevant commands.[42]

---

[41] Here Adams allows for "counsels" or advice, but the actual commands of God are the most narrowly construed condition of moral obligation.

[42] Ibid., 261.

Granted, Adams was not, in this passage, responding to Murphy's analogy, but I think his argument has force there as well. Traditional divine command theories postulate a direct connection between what is commanded by God and how the commands are to produce an intention in the agent on whom the command is directed; this falls in line with Murphy's postulate (2) above (the ought-implies-can principle). I like the way Adams responds to such a claim as Murphy's:

> The main benefit I can see in replacing divine commands with divine will in a theory of obligation would be avoiding the problems that attend the requirement that commands must be revealed or communicated in order to exist as commands. This benefit would depend on the assumption that the relevant divine will can be what it is, and impose obligation, without being revealed. But this yields an unattractive picture of divine-human relations, one in which the wish of God's heart imposes binding obligations without even being communicated, much less issuing a command. Games in which one party incurs guilt for failing to guess the unexpressed wish of the other party are not nice games. They are no nicer if God is thought of as party to them.[43]

Murphy may contend that God's wishes may be expressed, but the problem remains that it cannot be done as a command. So I see no good reason to maintain a DW view as opposed to a DC view in Murphy's analogy. In fact, if moral obligation is to obtain, then the requisite act of commanding is necessary to impose the obligation.

## A Closer Look at Speech-Acts

A good question to ask, and one that elicits concern over DW, is whether or not God's commands are speech-acts. I say this is a concern for DW not because the DW proponent must hold that God cannot speak but rather because DW does not capture what occurs when in fact God does speak. We have noted that Murphy and others hold that God's commands play merely an informative, not a normative, role and that God's will is what obligates. It is this claim that I want to consider, in light of a distinction drawn out in most accounts of speech-acts, namely that between the illocutionary act of speech and the perlocutionary act of speech. Consider this question: if God utters a command, can

---

[43] Ibid.

it be the case that the only thing that happens is that in uttering the command God *merely informs us of his will*? I will argue against this possibility.

In proper speech-act parlance we may ask "if God commands me to X":

1. What does the command of God say? And,
2. What does the command of God do?

According to J. L. Austin, speech-acts have three distinctive elements.[44] The *locution* is the set of words that is uttered, the *perlocution* is the effect of what is said, and the *illocution* is the message conveyed by what is said. What is important here is that in order for speech to be an act, certain conditions must be met because speech is ingrained in social customs and institutions. Take, for example, the following words uttered from God to Abraham:

(s) Abraham, sacrifice Isaac.

In uttering this statement several things have been done. A witness might report that God said to Abraham "sacrifice" meaning "take the life of Isaac in some way." This is the locution of the statement. Second, in saying to Abraham "sacrifice Isaac," God persuaded Abraham to sacrifice Isaac—this is the perlocutionary force of the statement. Further, one may derive from (s) that it was the speaker's intention to *command* Abraham to sacrifice Isaac, rather than to offer it as a suggestion or merely as a report of the speaker's desires. This is the illocutionary force of the speech-act.

The question now becomes whether or not moral obligation is derived from either the perlocution or the illocution of divine speech-acts, or perhaps both. I see this to be the issue because DW and DC cannot say the same thing here. If we hold to the DW view that commands are the information highway to God's will, then moral obligation obtained (at least logically) before any divine speech-act—and such a contention seems incompatible with what speech-act theory proposes. Divine speech, as it were, is the divine action of obligating, and the words of the commands are inseparable from the content of the commands. The DW view, of necessity, separates the content of speech from the content of action.

The DW proponent may at this point recur to the possibility of the "non-imperatival community" mentioned above and claim that placing the focus of obligation on speech-acts fails under this model—for it would then be impossible for nonimperatival communities to be moral. But this need not be the case. Speech-act theory allows for indirect speech, which can have the

---

[44] J. L. Austin, *How to Do Things with Words* (London: Oxford University Press, 1962), 101–3.

same locution, illocution, and perlocution as direct speech. I think indirect speech might be what a natural law theorist would want, but in this case we need only postulate that so long as divine commands supervene on the created order there is no problem. (It's not either divine commands or natural law; it is both, narrowly construed.) The difference between DC and natural law is that between special revelation (e.g., the Bible) and general revelation (e.g., the created order). The difference between these aspects of revelation is epistemic, not ontological. Both special and general revelation are divine speech-acts, namely two aspects of God's revealed will. Special revelation's normative force is more likely to seen as true by someone within a theistic tradition because of a commitment to some type of verbal inspiration. In fact, most theistic traditions have it that their sacred texts are inspired by God. No such theistic (epistemic) commitment is required from the natural law. It is my contention that if divine commands supervene on the natural law, then one may accept the normative force of the natural law and not reckon it to its source. But this difference is merely one of how God speaks, not whether God speaks. In other words, the medium of speech is not as important as the content of the speech, and proposing a "nonimperatival community" as a counterargument against DC on this point is strictly an ad hoc maneuver. Why should we postulate a logical construct where God, *qua* Creator, even considers the act of creating such a community?

Murphy argues that in order for an argument like mine (and Adams's) to pass muster, there must be a correlation between human speech-acts and divine speech-acts. If this connection cannot be made, then the DW proponent need not waver. Murphy argues, in tandem with Rawls, Simmons, and Searle, that conventional rules and social paradigms do not confer moral obligation except by way of a moral principle that "entails adherence to those rules is morally required."[45] Against such an objection one may not invoke moral obligation in terms of God's will without question-begging (Why obey God? Because God said so). Rather, we must construct an independent *moral* principle that implies that obligations resulting from divine commands are morally binding. What Murphy has in mind is that mere rules are not moral, nor are positional or institutional requirements moral obligations. Why is this objection so problematic? Because if no speech-acts generate moral obligations, then divine speech-acts do not generate moral obligations. But this objection is not, it seems to me, about speech-act theory but about God's authority, which is only manifested in speech-acts. If we can answer this concern, then I think the

---

[45] Murphy, "Divine Command," 6.

speech-act model regains its original force, which favors DC and not DW. Let us consider a response to this objection—which is another *tour de force* from Murphy.

Suppose we take the line that God's commands cannot themselves be sufficient reasons for obedience; why obey them? We could say that if we do not obey God, he will squash us like bugs; if we do obey, he will reward us handsomely. In either case these appeals, and any others like them, are independent of the content of God's commands, and this makes his act of commanding only one of a number of reasons for doing that action.[46] What Murphy argues is that the DC rubric fails to account for God's practical authority.[47] Interestingly enough, his mode of justification for such a view is that "authority-bearing acts are content-bearing acts: they are speech-acts with propositional content."[48] Here is where I think Murphy loses one of his major theses. Earlier I argued that if one holds to a speech-act view, then it is going to favor a DC construct at least insofar as the illocutionary force of the speech-act is concerned. Recall, DW loses the authoritative force of the illocution because the content of God's will is what obligates an agent unto action—especially if, as Murphy later argues, "practical authorities constitutively actualize reasons for action by their commanding acts."[49] Thus, if all we have in divine agency is a being that can, in a speech-act's perlocution, inform us of the content of his will, then it seems that humans can do something through speech-acts that God cannot. This is so because it implies that the full force of divine speech-acts is stunted in making something obligatory that does not rely on the speech-act being complete (locution, perlocution, and illocution). On the other hand, Murphy might well contend that his theory is complete and that humans can generate moral obligations merely through their act of willing, without any recourse to the content of their commanding. But here I recur to Adams's statement that this would be an unfair game.

So where does Murphy go to disconnect God's authority in commanding so that a DW construct is preferable? He argues it is not the case that God's omniscience, omnipotence, or goodness entails that he has practical authority over us.[50] I would like to consider what it means for an agent to have practical

---

[46] See Mark Murphy, "Divine Authority and Divine Perfection," *International Journal for Philosophy of Religion* 49 (2001): 168.
[47] Ibid.
[48] Ibid., 157.
[49] Ibid.
[50] Ibid., 161–74.

authority. If my take on the issue is effective, we will see that God is practically authoritative, and the DC has no reason to be ill-at-ease.

The question, it seems, is whether or not practical authority is a divine perfection, not whether divine perfections are what ground practical authority.[51] Hence, we cannot make an argument from God's omniscience to his authority because all we get out of the omniscience claim is that God knows what decisive reasons an agent has for acting, which merely "passes along" information to rational creatures, giving them decisive reasons to believe that the agent has decisive reasons to perform that action.[52] In other words, God's omniscience entails that he would not tell us to do something when there is not a decisive reason for us to do it.

A similar case can be made from his perfect moral goodness. If we look to morally good agents for insight into a situation, then looking to God for moral insight has some purchase; for *a fortiori* there is no one morally superior to God. Further, if we take the conjunction of God's omniscience (guaranteeing that he is not prone to epistemic mistakes) with his inherent moral goodness, then an even greater case seems to be made for God's practical authority. Murphy dissents, arguing that

> There is a difference between the claim that if God tells us what to do, then we have decisive reason to do it and the authority thesis, which is the claim that God's telling us what to do constitutes a decisive reason for doing it.[53]

In other words, the authority thesis entails the compliance thesis. If we hold that the compliance thesis means an agent has compelling reasons for an action, this does not mean that one of those reasons is that God has told him or her to do that action. If we seek the advice of an Aristotelian virtue ethicist who embodies virtue, then this gives us reason to think that the virtuous man or woman has better access to independently existing practical reasons for action.[54]

A final consideration is whether or not God's omnipotence entails practical authority. Murphy argues that God's omnipotence does not entail his practical authority, only theoretical authority; I want to consider why he makes this argument and why we should reject it. Certainly divine properties entail theoretical authority over agents, but that is not what is at issue here. Practical

---

[51] This is, at least, what Murphy contends is the key issue, 168.
[52] Ibid., 160.
[53] Ibid.
[54] Ibid., 161.

authority, writes Murphy, elicits a normative power over an agent, whereas theoretical authority does not.[55] Thus, if we think of omnipotence as a theoretical authority, it "may seem to deny practical authority to God is to deny God certain powers, which is tantamount to denying divine omnipotence."[56] If God cannot provide sufficient reason through his command for an agent to act, then God lacks a power that he could have and apparently does not. And what is worse, it seems that people have this kind of power—we might think of the power of a CEO over one of his minions as just such a power. Just as my previous concern with DW is that it enables human agents to do something through speech that God cannot, here we have the same concern for the DC proponent regarding divine making properties.

But I think there is a plausible rejoinder to Murphy's concerns; namely that practical authority is to be counted as a divine perfection—and this not *in virtue* of the fact that God is omniscient, omnipotent, and omnibenevolent. Rather, practical authority is an essential divine property. I think there are several lines of attack here, the first of which resorts to a distinction between direct and indirect speech-acts. If Murphy's concern is that the direct command of God does not provide an agent with any reason to act in a certain way, this need not worry the DC proponent; for we have allowed obedience to the natural law to mitigate this concern. Admittedly, such obedience is not in conformance with a divine command issued through God's literal obligation-generating activity by direct speech but rather conforms to a command given by indirect speech. Even Murphy writes, "It is plausible that states of affairs that constitute reason-candidates have their status as such only given certain features *of the world*—features about the nature of the created rational beings in those worlds, the nature of the forms of action available to those beings, the characteristics of those being's environment, and so forth."[57] Suppose the supervenience thesis works here; what does it say of my previous contention that God's practical authority is not in virtue of his omniscience, and so forth?[58] Under this construal God's practical authority follows perforce from his creating the world with goodness supervening on it—including the intellection of human agents. This is why the distinction between direct and indirect speech is so helpful. Murphy is simply wrong to argue that God's commands do not express compelling reasons for an agent to act. If we consider Abraham, it

---

[55] Ibid., 162.
[56] Ibid.
[57] Ibid.
[58] As a reminder, supervenience refers to a dependence relationship, where one thing depends on the other, or is derived from the other, in some way.

seems the only compelling reason he had to sacrifice Isaac is because God commanded it—*there is no other story to be told there*. But even if there were, the idea that God's practical authority is diminished by the fact that his direct speech does not have any purchase with most agents is not decisive in and of itself. We may still derive every element of a meaningful speech-act theory from the content of God's indirect speech. If Murphy's concern is that agents have decisive reason for action, this is just as compelling a case as any. For as every natural law theorist would want to propose, there are some things that we can't *not* know. In the order of ontology, this is because these features supervene on creation and have their being from God as their first cause.

I think my account effectively answers another of Murphy's concerns, namely that divine-making properties must, of necessity, have intrinsic maxima.[59] As the argument goes, if these properties do not have intrinsic maxima, then it is logically possible for God to be more perfect than he is. Thus:

> For A to be maximally great is for A to be maximally great in every possible world with respect to every perfection. For A to be maximally excellent in a world with respect to a perfection P is for A to exhibit P to an extent such that no being in any world exhibits P to a greater extent.[60]

Murphy's argument regarding practical authority may be characterized thus:

1. Divine perfections must have an intrinsic maximum.
2. Practical authority does not have an intrinsic maximum.
3. Therefore, practical authority cannot be a divine perfection.[61]

The first premise follows from Murphy's argument about intrinsic maxima—namely that no being can be God if it is possible that another being exhibit any of his attributes more perfectly than he. The second premise hangs on the notion that practical authority depends on two things: the number of rational beings over whom one is authoritative and the scope of the actions with respect to which one's dictates constitute reasons for action.[62] Additionally, since the possible beings and scope of actions may be increased, there is no intrinsic maximum. Thus, if practical authority does not have an intrinsic maximum, and divine perfections must have an intrinsic maximum, God does not have practical authority.

---

[59] Ibid., 169.
[60] Ibid.
[61] See William Wainwright, *Religion and Morality*, Ashgate Philosophy of Religion Series (Burlington, VT: Ashgate, 2005), 137.
[62] Murphy, "Divine Authority and Divine Action," 168.

Concerning this argument, its first premise may be questioned. William Wainwright argues that "one plausible interpretation of Murphy's first premise is that God is unsurpassable in the sense that (1) for each perfection which has an intrinsic maximum, God exhibits it to the utmost degree, and (2) for each perfection that lacks an intrinsic maximum, God exhibits it to a superlative degree and is such that no other possible being exhibits it to a greater degree."[63] This reading of the premise is problematic, however, for while it allows that some divine perfections need not admit of an intrinsic maximum, thus blunting the force of the objection, it leaves open the possibility that God might have been more perfect than he is. But this possibility need not be a concern, for if the argument has it as a logical possibility that another agent might exhibit more excellence than God, we need not accept this possibility as actually true. What we must conclude, it seems, is that for whatever degree of excellence any agent may exhibit, God exhibits it nearer to its upper maximum than any other possible being. Admittedly, I find it suspect that one denies that every perfect or excellent making property does not exhibit an intrinsic maximum, but that is not the concern here. The broadly logical possibility that an agent exhibit said features in greater fashion than God is the issue—and in no way must we say this (logically or otherwise).

Concerning the second premise, Murphy has confused a distinction between a being possessing a divine perfection and exercising a divine perfection.[64] William Wainwright argues, correctly I think, that we can distinguish between God's "creative power" and its exercise. To quote Wainwright:

> That God creates 5 billion rational beings in possible world w1 and 150 billion rational beings in possible world w2 doesn't entail that God has more creative power in w2 than in w1 since, while God has created 5 billion rational beings in w1, he could have created more.[65]

I suspect that even if one holds that God could have created a better world, producing more goodness in it than that of the actual world, such a possibility does not diminish his goodness in any way. Rather, it admits of a distinction between the possession of goodness as an intrinsic property of that being (in this case God), and the manifestation of that perfection through his creative power. Likewise, the distinction between the possession of practical authority and its exercise has some purchase here. Even if there is a concern that God

---

[63] See Wainwright, *Religion and Morality*, 138. Murphy's comments are to be found in Murphy, "Divine Authority and Divine Action," 169–71.
[64] See Wainwright, *Religion and Morality*, 139.
[65] Ibid., 139–40.

practices more practical authority in w2 than in w1, that does not mean he possesses any less in one world over the other. So I think that Murphy's objection as it stands is not enough to defeat what the DC proponent needs with regard to the content of God's commands *qua* practical authority.

## Conclusion

What we have been considering in this chapter is how a DC proponent can hold such a view to be superior to DW constructions. It has been my intent to substantiate most of what the DW proponent wants, especially DW accounts that ground moral responsibility as in some way deriving from God's antecedent will. But what we noticed is that DW views are incomplete, for the bridge between the content of God's will (a metaethical issue) and moral obligation (a normative thesis) resides in God's revealed will. To substantiate this claim we have given attention to how speech-acts are to be understood in a DC view and argued that DC is a more complete system to ground how it is, via speech-acts, God obligates through his commands.

CHAPTER ELEVEN

# Is God Morally Arbitrary or Morally Irrelevant?

In this chapter I am going to consider an argument that, if successful, seriously damages the plausibility of any divine command (DC) theory of ethics. Some consider it to be the earliest formulation of what a DC theory entails, only to subvert such a theory to a logical conundrum and utter defeat. I am speaking of the Euthyphro dilemma that comes from the Platonic dialogue *Euthyphro*. There we are invited to consider the ramifications of endorsing a strong theistic ethic. I like Bertrand Russell's formulation of the problem. He writes:

> The point I am concerned with, if you are quite sure there is a difference between right and wrong, you are in this situation: is that difference due to God's fiat or is it not? If it is due to God's fiat, then for God Himself there is no difference between right and wrong, and it is no longer a significant statement to say that God is good. If you are going to say, as the theologians do, that God is good, you must then say that right and wrong have some meaning which is independent of God's fiat, because God's fiats are good and not bad independently of the mere fact that He made them. If you are going to say that, you will then have to say that it is not only through God that right and wrong came into being, but that they are in their essence logically anterior to God.[1]

Even on a cursory reading we may see the force of the dilemma. If God loves right actions because they are right, then it follows that these actions are right independently of God's loving them. For instance, if God does not exist,

---

[1] Bertrand Russell, *Why I Am Not a Christian and Other Essays on Religion and Related Subjects* (New York: Simon and Schuster Touchstone, 1957), 12.

the actions that would be categorized as right would still be right. God, ontologically speaking, does not provide the foundation for ethics (as the objection goes). Further, "if the moral law were independent of God's will, then He no less than we, would be under an obligation to obey it."[2] Such a claim demeans any strong notion of God's freedom, even if it was the case that God created the world. For prior to creation these moral "brute facts" exist and God, whose very nature is to do good, must create the world such that those features supervene on creation (God is morally constrained to create the best possible world).

On the other hand, if right actions are right because God loves them, then it seems that any action God loves is right in virtue of God loving that action. If God does not have "good moral reasons" for his commands, then his commands are "from the moral point of view, completely arbitrary, and we have no obligation to obey them."[3] In a nutshell, advocates of DC need to do one of two things. They must either "admit that God's commands are not backed by any further moral reasons, while insisting that we nevertheless have an obligation to obey them," or "try to show that the moral values that rationalize God's commands are not independent of God and do not compromise His sovereignty."[4]

Of course, the Euthyphro dilemma becomes a more compelling story if one agrees that these two options, the arbitrary will formulation or the independence formulation, exhaust all of the possibilities. However, a number of other options are available to the DC ethicists that serve to counter this claim. One may argue that the logic of Socrates as presented in the *Euthyphro* is not sound, for it is based upon a false dichotomy; or one may make the claim that the mode of God's willing is his perfect nature. Each of these views requires unpacking. I will first argue that the logic of Euthyphro is faulty when one considers the dilemma in light of the doctrine of divine simplicity. After articulating the logical problem and providing a preliminary defense of divine simplicity, I will then turn my attention in the next chapter to other problems that confront such a doctrine. We will first consider whether or not postulating such a doctrine diminishes God's freedom. Then we will consider whether or not simplicity diminishes God's power.

It is my contention that the theist is on firm ground if he claims that God's goodness is best articulated through the doctrine of divine simplicity. According to divine simplicity, God's nature is not composed of different properties

---

[2] See Wes Morriston, "Must There Be a Standard of Goodness Apart from God?" *Philosophia Christi* 2 (1996): 127.
[3] Ibid.
[4] Ibid.

(e.g., omnipotence, omniscience). Rather, God is a being himself subsisting whole and entire with no differentiation of parts. If, for example, one looks more closely at Bertrand Russell's postulate, he makes an implicit commitment to the bifurcation between properties and the being that exemplifies those properties. However, such a bifurcation is not an essential theistic belief, for the doctrine of divine simplicity has substantial support in the annals of theistic literature (especially Christian). If the property/exemplar dichotomy is rejected, then one has good reason for arguing that the Euthyphro dilemma does not hold. I will now turn my attention to offering an account of divine simplicity and of how this doctrine resolves the apparent dilemma.

## THE LOGIC OF EUTHYPHRO AND DIVINE SIMPLICITY

Postulating a doctrine of divine simplicity as a defeater of the Euthyphro dilemma is not without historical foundation. In a relatively recent article, Norman Kretzmann argues that the Euthyphro is dissolved on just such a doctrine. According to Kretzmann there are two theories of religious morality that can be extracted from Euthyphro, theological objectivism (TO), Euthyphro's first horn, or theological subjectivism (TS), Euthyphro's second horn:

> (TO) God approves of right actions just because they are right and disapproves of wrong actions just because they are wrong; or

> (TS) Right actions are right just because God approves of them and wrong actions are wrong just because God disapproves of them.[5]

The important project is to show how Kretzmann thinks that (TO) and (TS) are resolved through simplicity, a doctrine which maintains:

> God is radically unlike creatures in that he is devoid of any complexity or composition, whether physical or metaphysical. Besides lacking spatial and temporal parts, God is free of matter/form composition, potency/act composition, and existence/essence composition. There is also no real distinction between God as subject of his attributes and his attributes. God is thus in a sense requiring clarification *identical* to each of his

---

[5] Norman Kretzmann, "Abraham, Isaac, and Euthyphro: God and the Basis of Morality" (accessed 11 August 2012); this version cited from an online text available at http://cavehill.uwi.edu/bnccde/_e&ae/nk.htm. This essay originally appeared in *Hamartia: The Concept of Error in the Western Tradition. Essays in Honor of John M. Crossett*, ed. Donald V. Stump, James A. Arieti, Lloyd Gerson, and Eleonore Stump (Lewiston, NY: Edwin Mellen Press, 1983), 27–50, and was reprinted in *Philosophy of Religion: The Big Questions*, ed. Eleonore Stump and Michael J. Murray (Oxford: Blackwell, 1999), 417–28. (TO) simply refers to moral values that exist independent of God and (TS) to the idea that moral values depend on God.

attributes, which implies that each attribute is identical to every other one. God is omniscient, then, not in virtue of instantiating or exemplifying omniscience—which would imply a real distinction between God and the property of omniscience—but by *being* omniscience. And the same holds for each of the divine omni-attributes: God is what he has. As identical to each of his attributes, God is identical to his nature. And since his nature or essence is identical to his existence, God is identical to his existence.[6]

More specifically, Kretzmann emphasizes the entailment of such a doctrine on identity statements, that "God is good" is more precisely phrased "God is identical with goodness."[7] To be more specific, God is goodness made real, not just the property of goodness. He is the reality of goodness.

It seems that one may hold a Platonic account and still derive the same identity claim, namely that "God is good" means that "God is identical with the [property of] goodness." Yet such a distinction is exactly what proponents of divine simplicity desire to avoid; for though God may be exemplifying the same properties, the point of simplicity is that these properties are descriptive of God's essence, not their own essence that God chose to exemplify (even eternally). Thus, we may delineate a distinction between kinds of identity claims. Borrowing from Frege, "there are two kinds of identity claims, uninformative, as in $9 = 9$, and informative, as in $9 = 3^2$."[8] The counterpart to our moral discussion obviously involves informative identity claims.

Consider Frege's famous analogy involving the morning star, the evening star, and the planet Venus. Given that these three names designate the same referent, then "it is true and informative to say that the morning star is identical with the evening star."[9] By identical he must mean to imply that both the morning star and evening star have all and only the same properties. Yet one may consistently hold that the morning star and the evening star are not altogether the same. For "if we focus on the designations rather than on the phenomena themselves, we say that the designations 'morning star' and 'evening star' differ in sense although they are identical in reference."[10] Thus we have two expressions with one and the same referent and yet have two different senses. The analogue to simplicity is quite forthright. We have God's goodness, God's

---

[6] See William Vallicella, "Divine Simplicity" (accessed 10 September 2006); http://plato.stanford.edu/entries/divine-simplicity.
[7] Kretzmann, "Abraham, Isaac, and Euthyphro."
[8] Ibid.
[9] Ibid.
[10] Ibid.

power, and God, respectively.[11] The purported strength of such a distinction is that "when God is conceived of as identical with perfect goodness, the kind of distinction that was crucial between (TO) and (TS) becomes a mere stylistic variation."[12] Thus we arrive at "simplicity counterparts" to (TO) and (TS), designated (PBO), "perfect being objectivism," and (PBS), "perfect being subjectivism":

> (PBO) God, conceived of as perfect goodness itself, sanctions certain actions just because they are right and rules out certain actions just because they are wrong.

> (PBS) Certain actions are right just because God, conceived of as perfect goodness itself, sanctions them; and certain actions are wrong just because God, conceived of as perfect goodness itself, rules them out.[13]

What we derive from (PBO) and (PBS) is an objective standard of good that is the sole criterion of moral rightness and wrongness, namely God. These standards follow from his nature, for he has these properties essentially. This is a marked advance from (TO) and (TS), which left us at the horns of the dilemma with no apparent hope of resolution. Now we may claim that (PBO) and (PBS) are two ways of saying the same thing: "actions are right if and only if goodness certifies them as such, and goodness certifies actions as right if and only if they are so."[14] God is conceived of as "the ultimate judge who is identical with the ultimate criterion itself."[15] Therefore, the bifurcation between (TO) and (TS) does not obtain under this construction, and the chasm between theological objectivism and theological subjectivism collapses. If there is no dichotomy, then there is no Euthyphro dilemma.

Of course, postulating the simplicity doctrine (henceforth SD) as a defeater of the Euthyphro objection is not without its problems, for the doctrine is highly controversial. Norman Kretzmann's presentation is no exception, for as William Mann argues:

> The solution is too good to be true.... Because he [Kretzmann] is willing to trade in the locution "just because" for the locution "if and only if". If those locutions were interchangeable, then we could express [the two propositions] slightly differently:

---

[11] Ibid.
[12] Ibid.
[13] Ibid.
[14] Ibid.
[15] Ibid.

(TO*) God, conceived of as a moral judge identical with perfect goodness itself, approves of right actions if and only if they are right and disapproves of wrong actions if and only if they are wrong.

(TS*) Right actions are right if and only if God, conceived of as a moral judge identical with perfect goodness itself, approves of them and wrong actions are wrong if and only if God, conceived of as a moral judge identical with perfect goodness itself, disapproves of them.[16]

What Mann has drawn out of Kretzmann's argument is the presumption that the "just because" clause in (TO) and (TS) record "genuine asymmetries."[17] Based on this presumption Kretzmann is able to claim that the two horns end up being equivalent. However, if there is a causal asymmetry that obtains between God's act of approval and the rightness of the action, the question of which of the two is prior may still be revised, which would undermine the resolution provided by Kretzmann. I think this objection is substantial for the SD proponent and requires further attention. Let us look closer at Mann's argument and see how the SD proponent might respond.

William Mann proposes a "modal analogue" to the discussion between objectivism and subjectivism, having to do with the relationship between God and necessary truths. The alternatives are that God either affirms necessarily true propositions because they are necessarily true, or necessarily true propositions are necessarily true because God affirms them. SD proponents would presumably want to restate these alternatives as follows:

(NPN) God, conceived of as omniscience itself, affirms necessarily true propositions if and only if they are necessarily true and denies necessarily false propositions if and only if they are necessarily false.

(NPG) Necessarily true propositions are necessarily true if and only if God, conceived of as omniscience itself, affirms them and necessarily false propositions are necessarily false if and only if God, conceived of as omniscience itself, denies them.[18]

Of course, the analogy between (TO), (TS), (NPN), and (NPG) is exact. (NPN) suggests that God knows all necessary truths, affirms their necessity,

---

[16] William Mann, "Modality, Morality, and God," *Nous* 23 (1989): 85.
[17] Ibid.
[18] Ibid., 88. I have renamed Mann's propositions to account for the biconditional relationship. Thus, (NPN) holds that God affirms certain propositions because they are necessarily true, whereas (NPG) holds that these propositions are necessarily true because God affirms them.

and cannot curtail their necessity. Further, the necessity of such propositions as 2 + 2 = 4 determines the content of God's belief. (NPG) implies on the other hand that it is God's willing 2 + 2 = 4 to be necessarily true that causes this to be so. How can it be that necessary truths are dependent on God, yet God cannot revise them?

It is fair to suppose that freedom (in this case God's freedom in creation) involves "the agent's ability to bring about the opposite outcome or allow the opposite outcome to occur," understanding freedom "as liberty of indifference."[19] Consider the proposition:

*2 + 2 = 4 if and only if God affirms that 2 + 2 = 4*

If we suppose the liberty of indifference applies to God, and not only contingent creatures, then we are forced to admit that God is not free with regard to the above proposition, for he does not have the power to actualize its negation. Following Mann, proponents of (NPN) affirm an epistemic variant of the proposition:

*2 + 2 = 4 if and only if God believes that 2 + 2 = 4*

Proponents of (NPG) affirm a volitional variant:

*2 + 2 = 4 if and only if God wills that 2 + 2 = 4*[20]

However, the dichotomy between the epistemic and volitional propositions never obtains under SD. Proponents of the epistemic thesis hold that beliefs are proper only in regard to how they correspond to the way the world is. But this presupposes there *is* a Platonic mathematical realm prior to the exercise of God's will as Creator. Under this construal God has a belief, in this case regarding the necessity of the proposition 2 + 2 = 4, and this belief is independent of his will. As such, God's knowledge regarding the proposition is strictly a matter of intellection; that is, God's beliefs about the proposition are mediated through something other than his creative will. But as Mann notes, and properly I think, there are two implications for SD in our discussion of epistemic priority. The first is the equivalence of God's "believing with God's knowing" and the second is "the identity of God's knowing with God's willing."[21]

---

[19] Ibid., 90–91.
[20] Ibid., 91, emphasis added in both propositions.
[21] Ibid., 92.

According to SD, God's believing 2 + 2 = 4 is God's willing that 2 + 2 = 4. As Mann explains:

> It is not as if there were two separate faculties in God, an epistemic faculty and a volitional faculty. It is rather that there is one divine activity, which in some respects from our point of view is more aptly called his believing or knowing, and in other respects more aptly called his willing.[22]

The proponent of SD affirms necessary propositions are unchangeable but also that God wills their content to be exactly what it is. Thus, says Mann,

> We can think of the necessary truths not as templates according to which even God must channel his activities in the act of creation, but rather as a part of the creative expression of this perfectly rational will.[23]

In holding that God is perfectly rational, the SD proponent holds that God's knowing will is the ground of knowledge of all true propositions, contingent or necessary, that they are true, and of all false propositions that they are false.

The epistemic variant of the original Euthyphro dilemma only works if one dissociates God's knowledge and will, which is exactly what SD does not affirm. Divine simplicity does not claim that God's understanding of necessary truths is logically prior to his willing them. In fact, there is no difference in these actions. There is an obvious distinction in the *descriptions* between his knowing and willing, but this does not entail that these are ontologically distinct; the descriptive distinction resides in *how we think about God*. Given this, there is no logical division between his knowing and willing. So the chasm between (NPN) and (NPG) is bridged on the simplicity doctrine, and the DC proponent need not accept the epistemic variant of the Euthyphro as a threat.

We have given sufficient attention to the logical problem of Euthyphro's dilemma and have shown that the doctrine of divine simplicity provides a sound defense against the problems posed in Euthyphro's disjunction. We have argued that the success of the disjunction relies on the mistake of believing we must prioritize either God's knowledge or God's volition, which actually are not distinct when one endorses a view of God as perfectly simple.

---

[22] Ibid.
[23] Ibid., 94.

## THE EUTHYPHRO AND NONDIVINE COMMAND THEORIES

There is a reason for thinking that no matter what framework we endorse as our moral position the Euthyphro dilemma may be raised. And of course there is no reason why a DC ethic should be rejected merely on the basis of the Euthyphro dilemma if a sufficient case can be made that everyone must give an answer to it. So why do I think that everyone has a Euthyphro dilemma? Part of the response hinges on the nature of the argument itself—but only in an implicitly epistemic sense. If we say that God is good, it seems we are using a pre-existing nexus of value concepts to make that claim, or so the objector proposes. I've tried to give reason as to why a simplicity doctrine resolves this concern; but even if it does not, I still think there is another line of response to be made—namely to consider the opponent's view and see if it fares any better with the same problems. Simply put, the concern is whether or not naturalistic accounts of goodness require an external, independent standard to which they conform. Upon closer inspection we will find that they do and that there is no compelling response to this problem; therefore the nontheist is in no better shape, at least as far as the Euthyphro objection goes, than the DC theorist. For example, suppose that we endorse a Platonic criterion of goodness where goodness is a property much like a brute fact. All we have done in postulating this entity is to move the question back one step. Granted, this view allays any arbitrariness—but it has in the meantime sacrificed efficient causation. Forms, ideas, and abstracta are all causally inert and do not cause things to be a certain way. How, then, do the Forms come to be as they are? There is also the lingering infinite regress problem, namely, why is it the case that these ideas may be postulated, but not verified, as the ultimate stopping point for values? It seems consistent to ask whether or not we can gauge these ideas or Forms by yet another standard of goodness that supervenes on them—and the infinite regress begins anew. If the Platonist may claim that the Forms are where the evaluations cease, then the theist is on firm ground in making the same claim about God. But as I've said, at least the theist may postulate not only that God defeats the infinite regress problem but that God also defeats the problem of causation and agency to bring about these states of affairs.

Perhaps a teleological ethic is on safer grounds—more specifically a utilitarian schema for determining an "ultimate criterion" for moral values. On this point I think Edward Wierenga is correct. He writes:

> We may note that if the objection [Euthyphro] is correct, it can also be applied against utilitarianism: "we must judge for ourselves whether an

act whose utility is as great as any of its alternatives is right. To judge this is to make a moral decision, so that in the end, so far from morality being based on utility, utility is based on morality."[24]

What is at issue here, I think, is the concern over who has last say in what grounds these values—what is the "stopping point" that provides the grounds of these values? The necessity of the stopping point just is that it provides resolution to infinite regress concerns, that values are not inextricably tied to other systems or accounts of evaluation. Thus, when we ask "what is good about . . ." we want the definitive account of good-making properties, not merely *an* account of these properties. As William Alston notes,

> Whether we are Platonist or particularist, there will be some stopping place in the search for explanation. An answer to the question "What is good about?" will, sooner or later, cite certain good-making characteristics. We can then ask why we should suppose that goodness supervenes on those characteristics. In answer either a general principle or an individual paradigm is cited. But whichever it is, that is the end of the line—On both views something is taken as ultimate, behind which we cannot go, in the sense of finding some explanation of the fact that it is constitutive of goodness. I would invite one who finds the invocation of God as the supreme standard arbitrary, to explain why it is more arbitrary than the invocation of a supreme general principle.[25]

In lieu of my argument, certainly relativistic theories of any stripe will not sufficiently allay the concerns of Euthyphro, nor will the most sophisticated system of noncognitivism suffice either. The purpose of this *reductio* is that it takes the problem to where it really needs to be—*not* prioritizing its implications only on one view. Through a simplicity doctrine I provided how a DC theorist might want to respond to Euthyphro's concerns; in this section I have provided a defense. Of course, the aim of this element is not to argue that since everyone has a Euthyphro dilemma DC is true. Rather, my aim in this section has been to sober up the minds of the objectors whose rejection of DC hinges on Euthyphro.[26]

---

[24] See Edward Wierenga, "Utilitarianism and the Divine Command Theory," *American Philosophical Quarterly* 21 (1984): 313.
[25] William Alston, "What Euthyphro Should Have Said," in *The Philosophy of Religion: A Reader and Guide*, ed. William Lane Craig (New Brunswick, NJ: Rutgers University Press, 2002), 293.
[26] For instance, Kai Nielsen.

## OTHER CONSIDERATIONS

Earlier I took specific steps to delineate a distinction between something being good and something being right. Recall that goodness is a value term that exists (logically) independent of actions that are categorized as right; right actions are those whose actualization follows in acting from the force of a rule rather than acting in accord with a rule. This highlights an important note in our discussion of Euthyphro. On a pragmatic level, it is a truism of evaluational development that some persons come to understand goodness through someone who embodies these properties rather than understanding the rules by which these properties are being governed. But to point out the obvious, what this says of the one acting lovingly, virtuously, and so forth is not that he does it out of compulsion; it may be his very nature to act in just such a way. If God's actions do have a moral component, it does not follow that he acted under the compulsion of a rule to overcome his hellish proclivities. It does not follow from anything I have postulated that an action is moral only if it is performed under obligation. Instances of supererogation defeat such a claim. Even so, if it were the case that acting morally is a byproduct of acting under obligation, it still would not follow that God's goodness is a moral fact about him. I reject such a claim because of its obvious absurdities—the most significant of which is that God is not "morally" good. However, I bring this up merely as a counterpoint to the claim that if we endorse the obligation model of goodness, it is logically impossible for God to be good.

Suppose for a moment that we allow for Platonic essences. All of the fears of arbitrariness are resolved, and so long as one endorses an account of divine goodness that makes it out to be an attribute like the goodness of any other thing, there is no problem with God being good. I think there is another concern besides the problem of God's aseity that requires attention here. It seems to be a leap in logic to infer that if Platonic Forms exist, then God depends on them to account for his goodness. Certainly this dependence relationship is not one of causal dependence—the Forms are causally inert. This is significant, for I think it is best to read the original assertion of the dialogue as a causal model. Consider again Plato's construction of the dilemma through the mouth of Socrates:

> Consider this: is the pious being loved by the gods *because* it is pious, or is it pious *because* it is being loved by the gods?[27]

---

[27] *Plato: Complete Works*, ed. John Cooper (Indianapolis: Hackett, 1997), 9. Here the dialogue centers on the pious, whereas we have been concentrating on the good. This distinction is not important, for the reasoning is based on the same concerns. Plato's gods were simultaneously endorsing mutually exclusive value claims on the same proposition.

We may now recast the argument in its logical form. In order for Socrates to succeed, the two possibilities must be held as a disjunctive dilemma—that if we endorse the first horn of the dilemma there are unacceptable consequences, and likewise if we accept the second horn of the dilemma. The conclusion based on this structure should be that one cannot claim *either* aspect of the disjunction to be true without falling into problems. Socrates comes to a different conclusion. Given the absurdity of the claim that the good is determined by the gods it must follow that the other horn is true, QED. But we've noted the problems of causation for Platonic models, so the causal line of argument is far from conclusive.

If we deny the relationship in the disjunction as one of cause and effect, we must then ask what the relationship actually entails. Perhaps we could postulate an identity claim as a rejoinder.[28] In doing so, another line might be provided that shows no disjunctive dilemma exists to be resolved. Euthyphro might have responded to Socrates by saying, "I have made an identity claim, similar to 'Jocasta is Oedipus' mother.' Am I required to say that she is Jocasta because she is Oedipus' mother, or that she is Oedipus' mother because she is Jocasta?"[29] Such an identity claim is not to be understood in terms of a causal relationship and provides sufficient reason to deny the conclusion of the dilemma.

The problem in postulating identity claims is that one must ground what kind of identity claim is being made. Here it seems to refer to a being's properties, and given our previous assertion of SD, this poses the question of how we are to understand properties and identity. Alvin Plantinga, contrary to SD, argues:

> If God is identical with each of his properties, then, since each of his properties is a property, he is a property—a self-exemplifying property. Accordingly God has just one property: himself. This view is subject to a difficulty both obvious and overwhelming. No property could have created the world; no property could be omniscient, or indeed know anything at all. If God is a property, then he isn't a person but a mere abstract object; he has no knowledge, awareness, power, love, or life. So taken the simplicity doctrine seems an utter mistake.[30]

James Hanink and Gary Mar argue that Plantinga's challenge misses the point. The "believer" confesses that God is both "person" and "Perfect

---

[28] This is the line of reasoning in Richard Joyce, "Theistic Ethics and the Euthyphro Dilemma," *Journal of Religious Ethics* 30 (1996): 53.

[29] Analogy borrowed from ibid.

[30] Alvin Plantinga, *Does God Have a Nature?* (Milwaukee: Marquette University Press, 1980), 86–87.

Righteousness," which allows for the conclusion that the property of Perfect Righteousness is a person.[31] Such a response will only work if one allows for the possibility that persons and properties are not distinct as a matter of conceptual necessity, which is what SD wants—at least regarding divine ontology. The alternative is that we have a being that (in this instance) either exemplifies Perfect Righteousness or Perfect Righteousness as essentially a part of his nature; that is, righteousness is an essential attribute of God but "not identical with Him."[32] Hanink and Mar contend that such a supposition is acceptable, that "God's uncreated but essential righteousness is dependent on him for its existence and identity in a way that does not make God's existence equally dependent on His righteousness."[33] This relationship is much like natural numbers, where the number one is an "essential member" of the set of natural numbers. The set cannot exist without the number one, nor can the number one exist without the natural number system. It is still consistent, though, to maintain that the system of natural numbers is "metaphysically more rich" than the number one.[34] By parity of reasoning, there is no righteousness without God and there is no God without righteousness. All this argument seems to show, though, is that if one holds to a bifurcation of persons and properties, the disjunctive dilemma of Euthyphro still does not follow. This is no small contribution, for it shows that even if the coherence of SD is questioned, the validity of the disjunction still remains problematic.

There is one more thing I would like to consider about the structure of Euthyphro, and this goes to the causal language integrated into the dialogue. If we have recourse to the assertion of Socrates and allow for the use of the term "because" in his original argument, it is not at all clear that the meaning of "because" is indefeasibly connected to God's reasons for approval—which is what the Euthyphro dilemma requires. Thus, what we are aiming at here is allowing for the claim that for some action, God approves of that action because it is good. If I approve of eggplant pontchartrain because it is the perfect blend of textured eggplant, pontchartrain sauce, and angel hair pasta, then these properties must be in the dish for me to discover them. These properties are a part of the dish such that they do not depend on my having eaten or even ascribed these properties to it. But as Richard Joyce has noted, some "because" claims are better understood as "in virtue of" relations rather than cause and

---

[31] James Hanink and Gary Mar, "What Euthyphro Couldn't Have Said," *Faith and Philosophy* 4 (1987): 246.
[32] Ibid., 247.
[33] Ibid.
[34] Ibid.

effect relations.[35] For example, if we say Allen is a bachelor because he is an unmarried man, we do not understand this as a cause and effect relationship. Allen is a bachelor in virtue of the fact that he is an unmarried man. Seemingly this relationship is symmetrical even in a materially equivalent construct. But certainly what is not gotten at here is that Allen is unmarried because he is a bachelor, where "because" means his being a bachelor is a reason for his being unmarried.[36]

One might argue that if God's reason for loving a thing is not grounded in the thing itself, then his love is arbitrary. But this need not be the case. It is compatible with our thesis that (1) an act is right because God wills it, and (2) God wills an act because it contributes to human flourishing. What this does not entail is that human flourishing is fundamentally what makes an act right. Proposition (1) expresses a metaphysical relationship whereby the rightness of right actions consists in God's willing them. And I think it is consistent to say that proposition (2) comports with my earlier thesis that DC and natural law may coalesce on a level of divine supervening. More explicitly, what DC and natural law both assert has its genesis in God's will. Part of natural law theory is that persons have a human nature that is contingent on God's creative will. Thus, when God exercised his creative will and brought human nature into existence, there was a blueprint for its full realization. Though I have disagreed with Hanink and Mar in other areas, this is one point upon which we converge, namely that DC and natural law form a structural unity; insofar that they do, the objection that the moral law is arbitrary fades. Hanink and Mar write:

> In willing human nature, God also wills the realization of human nature. Moreover, in the Decalogue—to take the central case—God's will operates legislatively. This realization of human nature is worked out in the conducting of human life. One's life is excellent insofar as one is rightly oriented toward the goods that constitute human happiness. One is virtuous insofar as one's conduct is habituated in obedience to God's legislative will.[37]

I think another important aspect of the Euthyphro problem rests on the theological distinction between the gods of Homer and Hesiod and the transition to the traditional Hebraic God of Abraham, Isaac, and Jacob.[38] None of the Hellenistic gods were, ontologically speaking, that than which none greater

---

[35] Joyce, "Theistic Ethics," 56.
[36] Ibid., 57.
[37] Hanink and Mar, "What Euthyphro Couldn't Have Said," 254.
[38] Ibid., 241.

## The Binding of Isaac

The narrative that most plagues DC theorists is found in Genesis 22, a narrative known in the Hebrew tradition as the binding of Isaac. There we find God commanding Abraham to sacrifice his only son, Isaac (Gen 22:2). Nothing in the narrative indicates that Isaac deserved death (as from the principle of forfeiture, for example), and nothing in the narrative indicates that Abraham was hesitant to perform the action. The text is explicit that Abraham's expectation was that both he and Isaac would be returning down the mountain together and that God would restore Isaac unto life (Gen 22:5; Heb 11:19). Abraham could reasonably project such an expectation because it was through Isaac that God was to number his ancestry as the stars in the sky, which would be impossible to do if Isaac was dead. Granted, this statement of blessing came to Abraham after he obeyed God in his willingness to sacrifice Isaac. My point here is that Abraham and Sarah had already received a message from God that this child would be a blessing; in this instance, it is revealed how Isaac would be a blessing. Abraham's expectation of Isaac's continued life is therefore reasonable. The implication of this narrative in our current discussion has to do with the arbitrariness objection. It is to this end that I want to concentrate my comments.

An important point is worth mentioning: it would be historically out of order for us to make an argument against child sacrifice from a conventionalist perspective. Robert Adams explains that the binding narrative is missing, "precisely the thought that it is, or might be, morally wrong for Abraham to sacrifice Isaac."[39] Further, its absence from the Genesis narrative "probably reflects a cultural background in which child sacrifice was a generally accepted practice and disapproval of this manifestation of a parent's generous piety toward a deity was not part of the religious repertoire."[40] I am merely trying to avoid a pitfall common in much of the discussion concerning this narrative. There would be no cultural backlash upon Abraham if the sacrifice had occurred, and we have no reason to think that "child sacrifice was and is a hideous evil in

---

[39] See Robert M. Adams, *Finite and Infinite Goods: A Framework for Ethics* (Oxford: Oxford University Press, 1999), 278.
[40] Ibid.

the life of any individual or culture that has practiced it, despite any religious virtues that they may have exemplified in the practice."[41]

Thus, what we need to provide is a plausible account of how the DC theorist might respond to the concern that God's command to Abraham was morally reprehensible in that it seemingly violates God's own prohibition against such actions.[42] I think an underlying problem in the debate between DC proponents and DW proponents is an incomplete application of the text. Most, if not all, of the attention has been given to what I call God's initial command. In Gen 22:2 God says to Abraham:

> "Take now your son, your only son Isaac, whom you love, and go to the land of Moriah, and offer him there as a burnt offering on one of the mountains of which I shall tell you." (NKJV)

Of course, if the act commanded in this verse were to be actualized, then Isaac's life would end. But one of the factors central to our discussion is the verse preceding this one and the second imperative following it. Consider the beginning of the narrative:

> Now it came to pass after these things that God tested Abraham, and said to him, "Abraham!" (v. 1 NKJV)

If we left this verse in isolation, then the content of the testing would be incomplete. In order to test someone there must be explicit content revealed from one agent to another. Let us call this the content of the imperative. The command may be "have no other gods before me," or the command may be "do not murder." But what is revealed is a specific way in which the agent is required to act. If God were merely to utter "obey me," then the follower may rightly question "with regard to what?" Hence, what we find in the moral commands are the revealed will of God explicitly stated as to how an agent may exemplify obedience.

Another consideration from the text is that the narrative identifies two commands from God. The initial command is for the sacrifice, and the second command is from the Angel of the Lord revealing that Abraham *is not* to sacrifice Isaac (Gen 22:12). Thus, in the span of twelve verses God expresses two imperatives to Abraham, one the antithesis of the other, at least with regard

---

[41] Ibid., 280.

[42] Canonically Exodus is after Genesis. I am not being anachronistic, for the injunction against murder is found systematically throughout the Bible, antedating even the written law (consider the narrative of Cain slaying Abel).

to the consequences of the command. Prima facie, one may suppose that in commanding logically opposite states of affairs God has shown his will to be arbitrary, but I do not think this is so. First, what I argued before is that DC provides the best case for how God's relationship to speech and its binding force works in speech-act theory. In the case of Abraham we must not confuse the objective of the command with the probable consequences of obedience to the command.

Every moral command imposed by God has as its root the same concern, namely whether one holds anything in a higher priority than one's relationship to God. In this case, the initial command tests Abraham concerning the content of his ultimate concern—either the life of his son or his belief in the primacy of God. But what is of interest here is that in commanding the binding of Isaac, God brought it about that Abraham was morally obligated to sacrifice him. Now one might argue that in imposing the obligation on Abraham to sacrifice Isaac, God desired to bring about the intention in Abraham to sacrifice Isaac. I think the narrative indicates something else—namely that in all circumstances where God places a moral obligation on an agent, the intent of the obligation is not necessarily to bring about a specific state of affairs per se (Isaac's death), but to bring about *obedience* with regard to the content of what is commanded. Thus, given that I previously argued that the sacrifice would not be condemned socially and that Abraham expected Isaac to be with him in some sense after the sacrifice, an account of what Abraham was obligated to do is needed. Second, we must give attention to the intention formation problem of the narrative. If God commands Abraham to sacrifice Isaac and creates the intention in Abraham to bring about the death of an innocent, is this not an instance of intent to murder—hence a violation of God's own law (and necessarily arbitrary)? Let us consider these in turn.

There is no textual reason to argue that Abraham balked at the command to sacrifice Isaac on the basis of social constraints or a belief in the finality of death. Abraham had neither of these concerns. What is more, such constructions miss the point that is central to the narrative. Even if we endorse a DW construct and hold that God's commands play only an informative role in moral obligation, we must take note of what is informed through the commands. If we have recourse to the story of the fall of Adam and Eve, God uttered a divine injunction against eating of the tree of knowledge. There is no conventional attack on eating of such fruit; in fact, not long after the divine command the serpent appears to Eve making an appeal that the fruit not only brings knowledge (a good thing) but as well makes them (Adam and Eve) as God is (Gen 3:5). Neither knowledge nor being like God can be a bad thing, especially insofar as these characteristics are divine traits. Recall that our primary aim in wrongdoing is "always some anticipated good."[43] This is not the level upon which we fault Adam and Eve. Rather, in eating of the fruit Adam and Eve violated a known command of God. The perceived goods of knowledge and godlikeness were held in higher esteem than God himself. Thus, when someone argues that God has no reason to command the things that he does, the theist is on solid ground to claim that the content of a divine command is to produce (reducibly) the same intention in every agent, only the byproduct of which has variation. What is this intention? To obey the known commands of God and have no other perceived good to be held in higher esteem than him. God's reason for commanding is to see this through in our moral agency.

A final note concerning this passage is in order. The binding of Isaac is instructive about how loving, not hateful, God actually is. Child sacrifice was a common practice in cultures around Israel at that time (e.g., Lev 18:21). The second command preventing the sacrifice of Isaac demonstrates the difference between the God of Israel and those of other religions. The binding of Isaac provided a stage on which that difference would be on display.[44]

## Conclusion

How does this impact our discussion of Abraham and Isaac? I think Abraham was confronted with the same problem as Adam and Eve—namely that when God commanded him to sacrifice Isaac, knowing the content of the command automatically meant knowing what it would be to fail the expectation of that command. We have no more reason to think that Abraham would not sacrifice Isaac merely out of knowing what it would be not to obey than we do for any social constraint placed upon him, especially since there was none. If we ask what the perceived good in such an action would be, the answer is the same here as it was in the narrative of the fall. For the "sake of standing" Abraham might have failed to sacrifice Isaac, and in doing so have failed to set aside a life that is "subordinate to God's edict," and instead "struck out on his own."[45] This means that Abraham could have seen a good in a personal, independent destiny aimed at becoming like God. In this case, it might just be that the binding narrative is one instance of control over life itself, namely that of Isaac.

---

[43] See Hugh McCann, "The Author of Sin?" *Faith and Philosophy* 22 (2005): 150.

[44] For a more thorough treatment on this theme, see Paul Copan, *Is God a Moral Monster? Making Sense of the Old Testament God* (Grand Rapids: Baker, 2011), chap. 5.

[45] McCann, "Author of Sin," 150.

So what of the second concern, that when God commanded Abraham to sacrifice Isaac he intended to bring about the intention in Abraham to take the life of an innocent (i.e., murder)? What we have argued, I think, sufficiently answers this question. When we differentiate the byproduct of obedience with obedience itself, these concerns are allayed. Abraham's decision to sacrifice Isaac was not simply intending the death of an innocent, and thus committing murder. Rather, the intention formation process is that in obeying the command Abraham decided to carry out God's will.[46] In fact, Scripture affirms such a conclusion. Of Abraham it is written:

> By faith Abraham, when he was tested, offered up Isaac, and he who had received the promises was offering up his only begotten son; it was he to whom it was said, "IN ISAAC YOUR DESCENDANTS SHALL BE CALLED." He considered that God is able to raise people even from the dead, from which he also received him back as a type. (Heb 11:17–19 NASB)

Consider also Patrick Lee's comments on Thomas Aquinas's view of the incident with Abraham and Isaac:

> One might object that in Abraham's case the death of Isaac is a condition for Abraham's executing God's project and therefore Abraham must intend the death of Isaac directly. But Thomas's argument is that the role of an executor is a special case. Acts we perform "on our own" are composed of act-in-intention and act-in-execution; but where a subject executes the intention of a superior, the whole act is divided between partners, with the result that the executor's intention precisely as executor, is no different from the manifest intention of the superior. Hence Abraham's intention is the same as God's: if God does not directly intend death, then neither does Abraham.[47]

It is not the case that God's intention was to secure the death of Isaac. If this was God's intention, he would kill Isaac anyway. Nor is it obvious that what God was doing in commanding the sacrifice was producing an intention in Abraham to commit murder. Rather, God set out to "test" Abraham with regard to the content of his faith. If all intrinsic moral evil is a replication of the fall of Adam, I think the test is best understood as whether or not Abraham would liken God to his status and Abraham unto his own. The decisive grounds for revealing this, in this case, just was the binding of Isaac.

---

[46] See Hanink and Mar, "What Euthyphro Couldn't Have Said," 249.
[47] See Patrick Lee, "The Permanence of the Ten Commandments," *Theological Studies* 42 (1981): 433–34. This quotation taken and adapted from Hanink and Mar, "What Euthyphro Couldn't Have Said," 261.

CHAPTER TWELVE

# Evil and the Worship-Worthiness of God

In this work I have defended the notion that God is necessarily morally perfect. As such, I grounded the good in his nature and argued that God is the best explanation of the existence of objective moral values. In other words, throughout this work I have accepted perfect being theology as my framework for both biblical and philosophical reasons. One may wonder, though, just what the theist has lost in arguing that, necessarily, God is morally good, as it may seem that I have vitiated two (or more) doctrines that are conceptually mandatory for any perfect being theologian. This is troubling, for if the doctrines utilized to make a case for theism are incoherent, then whatever else is derived from them loses their explanatory power. In other words, the previous discussions on the problem of evil have arms that reach beyond that discussion and into philosophical theology more broadly construed. Therefore, I consider it important to address at least a couple of those concerns.

Consider the problems of God's freedom and God's omnipotence, respectively. I argued that it is logically impossible for God to will (for himself) any evil state of affairs. Such a postulate seems to destroy any possibilities of moral freedom in God, if moral freedom is to be understood as the ability to will another (perhaps opposite) state of affairs than one does. Also, such a postulate seems to diminish God's omnipotence in that he does not have the power to actualize an evil state of affairs; God cannot, perforce, sin. Let us consider these two problems in turn, for it seems there is a dependence relationship between them. At least descriptively, God's will is anterior to his actions, thus I will place the discussion of God's freedom first and subsequently address the problem of God's power. Finally, I will consider how the responses to these concerns leaves open the possibility that the traditional God of theism is worthy of worship.

## Necessary Existence and God's Freedom

There are several reasons for wanting God to be maximally free. If God is determined by external conditions, then his moral autonomy is compromised. For he, no less than we, is morally evaluated by whatever these external conditions stipulate in conjunction with whatever state of affairs he actualizes. Such a view diminishes God's sovereignty and should be rejected. Our concern is of a different nature, for we argued against any independent criterion of value and proposed a model of God's activity that divorces him from any obligation, moral or otherwise. If we hold, however, that God acts necessarily as he does, then one may object that we have diminished God's freedom, and concomitantly bound him morally to a different determining condition, namely his nature. On this model it is consistent to say that God conceives of seemingly an infinite number of *possible* divine actions. However, there is logical necessity with regard to what God actualizes, for God is morally constrained by his nature to do all and only that which is right. What is meant by "constrained" is a bit elusive, but suffice it to say it is not compatible with a meaningful account of divine freedom. Thomas Flint explains the problem well:

> If God is a truly perfect being, he has no choice but to create (i.e. actualize) the best world he can create. Failure to do so would point to either a lack of knowledge or benevolence, and such lackings would be inconceivable in the case of "that than which none greater can be conceived." But if God's creative activity is thus determined by essential elements of his nature (i.e. his omniscience and benevolence), one can hardly label his acting of creating a free action and still remain a libertarian in good standing, for libertarianism insists that an agent performs a free action only when his activity is not determined by his nature.[1]

Flint's conclusion is quite problematic for our discussion; if God is not significantly morally free, then God is not a moral agent.[2] So, how might we

---

[1] See Thomas Flint, "The Problem of Divine Freedom," *American Philosophical Quarterly* 20 (1983): 255.

[2] This is Alvin Plantinga's language. He writes, "A world containing free creatures who are significantly free (and freely perform more good than evil actions) is more valuable, all else being equal, than a world containing no free creatures at all. Now God can create free creatures, but He can't cause or determine them to do only what is right. For if He does so, then they aren't significantly free after all; they do not do what is right freely. To create creatures capable of moral good, therefore, He must create creatures capable of moral evil; and He can't give these creatures the freedom to perform evil and at the same time prevent them from doing so. The fact that free creatures sometimes go wrong, however, neither counts against God's omnipotence nor against His goodness; for He could have forestalled the occurrence of moral evil only by removing the possibility of moral good." *God, Freedom, and Evil* (Grand Rapids: Eerdmans, 1974), 30. Plantinga's construction of freedom as the power to do otherwise certainly fails on our model.

understand divine freedom in light of our claims about the divine nature in response to the objection by Flint?

One suggestion, made by Thomas V. Morris, is to understand divine goodness as "God's acting always in accord with universal moral principles, satisfying without fail moral duties and engaging in acts of gracious supererogation."[3] Let us be clear, on Morris's "duty model of goodness" God has moral obligations to "universal moral principles." As he sees it, a logical problem arises when one jointly commits to three theses: (1) the duty model of divine goodness, (2) a libertarian account of free will, and (3) the claim that God is necessarily good.[4] From the notion that God necessarily acts as he does we may conclude, says Morris, "that God does not exemplify the kind of freedom requisite for being a moral agent with any duties at all."[5] This entails that there is no necessarily good moral agent, for "only free acts are morally characterizable as the satisfaction or violation of duties."[6] Let us adopt Morris's requirement for freedom, that "an agent S performs an action A at a time t freely only if no conditions exist prior to t which render it necessary, or unavoidable, in a broadly logical sense, and by doing so in fact bring it about that S performs A."[7] From our discussion so far there is nothing to prevent the DC theorist from accepting a libertarian account of free will, nor must we deny God's moral agency or goodness. For it is still coherent to suppose, even under the duty model of goodness, that God fulfills all three conditions. Morris, for instance, makes a distinction between two states of affairs, namely behavior which results from *obeying a rule* and behavior which *accords with a rule*.[8] This distinction allows us to split principles governing human moral agency and divine moral agency. Humans are bound by moral duty, the byproduct of which is that humans act "under obligation." It must be remembered, however, that there is an ontological distinction between human nature and the divine nature. God's will is "holy," to borrow a phrase from Kant. The goodness of God is distinct from the deontological category of being right, for being right requires an agent to bring about what is moral. Goodness involves no such requirement. It is to be recalled that the purpose of obligation is to draw an agent toward an action that he is not otherwise motivated to perform, for

---

[3] See Thomas V. Morris, "Duty and Divine Goodness," in *The Concept of God*, ed. Thomas V. Morris (London: Oxford University Press, 1987), 107.
[4] Ibid., 108.
[5] Ibid.
[6] Ibid., 109.
[7] Ibid., 108.
[8] Ibid., 109.

example, to draw the liar toward truth telling and the murderer toward sparing a potential victim's life.

Thus, one may hold that God acts necessarily as he does, acting "in accordance" with principles which would "express duties for a moral agent in his relevant circumstances."[9] Of course, under this construction God does not have any duties. Nevertheless, if God (for example) says that he will bless Abraham with a child, then Abraham will be blessed with a child. Morris explains:

> R. L. Franklin has characterized the purpose of promising as "that of committing a man reliably to future acts." God can certainly declare his intention to bless Abraham, thereby committing himself reliably to do so (where committing himself amounts to intentionally generating justified expectations in his hearers). The libertarian can hold that, in making this sort of declaration, God is doing something for his creatures with an effect analogous to that of promising, or that even in the analogous sense he is making a promise.[10]

William Alston has a promising approach that encapsulates what we have said about deontological terms such as *right* and *wrong* and ontological terms such as *good* and *bad*. He invites us to consider God's goodness as distinct from the goodness of human agents. If we understand God's goodness as, necessarily, God acting in accordance with his perfect nature, then the axiological values we have put forth regarding divine ontology and divine actions are merely descriptive propositions about his nature. Alston explains:

> If we want to say that moral goodness can be attributed to a being only if that being is subject to the moral ought, his moral obligations and the like, then we won't say that God is, strictly speaking, morally good.[11]

So, our purpose in this section is to offer an account of divine freedom that avoids the pitfalls of necessary perfection. We want to offer an account of freedom whereby God is maximally free, and hence relevant with regard to moral agency, and yet remain true to our thesis that God cannot sin.

There are two conceptions of freedom, says Timothy O'Connor, which pervade the literature on free will. The first is the "openness of the future" to alternative possibilities for our actions.[12] A person acts freely only if she could have

---

[9] Ibid., 117.
[10] Ibid., 118.
[11] See William Alston, "What Euthyphro Should Have Said," in *Philosophy of Religion: A Reader and Guide*, ed. William Lane Craig (Brunswick, NJ: Rutgers University Press, 2002), 289.
[12] Timothy O'Connor, "Freedom with a Human Face," *Midwest Studies in Philosophy* 29 (2005): 208.

chosen a different action. Suppose we are in line at Sweet Eugene's House of Java and are attempting to select from a number of options, say between their fine cappuccino and latte, and whether to have a biscotti to match. The decision to partake of the biscotti and cappuccino is indicative of the fact that agents with metaphysical freedom "are able to select from among significantly different alternatives."[13] What is significant to note in such circumstances—and we can imagine them being moral rather than culinary—is that freedom is not coextensive with the existence of the alternatives but is a matter of "self-determination." The alternatives are "indicators of the self-determination manifested by one's action, which is necessary for responsibility."[14] Thus, it is O'Connor's contention that the freedom relevant to moral agency is born from the one action that is chosen, and not from the metaphysical category of worlds-gone-otherwise.

A second notion of freedom, and one that is more central to our thesis, centers on the idea of self-mastery.[15] According to O'Connor,

> A person acts freely to the extent that he has control of his appetites and impulses and is able reliably to direct his more significant actions toward larger aims. A self-mastered person perforce has a great deal of self-knowledge, including especially knowledge of the factors that incline him to this or that course of action. A free agent knows himself well—knows his own stable purposes, desires, and beliefs—and reliably acts in a way that reflects in some way this self-understanding.[16]

Let us apply the concept of self-mastery to the doctrine of God. God has no conflicting aims or practical constraints to which he is subject.[17] Nor does it seem that God has any desires (at least as we usually use the term), for desire is a passive state that arises from something not fulfilled in the agent with the desire; this mitigates the notion that God could have any irrational impulses.

It seems that O'Connor is on good historical ground in making such a claim, for the notion of rationality is at the core of Kantian ethics. In fact, earlier I noted an argument for the tenability of a Kantian DC ethic based on such considerations. Our purpose here is not to endorse that specific argument but to consider how it advances our discussion on self-mastery. Kant wrote:

---

[13] Ibid., 209.
[14] Ibid., 209–10.
[15] Ibid., 210.
[16] Ibid., 211.
[17] Ibid., 212.

> If the will is not of itself in complete accord with reason (the actual case of men), then the actions which are recognized as objectively necessary are subjectively contingent, and the determination of such a will according to objective laws is constraint. The conception of an objective principle, so far as it constrains a will, is a command (of reason), and the formula of this command is called an imperative. All imperatives are expressed by an "ought" and thereby indicate the relation of an objective law of reason to a will which is not in its subjective constitution necessarily determined by this law. This relation is that of constraint. Imperatives say that it would be good to do or to refrain from doing something, but they say it to a will which does not always do something simply because it is presented as a good thing to do. A perfectly good will, therefore, would be equally subject to objective laws (of the good), but it could not be conceived as constrained by them to act in accord with them, because, according to its own subjective constitution, it cannot be determined to act only through the conception of the good. Thus, no imperatives hold for the divine will or, more generally, for a holy will. The "ought" here is out of place, for the volition of itself is necessarily in unison with the law. Therefore imperatives are only formulas expressing the relation of objective laws of volition in general to the subjective imperfection of the will of this or that rational being, e.g. the human will.[18]

Overall I am in agreement with Kant, except that previously I demarcated the good and the right in order to explain why a being who has a holy will does not have any moral obligations, and Kant does not do so in terms of this distinction. However, the picture that Kant paints of God, and which is of great use, is one where God is self-sufficient. To quote Mark Linville, "He [God] is not finite, dependent, or a being of needs. God lacks the desire for happiness. And lacking this desire, He lacks any inclinations that could conflict with the moral law. God has a holy will, a will incapable of any maxims which could conflict with the moral law."[19] Linville's conclusion is that the moral law (a lá Kant) for a perfect being is a law of holiness and not a law of duty. Further, the connection between God's reason and his will is derivative of that found in the categorical imperative. Since the will is the source of moral failure, reason

---

[18] Immanuel Kant, *Foundations of the Metaphysics of Morals*, trans. Lewis White Beck (New York: Liberal Arts Press, 1959), 29–31. This edited version quoted from Alston, "What Euthyphro Should Have Said," 286–87.

[19] Mark Linville, "Euthyphro and His Kin," in *The Logic of Rational Theism: Exploratory Essays*, ed. William Lane Craig and Mark MacLeod (Lewiston, NY: Edwin Mellon Press, 1990), 199.

must bind the will. In God, there is perfect reason and perfect will; hence no binding is necessary.

Let us further pursue this line of argument. It is a central tenet of perfect being theology that God is omniscient (i.e., has perfect knowledge of the past, present, and future). It seems reasonable, then, to hold that God has complete knowledge of his own actions as well as ours. If this is so, then God has knowledge not just about his actions, but about how he will value (likely to be understood as axiological value) actions. W. R. Carter explains very nicely:

> One surely is guilty of some sort of moral failing in the event that one realizes one is about to act maliciously (say), it is within one's power not to so act, and yet one proceeds to act maliciously. In such cases, the moral transgression lies, not merely with what one does (the malicious action), but with what one does not do (namely, decide to act). Accordingly, I am skeptical of the idea that there is such a world in which an individual ceases by way of moral failing to occupy divine office. No possible world is such that one of its inhabitants sins at t but also is omnipotent, omniscient, and wholly good at t—1.[20]

Carter's concern is to offer a reply to the claims of Nelson Pike on the problem of God's omnipotence, which we will take up in a moment, but the epistemic corollary fits our current theme. In order for God to sin, for instance, it must be the case that God perceives some good in the act of sinning. Prima facie, this good is self-directed, but it need not be the case that this is true (God could, for instance, perceive himself robbing a bank for the purpose of feeding the hungry, rather than for his own gain). But to endorse such a view as even plausible with God requires one of two things: (1) God can have a deficient intellect such that his understanding of the good in a situation is lacking, or (2) there is no direct connection between God's intellect and his will. The first of these assertions is immediately countered by the notion that as Creator and sustainer of every human action, God cannot be ignorant of those actions.[21] Further, it requires a concept of the good that is not intrinsic to God, and hence requires him to ponder the relevant merits of a given action as gauged by some standard. However, it seems we are on better ground to speak of a connection between action-directed intentions and their influence on the rational process; this goes more to a defense of the self-control thesis than the possible-worlds

---

[20] W. R. Carter, "Omnipotence and Sin," *Analysis* 42 (1982): 105. It should be noted that God's relationship to time is not my concern here, even though I understand it has profound implications for any theory of divine epistemology.

[21] I understand that open theism denies such a claim, but that is not my concern here.

suggestion. Since we have a model whereby God may will something (human action) morally and it not come about, what of God's intentions about his own actions?

First, it is to be noted that an intention "settles an agent on one course or another."[22] Otherwise stated, the agent is "committed to a goal," and the intention provides a "settled objective."[23] Thus, I propose that when an agent has an intention, the intention is "conduct controlling" and not merely a "potential influencer of conduct."[24] Hugh McCann proposes that the rationality of intentions "depends on whether the goals they embody are such that, by pursuing them, we gain an acceptable chance of changing the world in ways we believe are better."[25] Thus, when the agent settles on an objective, there is a presumption of "epistemic consistency" whereby it is possible for the plan to be "successfully executed without any of the agent's beliefs being false."[26] Consider this in contrast to the model of sin provided before. It follows from the concept of sin that there is a failure either of will or intellect. If God fails in his intellect, it seems a matter of a false belief regarding an action, and hence he fails the epistemic consistency requirement. If God fails in his will, then it follows from our model that (1) God is not rational with regard to intention formation, for he would have a belief about an action's merit and then do otherwise; and (2) God would fail the self-control paradigm, for he would be acting according to desires (which have no necessary positive aim) in contrast to his intentions, at least as we have construed rational intentionality. However, there is no reason for us to hold that God is culpable for these errors. God, as we have argued, is a perfectly rational being whose will is in complete accord with reason. To borrow from Aquinas, God knows and wills himself, that is, his actualized being. Aquinas writes,

> Hence as His essence itself is also His intelligible species, it necessarily follows that His act of understanding must be His essence and His existence. Thus it follows from all the foregoing that in God, intellect, and the object understood, and the intelligible species, and His act of understanding are entirely one and the same.[27]

---

[22] See Hugh McCann, *The Works of Agency: On Human Action, Will, and Freedom* (Ithaca: Cornell University Press, 1998), 197.
[23] Ibid.
[24] Ibid.
[25] Ibid., 199.
[26] Ibid.
[27] Thomas Aquinas, *Summa Theologica* q. 1, a. 14, ad 1.

But there is a greater issue here than first meets the eye; it's founded upon the claim that freedom is best understood as the power to do otherwise. The issue concerns God's act of creation. God, it is often argued, bears some responsibility for creating a sinful world given that he knew anterior to its creation that Adam and Eve would partake of the forbidden fruit (or pick your favorite sin). For, the argument runs, even if it is not within God's power to create a world of free creatures that always choose to do what is right, it was certainly within God's power not to create at all. Let us consider the implications of these concerns on our discussion of divine freedom, for it seems God is not in the bank-robbing business but is in the work of creation. Can it be said of God that he is somehow culpable for the sin of Adam? This problem is different from the one provided before, for there we were considering whether or not God could sin with regard to his own actions. Now we are considering whether or not God may be found guilty in some way for actions that he wills but does not directly perform.

It seems that part of the concern here derives from our earlier discussion pertaining to God's will and human actions, such that God as Creator and Sustainer of all things in some sense wills certain evil states of affairs; perhaps one has in mind the atrocities of Auschwitz or the genocide in Darfur. For the sake of consistency, we cannot deny that God wills these things to be, but this does not commit us to the view that in his willing there is a "joint exercise of agency" between the sinner and God.[28] Consider again Hugh McCann's analogy to make this point. God's relationship to humans is not "analogous to that of the puppeteer to the puppet—which would indeed destroy our freedom—but rather to that of the author of a novel to her characters."[29] The figures of the novel owe their existence to the author's creative imagination, and "they are born and sustained in and through the very thoughts in which she conceives them, and of which they are the content."[30] Persons, and for that matter all of the created order, are brought into existence and sustained through God's creative will.

The power of this analogy is that it identifies the assumption upon which the objection is based, namely that there is a causal nexus between God's creative will and human actions. But this is not the case. As McCann notes, the author of the novel cannot enter into the world of the characters and "pervert" their authenticity as agents. In fact, McCann argues, and I concur, that in creating us God does not "act upon us or produce any intervening cause—even

---

[28] See Hugh McCann, "The Author of Sin?" *Faith and Philosophy* 22 (2005): 149.
[29] Ibid., 146.
[30] Ibid.

an act of will on his part—that somehow makes us do what we do."[31] God, as author of the novel, comprehensively provides through his creative fiat the existence of our decisions and the manifestation of our actions. To be precise, God creates us "in our willing," and the relationship is not as "cause to effect but as will to content."[32] For the sake of clarity, imagine the state of affairs in which I decide to rob a bank. Under this construction, it is a matter of God's creative will that I in fact rob the bank. However, nowhere in my decision to rob the bank is God to be indicted, for all that we have in God's creative will is that God wills to grant existence to my act of deciding to rob the bank.

This leaves a second concern, namely whether or not God is to be indicted for the content of his creative will (or for his having created anything at all). Such a concern is to be likened to a reader finding moral fault in Thomas Harris for creating Hannibal Lecter cannibalizing his victims. And so, to answer this question, and here again I think McCann is correct, we have to consider what it is that makes wrongful willing wrong, or we have to know what constitutes the sinfulness of sin.[33]

Whether we are considering the narrative of the fall of Adam (Genesis 3) or chronologically prior to that the fall of the demons (Jude 6), the essence of moral evil is the same: the defiance of a divine command. To be more specific, in defiance of the divine command not to partake of the forbidden fruit, Adam and Eve acted exactly in the same manner as the fallen angels before them. The purpose of the defiance was to "achieve a certain kind of standing," an "independent destiny" whereby they would become like God.[34] Thus, we may agree with McCann's view that at its core every sin is the same—namely to set oneself in rebellion against God, deciding to do what he has forbidden us to do.[35]

## **NECESSARY GOODNESS AND OMNIPOTENCE**

Suppose that we are confronted with the following two competing claims on the goodness of an agent:

> (G1) A being that is unable to sin is better than a being that is able to sin but does not.

---

[31] Ibid.
[32] Ibid., 146, 149.
[33] Ibid., 150.
[34] Ibid., 151.
[35] Ibid.

(G2) A being that is able to sin but does not is better than a being that is unable to sin.[36]

The contrast between (G1) and (G2) brings forth the supposed tension that follows by entailment from our argument from God's moral perfection. (G1) is a precise rendering of the impossibility of God's sinning. Yet, if God is omnipotent, then how can it be the case that God is incapable of sinning? At first blush we are on better grounds arguing for (G2), for in doing so we do not lose any of the moral qualities of God, and on this model he still does not sin, nor do we compromise his freedom or power. However, something seems amiss under any view that has God as able to sin. So, let us first investigate why the implications of (G2) are incoherent and then turn our attention to a defense of (G1).

In order to defend (G2), one must first explain what it means for God to be able to sin. It does not seem that we will arrive at (G2) through conceptual analysis. The concept of sin means to miss the mark, either intellectually or morally (where this mark comes from is of vital significance). The mark certainly is not divine obligation in terms of some independent criterion; neither does it seem to be self-imposed obligation. The incoherence of a first-person imperative is twofold. If we recall, our notion of obligation is a normative thesis whereby an agent is drawn through the imperative to a certain action he otherwise would not perform. God has no need of such an imperative. Second, suppose for the sake of argument that God *did* need an obligation to draw him into action; there is no positive prospect of finding a source for obligation. It cannot be God, for the standard must be external to draw him to the action (for the defect is now within him and requires reconciliation to what is normatively right). Nor does it make sense to say that the imperative is a first-person command, for that is conceptually ludicrous (there are no first-person commands).[37] So it seems the idea of "calling God down" is not going to succeed based on a conceptual analysis of sin.

Second, and briefly, there are no biblical grounds for arguing that God has the ability to sin. In fact, the systematic testimony of Scripture is that God is both omnipotent and yet does not have the ability to sin. God "cannot lie," writes Paul (Titus 1:2 HCSB). "It is impossible for God to lie," explains the writer of Hebrews (6:18). Suffice it to say, Scripture is not committed to the thesis that God's omnipotence entails that God can do literally anything. So,

---

[36] Special thanks to Robert Stewart for helping me articulate this point.
[37] I am indebted to Hugh McCann for drawing this to my attention.

let us consider a third option, namely whether or not omnipotence logically entails the ability to sin.

Thomas Aquinas makes a distinction between two types of possibility, namely things that are logically possible and things that are possible in terms of an agent's abilities. Regarding the first, Aquinas writes:

> Everything that does not imply a contradiction in terms, is numbered amongst those possible things, in respect of which God is called omnipotent; whereas whatever implies contradiction does not come within the scope of divine omnipotence, because it cannot have the aspect of possibility. Hence, it is better to say that such things cannot be done, than that God cannot do them.[38]

Accordingly, "whatever implies a contradiction" involves the conjunction of two states of affairs that violate the law of noncontradiction. If something is impossible for God, it must also be logically impossible. Thus Aquinas thinks the dilemma is laid to rest, and argues:

> To sin is to fall short of a perfect action; hence to be able to sin is to be able to fall short in action, which is repugnant to omnipotence. Therefore it is that God cannot sin, because of His omnipotence.[39]

However, there is nothing provided yet that proves sinning is both impossible in terms of God's abilities and logically impossible; a contention that seems prima facie compatible with incarnation theology (consider Mark 1:13). Thus, it seems we need further clarification to make our point.

In Proposition 12 of his work *A Discourse Concerning the Being and Attributes of God*, Samuel Clarke argues that the properties of God are coextensive, and hence the properties of God's necessary moral perfection and God's omnipotence entail that God cannot sin. In a rather lengthy passage Clarke writes:

> Free choice, in a being of infinite knowledge, power, and goodness, can no more choose to act contrary to these imperfections than knowledge can be ignorance, power be weakness, or goodness malice, so that free choice in such a being may be as certain and steady a principle of action as the necessity of fate. We may therefore as certainly and infallibly rely upon the moral, as upon the natural attributes of God—it being as absolutely impossible for Him to act contrary to the one as to divest Himself of the other; and as much a contradiction to suppose Him choosing to do

---

[38] Thomas Aquinas, *Summa Theologica* q. 1, a. 25, ad 3.
[39] Ibid.

anything inconsistent with His justice, goodness, and truth as to suppose Him divested of infinity, power, or existence . . .

From hence it follows that though God is both perfectly free and also infinitely powerful, yet He cannot possibly do anything that is evil. The reason of this is also evident. Because, as 'tis manifest infinite power cannot extend to natural contradictions, which imply a destruction of that very power by which they must be supposed to be effected, so neither can it extend to moral contradictions, which imply a destruction of some other attributes as necessarily belonging to the divine nature as power. . . . 'Tis no diminution of power not to be able to do things which are no object of power. And 'tis in like manner no diminution either of power or liberty to have such a perfect and unalterable rectitude of will as never possibly to choose to do anything inconsistent with that rectitude.[40]

Clarke's argument offers a necessary gloss on Aquinas and allays much of the concern in the contemporary literature concerning necessary goodness and moral perfection.

If we mistakenly suppose that there is no logical connection between perfect goodness and omnipotence, or other perfect-making properties, then we *may* conceive of a being that brings about an evil state of affairs because it is in its power to do so. Such an argument has been put forth by Nelson Pike and warrants a closer inspection in light of Clarke's claims.

If we agree with Nelson Pike that the term God is a title, then with that title come necessary properties (omniscience, omnipotence, goodness). Also, if a being is God, then it follows de facto that that being is without sin. To make the assertion that a being is God and does not have these properties is, as Pike argues, "logically" inconsistent with the attribute ascription status of the title.[41] However, in contrast with Aquinas and Clarke, Pike argues that though the being that is God holds that title, it is logically possible that God might not have filled that status. Pike writes:

It should be noticed that this third assumption covers only a logical possibility. I am not assuming that there is any real (i.e. material) possibility that Yahweh, if He exists, is not perfectly good. I am assuming only that the hypothetical function "If X is Yahweh, then X is perfectly good"

---

[40] Samuel Clarke, *A Discourse Concerning the Being and Attributes of God* (1705; repr., Glasgow: Richard Griffin, 1823), Proposition 12.

[41] See Nelson Pike, "Omnipotence and God's Ability to Sin," in *Divine Commands and Morality*, ed. Paul Helm (Oxford: Oxford University Press, 1981), 68.

differs from the hypothetical function "If X is God, then X is perfectly good" in that the former, unlike the latter, does not formulate a necessary truth.[42]

In distinguishing between the title God and the person Yahweh, Pike argues that he has eased the tension between necessary goodness and omnipotence. It is logically possible for God to sin, a lá (G2), which makes no statement against God doing all and only things that are not morally evil. To do evil means that individual would not merit the title God. The being that is God has the "creative power" to bring about states of affairs the "production of which would be morally reprehensible."[43]

We should first note that the creative power of God is exactly what Clarke argued is coextensive with God's moral perfection, which is why the inability of God to sin is a perfect-making feature. This undermines Pike's claim on the logical possibility of God's sinning. Only if we divest the relationship of goodness and power do we obtain this possibility, and under that construction a being that is maximally powerful is not necessarily good. The difference between these two beings is that logical possibilities concerning God's nature change so that "if God is omnipotent, then He can bring about any state of affairs logically possible for an essentially perfect being to bring about."[44] Thus, we need not endorse Pike's claim that the title God entails such a possibility, nor need we endorse (G2) to alleviate the problem, at least as the problem confronts us now.

If we conclude that the argument from divine title does not work as is, then there still seems to be a lingering problem. Consider the following claim:

> The world simply cannot be such that it contains a being that is both (essentially) omnipotent and essentially sinless. Any being that is essentially sinless is such that there is no possible world in which it commits sinful actions. Since such a being cannot sin, it cannot be all powerful and so cannot satisfy one of the requisites of divine office.[45]

Such an assertion has merit if and only if the tenet of God's essential perfection is denied and a doctrine of God's contingent goodness is endorsed. As such, there are possible worlds in which the being that occupies the divine office (in the actual world) does commit a sin; the power of the agent, then,

---

[42] Ibid.
[43] Ibid., 72.
[44] Jerome Gellman, "Omnipotence and Impeccability," *The New Scholasticism* 51 (1977): 36.
[45] W. R. Carter, "Omnipotence and Sin," *Analysis* 42 (1982): 104.

is to be characterized as the ability to do otherwise. Such a claim seems specious for several reasons. First, suppose we agree that freedom is grounded in the power to do otherwise. There is nothing that logically commits us to the belief that the counterfactual entails that God commits a sin. Edward Wierenga notes, "God's freedom requires that he be able to do alternatives to what he does; it does not require that these alternatives be evil."[46] Second, rather than understand freedom under a counterfactual model, we previously argued that freedom is better understood in terms of self-control, or in Kantian terms a holy will. Given that we have already addressed this, let us consider the most damning objection to such a claim.

According to the argument from divine title, God's goodness is not an essential property of his being; it is only a property of the being that possesses the office of divinity, and in the actual world this being is God (Yahweh). Pike's argument implicitly entails that there are worlds in which God, or as he says Yahweh, does not possess the office because he is not perfectly morally good in that world.[47] We may suppose then, that there are worlds in which the divine office is unoccupied, for there are no beings in that world that are perfectly (or maximally) morally good.[48]

But we should recall that our commitment is to the interdependence of perfect-making properties, and the argument of God's necessarily being morally perfect follows therefrom. Given God's essentially perfect will, as we noted before:

> The only way for God to sin is for him to not have the power to carry out the dictates of that will. But to do so would be to "fall short in action." But God's power is precisely the power to do whatever His perfect will desires. Hence, for God to sin would necessarily be the result of weakness in creative power, and contradict His omnipotence.[49]

So, there are a couple of points here that we may score against our objectors. The first is that the objectors have yet to show, in any of our discussion, that there are beings with more power than God; rather, there are actions that finite beings do (and we've called these imperfect powers) that involve abilities

---

[46] Edward Wierenga, *The Nature of God: An Inquiry into the Divine Attributes* (Ithaca: Cornell University Press, 1989), 212.

[47] Such a claim is also compatible with Edward Wierenga's contingent DC theory, which holds that if it were to be the case that God commanded the gratuitous pummeling of Carl, then DC would not be true in that world.

[48] Or perhaps this being loses some other perfect making property that is a necessary condition of possessing the divine title.

[49] Gellman, "Omnipotence and Impeccability," 34.

that God lacks.[50] Earlier we noted that our discussion of God's freedom occurs logically before God's power, and it is precisely for this reason. As essential perfectionists, we are committed to the notion that God's actions are intentional, and hence a matter of his will. Further, given the connection between God's rationality and will, there is some end at which the action is directed. Thomas Morris sees the rationality/will connection to entail the following:

1. Agents can only do what they see as good.
2. To see evil as good is to be in error.
3. God cannot be in error, so
4. God cannot see evil as good, and thus
5. God cannot do evil.[51]

So it will help our discussion to further our claim on God's ability by clarifying what has been called a *successful act*, which is an act that is successful at producing the end to which it is aimed.[52] Concerning God's actions this entails that God must have both the capacity and the all-things-considered intention to perform that action. The distinction between God's will and God's power undermines the contention that *God lacks the power to perform this action* is identical with *God cannot perform this action*. One is a matter of God's willing and the other a matter of God's potency; any action that God "cannot do" may then be understood as God lacking the "will-power" to perform that action.[53]

So, we are committed to the view that to sin is logically impossible for God, and this is no diminution of God's freedom or power. With regard to the claims of Nelson Pike we may conclude that God is comfortably sitting on his throne, and the office is occupied. Let us now consider how this discussion has been drawn into the literature as to its effect on a pivotal soteriological issue, namely whether or not God is a being that is worthy of worship.

## On God's Being Worthy of Worship

In light of our discussion on God's freedom and God's omnipotence, we now have a background against which we might respond to the claim that God is not worthy of worship. The argument for this claim is to be understood thusly:

---

[50] I am indebted to Thomas Senor for this point. See his "God's Goodness Needs No Privilege: A Reply to Funkhouser," *Faith and Philosophy* 23 (2006): 428.

[51] Thomas Morris, *Our Idea of God* (Downers Grove, IL: InterVarsity Press, 1991), 51.

[52] Ibid., 428.

[53] Ibid., 429.

1. A Person is praiseworthy for an action only if he could have refrained from performing it.
2. A necessarily good being cannot refrain from performing good actions, so
3. A necessarily good being is not praiseworthy for any of his actions. If
4. God is necessarily good, then
5. God is not praiseworthy for any of his actions. But surely
6. God is praiseworthy for his good actions. So
7. It is not the case that God is necessarily good.[54]

Thomas Morris provides a nice review of the central concern held by many people, both theistic and atheistic, about essential perfection theology. What we want to say at the end of the day is that God is praiseworthy; however, what is proposed in (1)–(3) undermines our ability to make such a claim. We do not praise a calculator for telling us that twice two is four, nor do we praise God for his actions that could not be any way other than they are.

The success of this argument hinges on whether or not premise (1) is true, and we have given good reason to think that it is not. There is nothing in postulating God's necessary goodness that entails coercion or any causal conditions that "make" God who he is. Further, such a claim is successful only to the extent that the counterfactual model of freedom is successful. But we have denied this claim for two reasons. First, even on a counterfactual model it does not follow that the alternative action God perform be evil; it need only be different from the one actually taken. So even if we accept premise (1), there are still accounts of God's activity (logically speaking) that do not require only one state of affairs, *only one type of state of affairs*, namely those that are not blameworthy. But this says nothing against God's ability to refrain from instantiating a specific state of affairs; he could logically instantiate any possible state of affairs of equal (good) value.

Our argument against (1) undermines the claim of (2) as well, for what is required for (2) to be true is that God must be able to refrain from performing any of the good actions that he does in fact do. Thomas Morris argues that the success of (2) "trades on an ambiguity" between the following:

> (2') A necessarily good being cannot refrain from ever performing any good actions whatsoever, and

---

[54] Ibid., 56.

(2") A necessarily good being cannot refrain from performing any of the good actions he performs.[55]

Even if we were to agree that (2') is of concern, the answer resides in God's act of creation; nothing necessitated God's act of creation. But it seems Morris is right in claiming that (2") is the hook, and this, I think, we have shown to be wrongheaded in our argument against (1). Without (1) and (2) the argument does not go through. So we need not worry about (3) as it is based on premises that are unsound.

Another line of defense follows from God's actions that are supererogatory. Granted, the traditional understanding of supererogation is that it involves going "above and beyond the call of duty." At first blush this seems to rule out the possibility of any divine act of supererogation. However, I think the definition confuses the point to be made in the discussion. The very notion of obligation speaks of a normative claim on an agent to draw him to an action of good value. In other words, deontic statements of the sort made against murder and the like are statements about deficiency in the agent *before* any action ever obtains. The badness of an action consists not in its outcome but in the will of the agent to act in a certain way. The murderer is guilty of the offense before it obtains specifically because she willed evil—and this independent of whether or not the act fails or succeeds. So what we have is value before obligation, and supererogation is obviously a value-laden term. To argue that a supererogatory act is the byproduct of going beyond what one is obligated to do is categorically backward. It is better that we understand the nature of supererogation in terms of ontology and not in terms of the traditional normative requirement.

Consider the concept of grace. Grace is an unmerited act of favor from one person to another.[56] There is nothing in the action required; it is permissible but not obligatory. But we certainly would not say that when an agent is gracious he is acting under compulsion of some sort (normative or otherwise). Rather, the graciousness in an action is the byproduct of the goodness in the agent performing the action. Even more pointedly, what we find in actions of this kind is a total contrast from the deontological definition. Grace, it seems, exists only when something has gone wrong; there is a fracture in the relationship, and there is no positive prospect of amends. There is seemingly no prospect of recompense for certain wrongs—such as a woman who is the victim of a rape. In such cases what we have is that in order for there to be reconciliation, the victim gives twice—first as the object of wrongdoing and

---

[55] Ibid., 58.
[56] I am following the traditional etymology of the Greek *charis*.

then as the agent of amends. Money does not address the wrong done, even if it provides the victim with security of some sort, equally so imprisonment. Rather, the very nature of the goodness of grace is that it seeks to reconcile what has been broken from the other end—from the end of the victim and not from the end of the victimizer. All the more such a claim holds in divine-human affairs. If sin is irretrievably to set oneself in rebellion against God and fracture the divine-human relationship, the only possibility of reconciliation is through a divine act of grace. Admittedly, such grace may not be accepted, but that is a debate of a different stripe. All that concerns us here is that *in even offering reconciliation where otherwise there could be none* God has done something supererogatory.

There is still a second issue to be dealt with here, and that is the implication of the alternative-world model for the relationship between praise and blame. What the objector's argument provides is a strange notion of praise where blame is a necessary condition of praise's possibility; this strikes me as counterintuitive at best. The very success of the alternate-world model hinges on the notion of actions being *conceivably* distinct from what they are, but we are on good grounds to say that in the case of God the conceivability criterion is a bad guide to possibility. Nothing in that criterion says anything of the *kind of power* in the agent such as self-mastery (or control) or being maximally rational. Nor does it say anything of the relationship between reason and the will. The volitional element of agency is irreducibly characterized to the conceivability criterion, or worlds-gone-otherwise, and this supposedly to actions of diminished moral value; I praise you because I can conceive of a world where I could blame you. Let's just say this will not wash.

## Conclusion

I think the model we have proposed has a much more promising response to these concerns. We have shown how it can be the case that God's omnipotence does not entail that God can do everything, strictly speaking. We have also dealt with the more problematic issue of God's freedom and proposed a volitional model whereby God's freedom is best understood through the relationship between his intellect, his will, and a notion of self-control (or mastery). We have argued that God is not subject to impulses or desires, for these very concepts are passive in nature and show potency in God's willing and acting. Here we have argued that the praiseworthiness of God's actions may be understood as (1) their being supererogatory in nature or (2) their being in perfect harmony with actions that for humans would be characterized as moral. Thomas Morris, as we have noted, distinguishes between acting "in accord with a rule" and "acting from a rule" and holds that God does the former. I think the language is muddy, but it draws to light the difference between the "prescriptive" function of moral principles for human conduct and the "descriptive" element of divine activity.[57]

So it seems the argument against the praiseworthiness of God fails. There is no reason to think that power and freedom are incompatible with one another, nor that we should think that the concepts of freedom and power are self-referentially incoherent in divine ontology. Further, the very fact that God is Creator and Sustainer of every contingent being warrants praise in itself; "in him we live and move and have our being," as the Bible says (Acts 17:28). The debt of existence is no small debt, and God's acts of creation and offering of reconciliation are manifestations of his supererogation.

---

[57] Ibid., 60.

# Concluding Thoughts

This volume is an attempt to address two universal features of human experience, namely the problem of evil and the problem of suffering. Indeed, there is no one way to address these issues, for there are many problems *from* evil. Some problems from evil are logical in nature—does the existence of evil logically preclude the existence of an all-good, all-knowing, all-powerful God who is also Creator of the world (see chap. 2)? Does the vast amount and kinds of evil that pervade our world make it very unlikely that such a God exists (chap. 3)? Why isn't God more obvious either in our experience or through undeniable proofs for his existence (chap. 5)? More pointedly, why does God seem to be so distant when his comforting presence is the most needed, namely as we undergo suffering resultant from evil? What about the problem of hell (chap. 6)? It must be conceded that if hell exists it is the pinnacle of suffering both for its intensity and for its duration. Does hell make sense, especially in light of the Christian belief that God is loving and desires that none perish? What about suffering resulting from purely natural phenomena (chap. 7)? Even if free will explains some evil, it does not seem at first blush to account for these facets of our experience. Other problems from evil are less logical in nature and more existential—how do I address the evil that we find in our world, and how do I address the suffering, both personal and otherwise, that is in the world?

Accordingly, the first seven chapters of this book are not providing a single progressive argument that unilaterally addresses the problems from evil. The free-will defense is, in my estimation, a sufficient response to the logical problem of evil. However, the free-will defense is not a satisfying answer to the evidential problem of evil. Likewise, one can argue that the natural consequences argument has its place at the table of ideas. It is both intuitive and morally instructive that we must bear out the consequences of the choices that we make. The natural consequence argument does not, however, entirely address the suffering wrought from natural evil. More could be said, but this is sufficient to demonstrate that the problems from evil will not have a single answer that, like a universal acid, dissolves all problems once they are submerged in its logical snares. So, the first seven chapters of this book read differently because they are addressing different problems from evil.

In the first chapter I developed and defended the free-will defense against the logical problem of evil. There it was shown that an all-good, all-knowing, and all-powerful God is logically consistent with the existence of evil in the world. In the second chapter I addressed the evidential argument from evil. This argument states that the amount and kinds of evil we find in the world provide rationally compelling evidence to think it unlikely that God exists because there are no goods of which we are aware that provide a morally sufficient reason for God's permission of certain evils (e.g., the rape and murder of a five-year-old girl). Against this charge I developed and defended a view commonly known as theistic skepticism. Theistic skepticism states that there may be goods that are beyond our ken (goods known only to God but not by us) that provide a morally sufficient reason for God's permitting certain evils. Given our limitations to grasp the ways of God, we should remain skeptical that, even if they were explained, we would understand or accept God's moral grounds for permitting the most horrific events. One proviso I make in the discussion is to flesh out the implications of the doctrine of divine conservation. According to this doctrine, everything that exists results from God's activity of conferring existence on reality and upholding it in its being. Divine conservation applies to both moral and immoral states of affairs. What is more, divine conservation requires intentional action on the part of God; intentional action is a purposive action of an agent and thus is directed at some end (or teleology). The upshot of this argument is obvious, for I can know that God has an end for which he sustains all things in existence without having a clue as to what that end might be. This argument, if effective, strips away the possibility that there are gratuitous evils in the world, if we understand gratuitous evil to mean an evil for which there is no purpose (rather than being understood as an evil for which there is no outweighing good). I do not intend my development here to deny theistic skepticism but to give it a different shape.

Chapter 4, on the defeat of evil, is the most important chapter in the book. Here I noted two things. First, given that free will is the bedrock on which all meaningful relationships are developed, God's creation was opened up to the possibility of things going wrong. Free will answers *why* the world is broken. The defeat of evil provides an answer to the question *what now*; now that the world is broken, how can the problem of sin and its consequences be addressed? Defeat requires an active stance against evil, on both an individual and communal level. It is also worthy of reminder that partnership with God is essential for evil's defeat to come to fruition, for there are many things we cannot address without divine assistance. Moreover, given that the problem of evil and suffering begins with persons abandoning God for their own purposes, the notion of defeat insists on conversion as its proper place of focus.

The chapter on divine hiddenness (chap. 5) addresses the problem of God's apparent lack of obvious presence in our experience or through undeniable arguments. Building on the foundation provided by Paul Moser in *The Elusive God*, I noted several reasons to address these concerns. God has a morally sufficient reason to withhold his presence when persons approach him with a haughty spirit or when mortals make inappropriate demands of him. A direct experience of God is, at least according to Scripture, impossible for created beings, for a direct encounter with the unveiled God results in death. As a result, we can expect God's presence to be veiled, and thus less than obvious, in our experience—we see through a looking glass dimly.

The chapter on natural evil (chap. 7) provides several scenarios where suffering resultant from natural causes should not be typified as natural evil (judgment, chaos in nature due to abuse of free will). The essence of the chapter was to develop Stephen Layman's unique approach, which is to compare naturalism and theism in terms of explanatory power concerning this problem. For there to be natural evil, there must be a world in which it occurs, with beings of a certain type (conscious, able to feel pain) that undergo suffering from natural events. It was argued in this chapter that theism provides a better explanation for these features of the world than does naturalism and thus provides a more satisfying solution to the problem of natural evil than does naturalism.

The same type of reasoning applies to moral evil (chap. 9). It is difficult for naturalism to provide a robust account of the moral standard that adjudicates our use of the word *good*. However, if a loving and morally perfect God exists, then a meaningful account of objective moral values is provided. The irony is that evil then becomes evidence *for*, rather than *against*, the existence of God. The rest of the volume develops this theme in response to some new and interesting arguments from evil, namely the deontological problem of evil. This argument proposes that the states of affairs in the world indicate that God cannot exist, for in his permitting these things to occur he has violated moral duties. If God is perfect, the argument goes, then these states of affairs would not be in the world; these states of affairs are in the world; therefore, God does not exist. In response I argued that if God exists, then he is not subject to moral laws or moral duties. If he is not subject to moral laws or duties, then he cannot possibly fail to meet any duties, for he does not have any duties such that he cannot meet them. The rest of the volume addresses objections to this view, namely the usual naturalistic concern about grounding morality in God, the problem of divine freedom, and whether or not God is worthy of worship.

I am fully aware that there is more to the story than I have provided here. What is more, I recognize that some people are not looking for answers to these questions as they undergo suffering. In times of suffering we usually need the comfort of friends, not the counsel of scholars. However, these questions persist for a reason—we cannot help but ask such questions when the emotional element has subsided, and we try to make some sense out of our experiences. I hope this volume provides some helpful insights when that season of life arrives.

# Name Index

Adams, Marilyn M.  *82, 87–91, 106, 108*
Adams, Robert M.  *54–55, 147–55, 157, 165–67, 169–70, 191*
Alston, William  *7, 9, 12, 23, 25–28, 30–31, 134, 186, 200, 202*
Aquinas, Thomas  *1–2, 38, 85, 106–7, 154, 162, 195, 204, 208–9*
Arieti, James A.  *179*
Austin, J. L.  *168*

Bobik, Joseph  *1*
Broadus, John  *95*
Buckareff, Andrei  *103*
Budziszewski, J.  *146–47*
Buwalski, Shawn  *99*

Cain, James  *103*
Carter, W. R.  *203, 210*
Chappell, T. D. J.  *39*
Chisholm, Roderick  *44–45, 48*
Clarke, Randolph  *3*
Clarke, Samuel  *208–10*
Copan, Paul  *102, 117–18, 131, 138, 148–49, 155, 194*
Craig, William Lane  *156*

Erickson, Millard  *92*

Flint, Thomas  *198–99*
Frankena, William  *137*

Gellman, Jerome  *210–11*
Gerson, Lloyd  *179*
Gomes, Alan  *94–95*
Gould, Stephen Jay  *129–30*

Habermas, Gary  *84*
Hanink, James  *188–90, 195*

Hanson, N. R.  *62, 66*
Hare, John  *50*
Hart, David B.  *48*
Hasker, William  *54*
Henderson, David  *39*
Henry, Douglas  *76–77*
Hick, John  *13, 82*
Himma, Kenneth E.  *103*
Howard-Snyder, Daniel  *62*

Joyce, Richard  *188–90*

Kane, Robert  *3, 103*
Kant, Immanuel  *145, 199, 201–2*
Kelsey, Morton  *82*
Korsgaard, Christine  *142*
Kretzmann, Norman  *179–82*
Kvanvig, Jonathan  *27–28, 67, 74–76, 78*

Layman, C. Stephen  *113, 118–22, 128–29, 219*
Lee, Patrick  *195*
Lindström, Fredrik  *50*
Linville, Mark  *202*

Mackie, J. L  *15–16, 19–22, 108, 139, 144*
Mann, William  *181–84*
Mar, Gary  *188–90, 195*
Marshall, I. Howard  *84, 86*
Martin, Michael  *137, 144–46*
McCann, Hugh  *3, 34, 43, 46–49, 51, 56, 97, 161, 194, 204–7*
McGrath, Alister  *124–27*
Moore, G. E.  *137–40*
Moreland, J. P.  *84*
Morris, Thomas V.  *62, 64, 199–200, 212–14, 216*
Morriston, Wes  *178*

221

Moser, Paul   *67–69, 71, 73, 78, 219*
Murphy, Mark   *85, 157–67, 169–75*
Murray, Michael   *7, 10, 148, 152, 179*

Nielsen, Kai   *139, 186*
Nietzsche, Friedrich   *61, 66*
Noland, James R. L.   *58*

O'Connor, Timothy   *3, 200–201*
O'Donovan, Oliver   *57*

Peterson, Michael   *20*
Pike, Nelson   *203, 209–12*
Pinnock, Clark H.   *93*
Plantinga, Alvin   *5, 16, 18–19, 21–22, 108, 133, 135–36, 188, 198*
Plug, Allen   *103*
Polkinghorne, John   *127*

Rawls, John   *142, 169*
Rea, Michael   *7, 10*
Rees, Martin   *125*
Reichenbach, Bruce   *11*
Rowe, William   *23, 25–27, 32–33, 40, 121*
Russell, Bertrand   *177, 179*
Russell, Bruce   *24*

Saville, Andy   *91*
Sayre-McCord, Geoffrey   *138*

Schellenberg, J. L.   *63, 66–67, 74, 76–77*
Senor, Thomas   *212*
Seymour, Charles   *98, 100, 103, 106, 108*
Sinnott-Armstrong, Walter   *156*
Spencer, Jeff   *95*
Spiegel, James   *36*
Stevenson, C. L.   *141*
Stewart, Robert   *207*
Stump, Donald V.   *179*
Stump, Eleonore   *31, 179*
Swinburne, Richard   *104, 119–20, 148*

Talbott, Thomas   *82–83, 106–7*
Taylor, Richard   *155–56*
Tooley, Michael   *133–34, 136*
Trakakis, Nick   *115*

Vallicella, William   *180*
Vanier, Jean   *48*

Wainwright, William J.   *50, 139, 142, 150, 153, 173–74*
Walls, Jerry   *105*
White, Lynn Jr.   *39*
Wierenga, Edward   *185–86, 211*
Wright, Christopher   *57*
Wykstra, Stephen   *29–30, 134*

Yandell, Keith   *55–56*

# Subject Index

**A**
animal suffering  *23–26, 121–22*
annihilationism (Christian)  *81, 91–97*
axiological arguments  *133–34*

**C**
categorical imperative  *145*
Christian universalism  *81–91, 93–94, 111–12*
cognitive idolatry  *70–71, 78*
cognitively robust theism  *69–70*
consciousness  *122–24, 128–31*
consequences  *9–11*
constructivism  *142–43*
cooperation with God  *49, 58, 72–73*

**D**
defense  *6*
deontological arguments  *133–36*
deterrence  *7–8*
disposition  *47, 50–54, 68*
divine command ethics  *157–75, 177–95, 201–2*
divine command theory  *150–54*
divine command theory (of ethics)  *136*
divine concealment  *65–67*
divine will  *161–75, 192–93*
dominion  *38–40, 57–58*

**E**
epistemic hiddenness  *74–76*
evidential arguments  *23–41*
evolution  *13–14, 123*
expanded standard theism  *32–33*

**F**
fine-tuning  *124–28, 131*
freedom (of God)  *197–216*
free will  *5, 8–11, 18–22, 31, 47, 52–53, 113, 115–17*

freewill defense  *18–22*
free-will theodicy  *8–11, 87–89*

**G**
grace (of God)  *214–15*
gratuitous evil  *34–35, 41*

**H**
human cooperation  *46–49*
human suffering  *23–26, 31–32, 35–37*

**I**
ideal observer theory  *145–47*
illocution  *168–70*
incorporeality  *64*
intention  *3*

**L**
libertarian freedom  *18, 99–100, 102–4, 108, 199–202*
locution  *168–70*
logical problem of evil  *15–22*

**M**
metaphysical naturalism  *118–24, 126–31*
metaphysical theism  *118–31*
moral evil  *2–4, 19–20, 113*
multiverse theory  *124–28*

**N**
natural evil  *4–5, 12, 113–24, 130–32*
natural-law theodicy  *11–13*
natural suffering  *114, 121*
necessary goodness  *206–15*
noetic effects (of sin)  *67–71*

**O**
objectivity  *138–56*
omnipotence  *206–12*
omnipresence  *64*
omniscience  *203–4*

223

## P

participation (in the defense of evil)  46
perfect-being objectivism  *181–84*
perfect-being subjectivism  *181–84*
perlocution  *168–70*
Platonic essences  *187–89*
pleasure  *44–45*
possible worlds  *19–21, 38*
preemptive annihilationism  *110–11*
privation of good  *1–2*
punishment theodicy  *6–8*

## R

reasonable nonbelief  *63, 76–78*
rehabilitation  *7*
restricted theism  *33–34*

## S

sanctification  *50*
simplicity doctrine  *181–84, 188–89*
simplicity (of a worldview)  *119–20*
soul-making theodicy  *13–14, 37, 49–58*
speech-act theory  *163–75*
suffering  *4, 43–49, 51–58, 72–73, 95–96, 102–7, 113–15*

## T

temptation  *2–3*
theistic objectivity  *147–50*
theistic skepticism  *28–30, 126–27*
theodicy  *5–6*
theological objectivism  *179–83*
theological subjectivism  *179–83*
traditional view (of hell)  *82–91, 96–106, 110–11*
transcendence  *64–65*

## W

worship of God  *212–16*

# Scripture Index

**Genesis**
1:26–27  *38*
1:28  *38*
3  *4, 9, 109, 206*
3:1–6  *96*
3:5  *193*
7  *117*
19  *117*
22  *191*
22:2  *191–92*
22:5  *191*
22:12  *192*

**Exodus**
7:14  *101*
8:15  *101*
8:32  *101*
9:7  *101*
9:12  *101*
9:34  *101*
10:1  *101*
10:20  *101*
10:27  *101*
20:17  *68*
32:34  *6*
33  *65*
33:19–23  *66*
34:29–35  *66*

**Leviticus**
18:21  *194*
19  *162*

**Numbers**
16  *117*

**Deuteronomy**
29:20  *92*

**1 Kings**
21:10  *100*

**Job**
1  *5*
1:16  *5, 115*
1:18–19  *115*
41:1  *118*
41:14  *118*
42:2  *83*

**Psalms**
1:4  *100*
9:5  *92*
23  *104*
37:9–10  *93*
37:20  *93*
51:1  *100*
51:3  *100*
58:3  *100*
58:10–11  *107*
63:11  *107*
68:1–3  *107*
69:28  *92*
78:45  *95*
94:16–23  *107*
14:21  *118*
14:29  *118*
143:12  *92*

**Proverbs**
10:25  *93*
11:10  *92*
12:7  *93*
24:20  *93*

**Ecclesiastes**
9:3–6  *104*

**Isaiah**
1:28  *92*
1:30–31  *92*
6  *65*
6:1  *65*
6:3  *65*
13:11  *6*
21:3  *100*
48:11  *109*
53  *36*
57:20  *100*
59:12–13  *101*
65–66  *104*

**Jeremiah**
17:9  *101*
21:14  *6*
48:28  *95*

**Lamentations**
3:22  *83*
3:31–33  *83*

**Ezekiel**
44:10  *100*

**Matthew**
5:22  *68*
5:48  *85, 162*
6:19–20  *95*
7:6  *102*
7:13  *93*
7:13–14  *85, 162*
8:11  *104*
8:12  *86*
10:15  *96*
10:28  *93*
11:21–22  *96*
11:29  *104*
18  *105*
18:15–20  *36*
18:21–22  *37*
22:39  *109*
23:24  *72*

225

23:37  *100*
25:31–46  *86*
25:35–36  *72*
25:40  *72*
25:41  *94*
25:46  *94*
27:45–46  *71*

**Mark**
1:13  *208*
9:47–48  *94*
10:17–25  *100*
12:30  *68*

**Luke**
1:70  *94*
12:47–48  *96*
13:22–30  *84*
17  *105*

**John**
3:16  *93*
4:24  *64*
6:44  *83*
12:24  *95*
12:32  *83*
14:9  *72*

**Acts**
17:28  *216*

**Romans**
1:18–25  *70*
1:20  *66*
1:21–32  *101*
1:26  *101*
1:28  *101*
2:8–10  *86*
2:15–16  *101*
05  *86*
5:18  *83*
6:1–2  *57*
6:6  *57*
8:11  *103*
8:19–23  *103*

**1 Corinthians**
2:14  *88*
5  *105*
13:4–6  *109*
13:6  *107*
15:54–57  *47*

**2 Corinthians**
1:3–4  *48*
1:4  *72*
2:15–16  *93*
5:17–20  *90*
5:19  *83*

**Galatians**
3:27–28  *86*
5:20  *68*

**Ephesians**
2:6  *88*
2:12–13  *112*
2:19  *112*

**Philippians**
2:10  *91*

**2 Thessalonians**
1:8–10  *7*

**1 Timothy**
1:17  *94*
2:3–4  *85, 162*
2:4  *83*

**2 Timothy**
3:8  *95*

**Titus**
1:2  *207*

**Hebrews**
1:3  *72*
4:15  *3*
9:27  *84*
10:29  *96*
11:17–19  *195*
11:19  *191*

**2 Peter**
3:9  *83*

**Jude**
6  *65, 206*

**Revelation**
5  *104*
7:15–17  *103*
14  *95*
14:9–11  *94–95*
20:10  *94*
21:8  *104*
22:12  *96*
22:15  *104*